Complete Guide to Lake Fishing

Other Books by the Author

HOW TO CATCH TROPHY FRESHWATER GAMEFISH
THE BROWN TROUT FISHERMAN'S GUIDE
STEELHEADING FOR EVERYBODY
GREAT LAKES STEELHEAD FLIES *(limited edition)*
TROUT FISHERMAN'S DIGEST
A CHILD'S INTRODUCTION TO THE OUTDOORS
THE SMALL-BOAT HANDBOOK
DARDEVLE'S GUIDE TO FISHING
THE FLY HATCHES
GETTING HOOKED ON FISHING *(with Jerome Knap)*
SHAKESPEARE'S GUIDE TO GREAT LAKES FISHING
SEA RUN *(contributing author)*
HOW AND WHERE TO FISH THE GREAT LAKES

AN OUTDOOR LIFE BOOK

David Richey

Complete Guide to

LAKE FISHING

Drawings by Dana Rasmussen

Outdoor Life Books

Crown Publishers, Inc.
New York

Copyright © 1981 by David Richey
Published by Book Division, Times Mirror Magazines, Inc.

Library of Congress Catalog Card Number: 79–4711
ISBN: 0–517–545136

Manufactured in the United States of America

To Ben East,
the dean of outdoor writers.
I owe him a great deal.

Contents

Acknowledgments

The Complete Guide to Lake Fishing could never have been written without the help and co-operation of others. I'd like to thank my wife Kay for her dedicated research and photos; Ben East for his faith in me and his tips down through the years; and Henry Gross, an editor's editor and friend. Also, Jim Daubel, Billy Westmorland, Les Sandy, and Dan Gapen. Also, Bransons Lodge, Air Canada, Air New Zealand, New Zealand Travel Bureau, Canadian Government Office of Tourism, Spence Petros at *Fishing Facts* magazine, Evinrude Motors, and Luhr Jensen & Sons. If anyone has been forgotten, my sincere apologies are offered.

Preface

My introduction to lake fishing occurred some thirty-five years ago when bass boats, sonar units, and the language of structure fishermen were nonexistent. Mine was the simple pleasure of fishing for bluegills and sunfish with a cane pole, an 8-foot length of line, and a rusty hook baited with a small red worm. Whenever the bobber ducked under, my heart throbbed faster; a swift upward swing of the pole sent a saucer-shaped gill flying over my shoulder to land on the dock. I would pounce on it like a kitten hassling a yarnball.

Lake fishing was an unsophisticated sport in those days, but times have changed. Fishing has become a science; the electronic equipment used on today's lakes would astound the fishermen of yesteryear. Modern lake fishermen have their own language, specialized equipment, and a host of new techniques that take fish with regularity.

Fortunately, new waters are being created at a rapid pace—

reservoirs, impoundments, and strip-mine pits—enabling anglers to experiment with these new methods. At the same time, new species of gamefish are being introduced into fresh water. Not too many years ago coho and chinook salmon were introduced into the Great Lakes from their native Pacific Ocean. In the last ten years, striped bass by the millions have been planted in reservoirs across the country. These new opportunities make it imperative for anglers to learn more about the habits and habitat of the gamefish they seek and to realize that lakes are as different from one another as human fingerprints. Indeed, reservoirs, farmponds, natural lakes, and strip-mine pits have only one thing in common—they all hold fish.

This book explains the differences among the various types of fishing waters usually lumped under the heading of "lakes." The emphasis throughout is on bottom conformation—that is, structure. Through an understanding of structure, anglers can learn to gauge the feeding habits and seasonal movements of gamefish. A chapter on each of the major species explains the best lures and techniques to use at different times of the year. Thus, combining a knowledge of lake types and the techniques appropriate to the species, readers have a better chance of catching more—and bigger—fish. Essentially that's what most anglers have in mind when they push off from shore. I hope this book will help them to do just that.

DAVID RICHEY
Buckley, Michigan

Underwater Structure

My first pass around Michigan's Manistee Lake had been a lesson in frustration. My Flatfish hung up continually in shallow weedbeds or on submerged slabdocks left from the lumbering days. So I beached the boat, went back to my car, and picked up the sonar unit I'd left behind in my haste to begin fishing. I clamped it to the gunwale and took another trip around the lake. Now I had a clearer picture of the bottom. On my next pass around the lake, I trolled my lure at the proper speed and depth. I felt a smashing strike and soon a mint-silver steelhead was dancing in circles behind the boat. I landed the fish after a fifteen-minute struggle and went back to trolling. The next pass produced another strike, as did the third circuit. I landed both fish. One steelie weighed 15 pounds.

My success after using the sonar unit hinged solely on my ability to *interpret* the bottom of the lake. I was able to troll my lures accurately without hanging on underwater obstructions. The sonar enabled me to fish deeper water and follow the curving dropoff. A sonar unit isn't a crutch for bad fishing habits, but it is a precise fishing tool designed to interpret the bottom of a lake—that is, its "structure."

Structure is any underwater formation (or object) that fish use. It can be gravel, weedbeds, or a sandbar with a sharp point and dropoff; an underwater hump, shoal, or reef; flooded timber; an old river channel; a dam face or flood-control device. To be successful, you must interpret the structure of the lake you're fishing. You should be able to determine whether the bottom consists, in whole or part, of silt, sand, mud, rocks, gravel, muck, brush, submerged trees, or exposed rock formations. Whether the lake is deep or shallow. Whether it contains an inlet or outlet. Whether it is smooth-bottomed or contains ledges, dropoffs, underwater humps, or stair-stepping rocky faces.

A knowledge of structure will help you to determine the movements of gamefish. As they move from deep to shallow water, they follow changing bottom contours, sharp dropoffs, or weedlines. Many forms of structure are present in lakes, and you should learn to differentiate among the various types. Following is a glossary of structure terms. Some bodies of water will contain most of these elements, or they may contain only a few. Observant anglers can readily spot the various types of structure, and then learn how fish move toward them. Then they must learn how best to fish each one.

Breakline.   This is an area with a sudden depth change, from shallow to deep water. A few examples would include the extreme edge of a sharp dropoff, a ledge, or the edge of an old river channel. Some lakes have weedlines that suddenly drop off into deep water. This would be both a weedline and a breakline.

Break, or break on structure.   A break on structure refers to any object on bottom that fish use during migration. Examples include any sunken object such as a deep-sixed boat, rocks, boulders, submerged logs, weeds, old stump fields, underwater humps, or nearly anything else of this nature.

Weedlines. Many different types of aquatic vegetation are found in lakes. Among the most common are cabomba, broadleaf cabbage, sand grass, chara and nitella (advanced forms of algae), coontail, duckweed, water milfoil, American elodea, horned pondweed, waterstargrass, southern naiad, brittle naiad, leafy pondweed, Sago pondweed, small pondweed, curlyleaf pondweed, American pondweed, Illinois pondweed, floatingleaf pondweed, largeleaf pondweed, waterthread pondweed, water buttercup, or bladderwort. Some weedlines are formed by emergent plants such as cattail, sweetflag, American lotus, spatterdock, water lily, watershield, arrowhead, creeping waterprimrose, water smartweed, bulrush, and waterwillow. Gamefish use weedlines for cover, and for a "landmark" that directs them toward shallower water. Anglers should study the various types of water weeds in a lake.

We've all seen anglers troll religiously along the edge of a weedline. They may take a gamefish infrequently, but they seldom catch many, simply because most are fishing far too shallow to interest feeding fish. It's important to learn that regardless of which type of structure is being fished, most species will not strike well unless they have a *direct and immediate access to deep water along the breakline.* A shallow weedbed surrounded by a large mud flat and shallow water doesn't produce the desired results because gamefish will seldom enter such an area to feed. Their sanctuary is too far away and extremely difficult to reach if danger threatens. Deep water means safety to most gamefish. Small fish, such as panfish, will often be found in shallow water, but when they become palm-sized, they begin living in deep water. They will then work into the shallows only along select avenues. Weedlines can be productive along either the deep or shallow sides, depending upon the species and the season. This will be covered in individual chapters elsewhere in the book.

Brushlines. A brushline is a line of submerged brush located along a

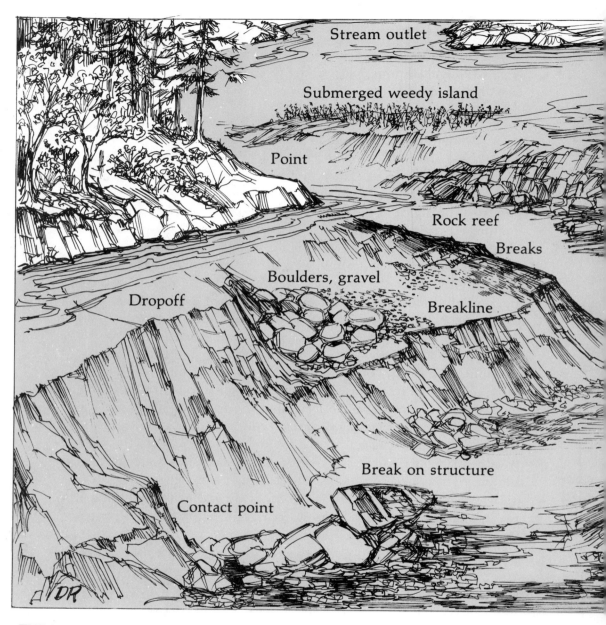

THE MAIN TYPES OF STRUCTURE IN A LAKE

deep-water edge. Such areas are common in many northern lakes or in flooded reservoirs where brush has been submerged by the rising water tables after impoundment. Such areas are capable of holding large numbers of gamefish at certain times.

Contact Point. A contact point is a feature structure where fish make their initial contact when moving from deep to shallow water. Such areas are often the sharpest breaks on structure, such as a cut, a narrow finger jutting deeper into the breakline, or that area where the break is closest to deep water.

Contact points remain in much the same locations for many years until flood conditions, removal, or deterioration sets in and they disappear. It's fair to assume that a productive contact point will provide good fishing for long periods of time. Succeeding generations of gamefish will move onto the same structure via contact points.

I knew an angler who once made a contact point on a northern Wisconsin walleye lake. He used a sonar unit to locate the deepest jutting point on a breakline where the water dropped from 15 to 23 feet. He closely measured the distance from shore, triangulated the exact position with three shoreline locations, and placed a one-ton load of medium-size gravel on the winter ice. The spring thaw sent the gravel crashing to bottom where it remains to this day. Last summer, I fished the spot two days after a high-pressure center moved through the area, and I caught fish on nearly every cast. The action lasted one hour, then died off. I returned the next day for another one-hour walleye session, and came away with a limit catch of 5-pound-or-better fish.

If this fisherman had dropped his gravel load in a different area, one where walleyes were never found, the story would have had a different ending. Knowledge of gamefish habits, bottom contours, and other structure formations can enable anglers to make contact points in prime locations. These spots can deliver superb sport. Unfortunately, they can easily be overfished by greedy anglers.

Dropoff. A dropoff is any area in a lake where the bottom contour changes from shallow to deeper water. Such areas are often visible from the surface by a change in water color. A dropoff affords easy access to the sanctuary of deep water for migrating gamefish. Dropoffs can be gradual or abrupt, depending on the type of lake. Sharp dropoffs usually produce far superior fishing prospects.

Migration routes.   These are avenues that sportfish follow as they move from deep water into the shallows, or from shallow to deep water. Such routes often work from deep sanctuary water, up to a contact point on a breakline, and along the breakline to a break on structure. There, the fish scatter in one or several directions to feed (this is called a scatterpoint).

Scatterpoint.   A point on the lake where gamefish begin separating. The schooling tendency of some species changes at this point, as fish travel loosely and not in a group. Such areas are often distinguished by breaks on structure, such as rocks or boulders at a depth where gamefish scatter to feed.

Color line.   A color line is a rapid, distinct change in water color as the depth increases. Oldtime anglers used color lines to locate dropoffs or breaklines. Such color changes often have a direct effect on gamefish and how or when they feed. Trout and salmon often feed along the deep-water edge of color lines. Shallow edges of this line produce no strikes, while the deeper portion produces excellent fish activity. Gamefish seem more tolerant of lures along the deep-water edge than near inshore waters.

Color lines are also present wherever a river or stream enters a lake. Often a stream flow is somewhat darker than lake water, and inflowing currents deliver food to hungry gamefish. This is often an overlooked location in many lakes, especially in spring and fall.

Points.   A point is as variable as Michigan's weather. Some points are long and tapered, and jut directly into deep water. Such areas are often the best fish producers of all. Other points are slow, tapering protrusions into the lake with shallow water on all sides. These are seldom worth fishing, although they can be productive after dark when some gamefish lose their inherent caution and move inshore to feed.

A wide, flat point (often called a bar) is a poor choice for anglers, especially when the tip of the point is located some distance from deep water. Those points that extend into a flat area with no appreciable drop in depth are likewise of little value. They remind me of the old chestnut about the town tease; they promise a lot, but deliver very little.

Anglers motor slowly through a flooded forest on Lake Sam Rayburn, a large Texas impoundment, using a sonar unit and contour map to locate good fishing holes.

Underwater humps. An underwater hump is just what it sounds like: a vertical uplifting of the lake bottom. Many humps are rounded and circled by flat, unbroken lake bottom. Such locations are not attractive to gamefish because the surrounding bottom does not have any breaks that can lead the fish to the hump.

The finest type of underwater hump is one with a point extending out to it, or a series of contour breaks that can lead gamefish to the area. Most productive humps are those with deep water on at least one side. A favorite hump of mine is found on a nearby brown-trout lake that always produces fast action, but only on the deep-water side. The shallow, flat side has never produced a fish, although I've fished it on occasion.

A peculiarity of most gamefish is that they rarely work up the shallow side of an underwater hump, feed on top, and then swim down the opposite side: Instead, they move up the deep-water side to the top, feed, and then head back into deep water. I've witnessed this particular movement pattern often on a chart-recording graph.

It should be noted that most fish species are especially shy while feeding on top of an underwater hump. Engine throb, thumping anchors, and too much fishing pressure will drive fish deep. Keep noise and surface activity to a minimum. If possible, make long casts with appropriate lures and work the top and deep-water edge. It's a tactic that can pay off with hefty stringers.

Sandbars. A sandbar can be a particularly attractive piece of underwater real estate for some gamefish. Sandbars usually offer changing conditions. In one year, their formation may attract migrating fish. The next year, they may be flatter than day-old beer.

Wind and wave conditions have a definite effect on sandbars. Currents and wave action can form underwater ridges and sharp points that serve as key migration avenues for feeding gamefish.

Look for sandbars with deep water at one end or the other, or along one edge. They will attract fish, if some break on the structure is present. I've seen cases where spring floods have washed several tree stumps onto a sandbar. The sand washes away under the stump and it settles slowly into deep water. A break (stump or some other obstacle) on a deep-water structure like a sandbar can provide fish with a contact point. Good fishing will be found nearby.

Boulders, rocky bottom, gravel.   Any rocky area—whether it be an underwater ridge of boulders, jagged or smooth rock, or gravel—can be productive, or it can be a dud for structure fishermen.

Smooth rock areas with little change in bottom depth seldom hold fish. But the same lake—with jagged edges, limestone outcroppings, and ledges *with access directly to deep water*—can attract excellent fish movements around structure.

Smaller rocks spaced periodically along bottom are seldom important to a structure fisherman unless the rocks *lead the way* from deep to shallow water, and point the fish toward a safe, easy migration route to the shallows. These rocks or boulders, when found on a sloping bottom contour with sharp breaks in between, may be one of the steadiest fish-producing areas in a lake.

Gravel or crushed rock seldom attract many gamefish unless for spawning purposes. Then the area can provide good fishing during the spawn. However, many states and some provinces have closed seasons during this period.

Deltas.   A delta occurs in lowland or flatland reservoirs that were created by damming a stream. The delta area on a reservoir is characterized by flat bottomland on each side of the original streambed. Some delta areas had mature forest on each side of the stream; some had fertile farmland spread out over the flat land; and some were forested and the timber cut before flooding occurred.

Many delta areas had distinct ridges running parallel to the edges of the old stream channel. The land then spread out along one or both sides of the channel. These flats help distinguish this type of underwater structure.

One of the key points to look for in any delta is good structure in the form of breaklines, breaks on structure, or contact points *a short distance* from the deepest water, which is always the old river channel. Gamefish simply won't move very far to reach shallow water if an easy avenue of access isn't open to them. Fish need to see a continuing path from deep to shallow water. This path must follow prescribed routings. For example, fish may move from the ridge bordering the river channel up a narrow finger of submerged land, until they make contact with brush or other timber in shallower water. But they won't do this if they have to swim too far.

An underwater hump that dead-ends onto a broad flat should not be fished. Gamefish will not go down the back side of a hump into shallow water unless cover is present, and only then if deep water is located nearby.

Cuts, or narrow indentations with deep water that extend from the river channel up and over the ridge and into the flat, shallow area, are one of the best spots to fish in a delta. Any breaklines along the edges of these cuts are often traveled by migrating fish following them from deep water.

I mentioned Michigan's Manistee Lake earlier in this chapter. The mouths of the Manistee River, and to a lesser extent, the Little Manistee River, have small deltas. Some of my finest steelhead fishing has taken place along the deep-water edges of dropoffs and along small cuts that meander from deep water up into shallow water. These fish do not feed actively, although they will strike savagely. Narrow indentations into the main delta area offer some of the best spots to troll.

A reservoir contains several hotspots in a delta situation. One of the better choices would be any area where two or more streams or channels merge. These spots are usually full of breaks—areas where a gamefish can leave the relative safety of the old river channel, and move shoreward. Impoundments can create *small* furrows in the earth. Upon flooding, the furrows remain and form small breaklines that fish can follow to shallower feeding grounds. These old cuts in the earth are prime locations for most species of fish, especially largemouth bass.

Boats, Motors and Accessories

Lake fishing requires a lake-fishing boat. This may seem to be obvious, but many anglers make do with whatever they can rent, tow behind the car, or borrow from a fishing buddy. Often the craft is too large or too small, and equipped with so many gadgets the fisherman can't cast or troll without tangling his line. These boats can make it extremely difficult to land a lunker.

Choosing A Boat

Choosing a boat and motor for lake fishing is as time-consuming as buying an automobile. It's difficult for me to recommend brand names here because I don't know where you'll be using your boat. Some anglers enjoy fishing on the Great Lakes or large impoundments, where speed is necessary to outrace a storm or to move to another fishing area. Others might be content fishing on lakes totaling less than 1000 acres. Others may wish to use their boat on a farmpond or strip-mine pit. The needs are endless, as are the hull and motor combinations.

It's important to buy a boat and motor for lake fishing that will be safe and seaworthy on the water you're planning to fish most often. Use sound judgment and never take the craft to waters where sudden storms and high, vicious waves can tear it apart. Rough water has an awesome power.

I've fished the Great Lakes often in my 17-foot Boston Whaler, but I pick and choose my days. I've trailered it to Tennessee and fished several reservoirs and backed it down ramps leading to Wisconsin muskie lakes. It has helped produce nice bass from small lakes where ramps weren't available and I had to launch across a sandy beach. The best advice I can give is to opt for a 16- or 17-foot boat for most *inland* lakes.

Many boat owners make the mistake of buying an engine much too large for their needs. Outboard manufacturers have now boosted their ratings to 300 horsepower, and who knows where it will end. There's little need for engines this large, especially on smaller inland lakes. An angler is much better off going with a 25 to 35 h.p. engine, regardless of the manufacturer. These outboards are capable of quick starts, slow trolling speeds, and have enough horsepower to hurry you down the lake to a new fishing hole. Anything larger will not troll slowly without fouling up the sparkplug. A smaller motor will not have the power needed to move you rapidly from one spot to another.

It's critical that new-boat buyers sit down with a dealer and explain their needs. Don't be conned into purchasing an engine and boat that will be too large to launch by yourself. It's a common trait among some boat dealers to sell a craft that makes them more money, but isn't suitable for the task intended. Stick by your guns and you should be able to purchase all-new equipment—boat and motor—for about $2000, and possibly less if you shop around.

A bass boat or a fiberglass tri-hull is adaptable to lake fishing, provided that you don't overload it or use an oversized outboard engine. A common mistake is to load such a craft with unnecessary gear, and an engine boasting at least 100 horsepower. Then the boat becomes unwieldy and difficult to control. I've used many fiberglass hulls through the years, and most have worked well. I've caught lots of fish from such boats, but I have always felt that they were too large and difficult to turn sharply when I wanted to follow a certain breakline.

One item I like to use on bass boats is an electric trolling motor. This piece of equipment is like the difference between a Ford and Cadillac when attached to the front of a boat. I prefer using a model with foot controls, and in the largest size possible. The larger units pack

The ideal fishing boat—a 16-footer with deep-vee aluminum hull, a flat floor, and a 25 horsepower outboard motor.

more thrust, and have a forward and a reverse switch that enables anglers to move forward, backward, or change directions. The only drawback is that electric motors do drain the energy from storage batteries. They must be recharged after nearly every trip.

For most anglers, I would recommend a 16-foot, deep-vee aluminum hull, with a flat floor for ease in standing and fighting fish, and an outboard with 25 to 35 horsepower. The craft should be equipped with either a sonar unit or chart-recording graph, and an electronic water thermometer. The only other tackle needed should be rods, reels, and one tackle box. A landing net and stringer complete the basic lake-fishing package. A cooler is helpful if space permits.

Outfit the boat with splashboards for backtrolling. These boards go across the stern and nearly envelop the outboard. Backtrolling means just what it says: trolling in reverse instead of forward gear. The boat turns more rapidly in reverse and the angler is capable of staying on structure far better than when forward turns are made. It also enables fishermen to slow the boat down to a crawl—a big plus if you're going after certain gamefish.

Splashboards are usually bolted onto the stern in such a manner so that the reverse trolling procedure doesn't kick water back up into the boat. The angler stays dry, an advantage when you're trying to pick up walleyes on a cold, gray November day. These devices can be ordered from Northwoods Tackle Division, P.O. Box 609, Menomonee Falls, WI 53051. Most are made of heavy-gauge plastic that can be molded to the exact fit of your boat's stern. They're worth their weight in gold if backtrolling is your bag.

Electronic Gear

Sonar units have swept the fishing scene by storm. I purchased a Lowrance Fish Lo-K-Tor years ago and still own the unit. This type of flasher, or a HumminBird, Ray Jefferson, Heath Kit, or other model, is about all the average angler needs. A common problem with any flasher is that the angler devotes too much time to watching the dial and too

A small bass boat powered by an outboard and an electric motor is a good choice, provided it is not overequipped and overpowered. These anglers have limited their gear to the essentials.

little time thinking out fishing problems. I've seen more than one case where two boats trolling toward each other have either collided or narrowly missed having an accident because the occupants of both boats weren't watching where they were going.

I use my sonar unit sparingly, only to obtain the feel of the bottom contours. I do carry several marker buoys to mark trolling runs or possible casting areas. A sonar unit (flasher-type) shouldn't be purchased with the idea of finding fish. I use mine solely to keep track of the depth and any changes in bottom contours. A flasher will not reveal those little humps or indentations on structure where fish often hide. The only way to locate these breaks on structure is to fish them thoroughly and feel your way along. A good man with a rod, reel, and lure can often tell you more about bottom contours than any sonar unit ever built.

I also own a Vexilar Sona-Graf, which I use often when fishing the Great Lakes for salmon and lake trout. I have used this rig in smaller lakes, but the strong sound waves often spook fish away from the boat. It's actually possible to see fish scooting off while watching a chart recorder do its job. They often move as soon as the sound waves strike them. A common occurrence on the Great Lakes is to locate a school of salmon. Good fishing can be had while only one or two boats are fishing. If you reveal the location of your hotspot and more graph-equipped boats find the school, the salmon will disappear. Some of this is due to fishing pressure, but some fish also spook because of increased sound waves going down through the water.

Chart-recording graphs or flasher units can help fishermen, provided that they understand the principles of each unit, and if they are used in a logical, sparing manner. Locate the best structures, triangulate them with shoreline or floating markers, and turn the unit off. You'll catch more fish.

The previous remarks may lead some readers to believe that the good ol' boy from Michigan has lost his senses. Everyone *knows* that the sonar unit is the key to catching fish. Well, that's not true, and I'd argue the point with anyone. Such units have never directly caught a

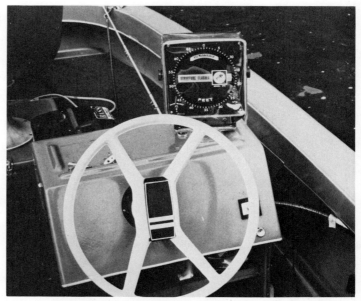

This Humminbird sonar unit, called a "structure flasher," is used by many lake fishermen. If used sparingly, to obtain the feel of bottom contours, a sonar can be a valuable aid.

Tom Mann, professional bass fisherman and lure manufacturer, uses a float tube and Humminbird Fish Tracker to find gamefish in small lakes and ponds.

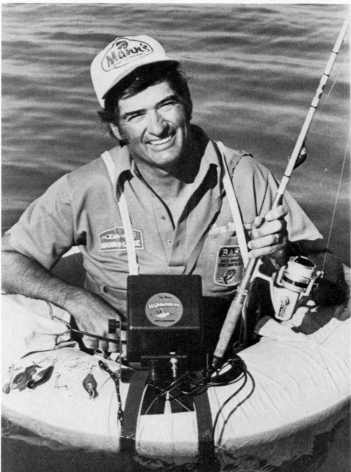

These fishermen have a chart-recording graph mounted on the dash near the wheel. The unit indicates depth and the presence of fish.

fish, but they do help pinpoint good structure where gamefish can be caught. Even more fish would be caught if anglers obtained a feel of the land, so to speak, and then relied on fishing skills and know-how rather than electronic equipment.

Four anglers proved this one day to my satisfaction. I teamed up with three other guys, both equipped with the same gear. We were all equal in fishing ability. One boat was to use its sonar unit all day, while the other boat used their flasher only to locate good structure.

We found a good breakline at the tip of a submerged reef on a northern Minnesota lake. We had caught fish the day before at both ends of the reef. It was the fourth day after a front had passed by, and the weather was changing again. Clouds were building, and the temperature was dropping. The walleyes were moving.

One boat with two anglers picked one end of the reef, while the other boat fished the opposite end. One group was to keep their unit on all day, while anglers in our boat used the flasher to find and mark the breakline. Then we'd turn it off. Both groups used the same lures that had worked well the previous day. Our agreement was to fish four hours at one end, break for lunch, and then switch locations and fish another four hours.

It was dramatically proved to me that the boat that didn't use the flasher constantly was able to harvest more walleyes. We backtrolled with Lindy rigs baited with leeches, anchored and cast jig-minnow combinations, and caught walleyes all along the structure. The four-hour morning period produced ten keeper-size walleyes for our group (we weren't using a flasher), while the other fishermen landed three smaller fish.

That afternoon, we switched locations and repeated the process. Again the group that used the flasher sparingly caught the most fish.

Such tests are not conclusive, but they do suggest that too much use of sonar units can lead to poor fishing. Sound waves spook more fish than is commonly believed. Marker buoys—placed at tips of structure, above protrusions along edges of weedbeds, or off the tip of a point or reef—don't disturb gamefish nearly as much as a sonar unit.

Electronic water thermometers are the only other piece of equipment I carry when lake fishing. They do not disturb the fish and can be valuable on stormy days.

Matching your boat and motor is essential. It's every bit as important as matching the rod and reel. A properly equipped boat, one without an overabundance of electronic gadgets, makes fishing a real joy. A good fishing rig can literally help you catch more fish than a poorly equipped craft. Too much gear, too little move-around space, and too many people in a boat reduce your efficiency on the water. Keep a boat simple, take only what's absolutely needed, and learn to think out fishing situations. You'll be a far better angler.

How Weather Affects Lake Fishing

Local weather patterns can greatly influence an angler's success on any lake, at any time. Weather is so changeable that even television weathermen are seldom right. I've seen too many fishing trips ruined by completely unreliable weather reports.

I've learned how to adapt to whatever the day brings. Whether it's raining, snowing, or clear, I go fishing and attempt to learn something new about how varying weather conditions affect fishing. Some of the information I've gathered over the years should help most lake fishermen.

Prevailing weather conditions can directly affect fish movements on any given body of water. Clearwater lakes are more seriously affected by cold fronts or clear, sunny skies than are dark-colored lakes with warmer water. Poor fishing conditions usually remain longer on cold, clear lakes than in any others. The reason for this will be explained

23

later in this chapter. The important point to realize is that weather does have a direct effect on fish, fishing, and the lakes. This knowledge can be used by anglers to increase their catches, but a fisherman must be willing to travel and to adapt to existing circumstances, or to plan ahead to cash in on optimum conditions when they occur.

Lake fishermen should know about more than the air temperature. In fact, air temperature is usually the last item to be considered. My pappy once told me the best time to go fishing was whenever you can get away. I've stuck with this philosophy through the years, but now I consider other factors besides the outdoor thermometer.

Lake fishermen should also consider the following: prevailing light conditions, warm or cold fronts, high and low pressure centers, how long the prevailing weather has held in an area, how much longer it's expected to remain, what the incoming weather holds in store, wind direction and velocity, and water color.

The sun, for instance, represents one of the biggest bugaboos to lake fishermen. Many anglers prefer fishing on bright, sunny days, regardless of whether they catch fish or not. This thinking goes entirely against the grain of structure fishermen. They know that a bright sun and high skies are not the best fishing conditions.

One June three years ago, I fished in northern Wisconsin on and off for four days. A high-pressure center had moved over the lake I was fishing and held in a stationary pattern for the entire time we fished. Midway through the fourth day storm clouds rumbled on the horizon and moved toward me. I had found an excellent break on structure in 15 feet of water off a narrow, sloping point jutting into the lake. This promised to be the best spot on the lake once walleyes began their shoreward migration.

The wind picked up, tree leaves rattled, and whitecaps were forming on the lake. Cloud cover moved in, the light intensity decreased, and we began working jig-minnow combinations along the tip of the point and near the break on structure. This break was a collection of fairly large rocks that fronted deep water—a perfect place for walleyes to contact the breakline.

Thirty minutes before the storm broke the walleyes made contact with the breakline. My wife Kay hooked the first fish, a 5-pounder. My second cast resulted in a hookup with a similar-sized walleye. We banged cast after cast into that area and boated nine fish. The smallest weighed 4 pounds; the largest weighed close to 8. The fishing turned sporadic and then died as lightning flashed across the darkened sky. Our fishing was done for the day, but that thirty-minute period more than made up for the endless hours we'd spent fishing during the previous days. Some might contend that we'd made a lucky catch, but I'd rather chalk it up to experience and planning.

The key factors behind this success story were that we had located a good break on structure and were fishing when the walleyes made their shoreward move. The decrease in barometric pressure just before the storm struck was another factor in our favor. The biggest piece of luck we had was when the cloud cover moved into the area with the storm.

The larger specimens of any freshwater species do not enjoy feeding or migrating under bright skies. A dark day, or one with intermittent cloud cover, contributes much more to fishing success than a boxful of lures or a lucky rabbit's foot.

Since sunlight plays such an important role in the success or failure of any lake-fishing trip, this shall be covered in detail.

Fish cope with intense, direct sunlight by heading for cover. A walleye may seek depths where the sun's rays are not a factor, while largemouth bass may nose into a heavy mat of weed growth. Fish, however, feed nearly every day, regardless of the weather. The determining factor is where and at what depths they will choose to eat, and how long they will feed. This is, in part, determined by the influence of sunlight.

Sunlight, or lack of sunlight, is often dictated by a high or low pressure center. The first two or three days after a front moves into the area can seriously reduce catches. The exception to that rule is when the front has been in a stable position for three days and *if* cloud cover begins moving into the area. Some anglers I know scan the long-range weather forecasts published in newspapers. They've learned to spot a change forming and are ready to capitalize on it when the new front arrives. I used to call the U.S. Weather Service at the local airport and talk directly with the weatherman in an effort to cash in on weather changes. That source dried up when the weatherman quit his job and decided to sell insurance.

One of the basic tenets of lake fishing is to determine weather frontal movements, and then be able to apply your weather knowledge in a manner that will produce gamefish. The secret here is to plan ahead for a fishing trip on those days when skies are dark or overcast. Avoid the typical sunny days that may be good for outdoor photo-taking, but poor for fishing success. Many lake fishermen labor under the misconception that bright days are the best times to fish. Actually bad-weather days often generate the hottest action.

I remember dozens of fishing trips where a sudden change from a high to a low pressure center, overcast skies, and spitting rain gave me the action needed to produce fish and photos for magazine articles. Nasty weather doesn't mean an angler should risk life and limb to fish when conditions are hazardous. If whitecaps are breaking over the bow of your fishing boat, you've overextended your welcome and should have been on shore long before it became too rough to fish comfortably.

Here's an example of how spitting rain can trigger fish movements. In an upstate New York lake I used to fish, I nicknamed one spot "The Rain Hole," an apt title for water where I caught smallmouths only at the very beginning of a rain shower. One could fish the lake for hours during other periods, but when skies clouded over and you could first smell the rain coming, smallmouth bass made their move onto that structure. Fishing was tremendous for fifteen minutes or so. As soon as the rain fell heavily, the action would stop and it was time to go home. It was possible to catch at least five fish during that brief spell; most would be 4- and 5-pound lunkers.

Lowered light intensity on the water is one sure-fire trigger that puts gamefish on the prod. Sometimes a cloud may block the sun for only thirty minutes, but that half hour period may offer some of the hottest sport of the day.

Gamefish also respond differently to light during cold weather. Icefishing for trout or northern pike can be a time-consuming sport with little reward during an overcast day. I've seen many cases where a bright sun peeking through cloud cover can trigger a wild feeding spree. Keep these sunlight case histories in mind and relate them to some of your own experiences. Sunlight on winter ice can increase oxygen in the water, and stimulate feeding activity.

Weather changes are a basic factor in any lake fisherman's life, regardless of locale. North America goes through four climate changes, even in Arctic polar regions. The seasons may be longer or shorter in some regions, but changes do occur. With these changes come weather pattern variations that influence directly the lake, the fish, and the fishing.

These variations should affect an angler's strategy. One method may produce during summer months, but fall flat on its prat during the fall turnover period. Changing weather patterns can seriously affect the time of day when gamefish make their push on a particular piece of structure. One time, I fished Tennessee's Dale Hollow Reservoir for muskies on a bright midsummer day. The fish were holding deep to avoid the harsh glare. We trolled deep-diving Bombers along stair-stepping ledges and off deep-water points. My next trip to the same area was in the early spring, to fish for white bass. A fisherman cornered me one day and berated me for writing about a technique that failed to produce. What he didn't realize was that muskies at that time were heading into shallow, muddy bays for spawning. He hadn't been fishing anywhere near where the fish should be at that time of year and under those weather conditions.

Frontal systems are an angler's best friend, if he knows how to use them. A front can be associated with either a high or low pressure center; both can work for or against the fisherman. A front is merely an area where two conflicting air masses come together. In some cases, it will be a high or a low. Fronts may contain either cold, dry air or warm, moist air. Frontal systems normally pass across North America in a west-to-east pattern, although a glance at a weatherman's map will show that such fronts can dip north or south, almost at will. Cold fronts have been the key to much of my fishing success, although the word "cold" doesn't necessarily mean a drastic temperature drop. It can be merely a downward shift of 2 or 3°. In spring, fall, or winter, it can mean a decided lowering of the air temperature. The temperature drop rarely means as much to fishermen as does the change in pressure that accompanies such a front. Fronts are usually accompanied by cloud cover, the other deciding factor that gets gamefish moving.

A typical situation occurs throughout the country whenever two fronts collide. A front with warm, moist air banging heads with a front containing cooler air will generally trigger thunderstorms, squall lines, rain, and possibly snow in northern regions. The best fishing will occur *before* the two fronts tangle; the reason—darkened skies and a change in barometric pressure. The amount of light is—again—the principal reason for increased fish activity.

After a storm passes, or after a cold front moves through an area, we are usually treated to clear skies with good sunlight. This is not a good time for fish movement.

The typical reaction of gamefish to a front is to move onto good structure before two fronts collide. They will probably feed, or at least strike readily to a properly presented lure or bait. After the fronts mix, the fish will usually head for bottom and may stay there for several days. Fishing won't improve until the weather moderates and temperatures begin to rise. This is usually accompanied by some high clouds. Three days is usually the maximum time gamefish will remain inactive.

Many fishermen plan trips around weather forecasts, and choose to wait until after a storm passes, when the weather is more stable. That may be fine for Joe Fisherman, but it means absolutely nothing to the fish. Anglers often labor continuously under this misconception.

Several years ago, when I first started catching brown trout from Lake Michigan, I noted that the hottest days in June or early July

Partially overcast skies in the evening tell anglers that a frontal system is on the way. Darkened skies and a change in barometric pressure usually spur gamefish movement. This period before two fronts collide is one of the best times to fish.

seemed best for fishing. If the sky was overcast, and it was so hot and muggy that you seemed to drink a thousand soft drinks, the browns were biting hard. Limit catches of five fish each for two anglers were common, but only for a few days. We'd knock 'em silly prior to a frontal system moving through and then we'd fish for two or three days and catch only one or two fish despite our fourteen-hour-per-day efforts.

I've since learned that hot, sultry days during midsummer can trigger some of the finest fishing of the year. Think back to those hot summer days when fish were taken everywhere, and good catches were made by most anglers. Next year, try to plan a fishing trip during some of the hottest days, particularly if cloud cover is present.

Lightning and thunder are fun to watch from indoors, but they don't help fishing. I've sat through many rainstorms and caught fish, but I've never caught fish with lightning flashing, and thunder making drumrolls in the heavens. It's a scary—and dangerous—time to be on the water. Many fishermen have been struck by lightning, or had close calls during thunderstorms. I'll do my fishing under better conditions.

When gamefish move after a two-front collision, it will be for only a short distance and just for several minutes. The fish then retreat to deep water. The first fish movement normally occurs on the second day after a front passes through your area.

It requires another day, sometimes two, before enough cloud cover builds up to filter out some sun rays. On the third day after a front moves through, you'll note increased activity and better catches. You'll probably see more clouds, and possibly a "two-tiered" layering of clouds, which filters sun rays twice before they strike the water. This is the best possible situation for fishing.

Certain gamefish species are less affected by frontal changes than others. A lake containing trout, largemouth or smallmouth bass, northern pike, walleyes, and panfish would show each species moving at various times. The reason behind this is that the changes are more noticeable to some fish than others. Northern pike are often the first gamefish to move and feed during a change. Trout will move as well, although not as early as pike. Bass seem to be most affected by a cold front moving into an area. It's not uncommon for these gamefish to cease all movement for three or four days, depending upon the severity of the weather change.

How do most gamefish move onto structure after a cold front passes through? Their first migrations are short and tentative, perhaps only moving up on structure for 5 or 10 feet. The next day's movement may show a lengthier movement and a longer stay on structure. On the third day, if light is filtered through heavier clouds and a warming trend of the air temperature prevails, the fish may move all the way from a deep-water sanctuary into relatively shallow feeding zones. Each kind of gamefish differs in the way it approaches structure. This will be covered elsewhere. Just remember that the first moves are short and last only a few minutes. As time passes, all movements become longer and fish are present for extended periods. The smaller fish of a species are usually the first to move, and they often stay longer. Big fish usually hold back and are more reluctant to move and feed until all conditions are favorable.

Sudden barometric pressure changes are noticed by all wildlife, including gamefish. A lowering barometer signifies a low-pressure center moving into an area, while a rising barometer denotes clearing skies and a rise in temperature. Each affects sportfish, and good fishing can be done in each case. It's simply a matter of knowing when to fish, and where.

We've learned that a dropping barometer is accompanied by cloudy skies, a reduction of sunlight striking the water, and a fish movement immediately prior to precipitation—either rain or snow. We also should have learned that a rising barometer indicates a clear sky with a warming trend. This generally means poor fishing for a period of two to four days on the average. At such times fish deeper than you would normally.

I'd like to refer again to my Lake Michigan brown trout fishing experience. Hot, muggy days spaced three or four days after a cold front moved through produced our fastest action. What happened to those same brown trout the day after a cold front moved through? I've spent many days fishing on such occasions, and my chart-recording graph would show the fish suspended in 50 or more feet of water, or smack on bottom. They were not found along shoreline structure such as points or dropoffs—they had moved to deep water. I could troll every lure in my box through the suspended or bottom-hugging trout, and strikes would be few and far between. This example could easily apply to almost every gamefish found in fresh water.

Water temperature isn't as big a factor in a gamefish's migrations as is commonly thought. I once believed that water temperature was the deciding factor in determining at what depth a fish is found. All gamefish are as comfortable in 40° water as they are in 70° temperatures because they are cold-blooded. They can adapt to water temperature. However, their metabolism is such that certain temperature ranges are better for feeding purposes. This will be covered in a specific chapter elsewhere in the book.

Although a change in water temperature does send fish on feeding sprees, it rarely affects fish migrations except in spring and fall when trout or other anadromous species are moving shoalward to spawn. This, in a strict sense, can be a migration triggered by water temperature. Gamefish seldom migrate strictly for food except, in winter, to reach a warm-water outlet where baitfish have congregated.

The Role of Wind

Wind direction plays an important role in the mixing of water levels during the summer, when some lakes stratify into three distinct levels. The wind's velocity and direction have a direct bearing on where some gamefish feed, and when they feed.

Walleyes are known as "dirty weather" fish. Rain, wind, rolling waves, and a falling barometer accompanied by a cold front will put them on the feed. George Yontz, an old fishing buddy of mine who's now dead, once told me, "Walleyes will always feed along the downwind shore in a stiff wind, particularly if the barometer is falling and weather is making." I fished with him one day on Michigan's Burt Lake, after the wind had been howling for two days. We caught walleyes that were feeding in extremely shallow water; every fish was a trophy. Try fishing downwind areas on large, shallow lakes when the wind turns the waves putty-gray. The fish feed voraciously in knee-deep water, provided that they have quick access to deep water. This is still another case of fish feeding under dark skies after following the "road signs" up from deep to shallow water. It would be useless to look for them in these areas at any other time.

Wind often provides food for trout in lakes. A nor'easter, or a wind from any quarter that lasts for a day or two, will churn up silt beds and release many nymphs. These nymphs will drift wherever the current or wind blows them, but it's always downwind. I've had several good days on some trout lakes where rainbows, browns, or brook trout would feed exclusively on the bonanza of wind-blown insects. It may be tough flycasting, but the reward can exceed the effort.

Weather patterns should be studied by lake fishermen. Changing weather can either make or break a fishing trip. Unfortunately, many anglers prefer fishing on days when the odds are against success.

Perhaps this chapter will change that habit.

CHAPTER

What Is a Natural Lake?

Natural lakes are fairly abundant in North America. Often called seepage lakes, they are usually spring-fed, or fed by precipitation or ground-water runoff. If they contain sufficient mineral content and heavy weed cover, natural seepage lakes can hold almost any species of fish.

Natural lakes are often categorized by their age. There are oligotrophic (young) lakes; mesotrophic (middle-aged) lakes; and eutrophic (old) lakes. Let's examine each type in turn.

Oligotrophic (Young) Lakes

Picture yourself on a Canadian lake, preferably on a windswept point where ledgerock outcroppings are common and whiskey jays circle over your evening campfire. A whitewater stream crashes into one end of the lake and a shallow feeder stream connects that lake with another over a spruce-studded ridge. This, by our standards, is an oligotrophic lake. Lake trout, pike and walleyes, a few smallmouth bass, and whitefish probably inhabit this lake. These lakes are about 12,000 years old, young by geological standards.

A young lake is low in nutrients—those enriching factors that quickly age a lake. Oligotrophic lakes are rocky waters with exposed rock walls, large boulders or heavy ledgerock, and steep shorelines that are usually dotted with evergreens or birch.

Such steep-sided lakes have sharp dropoffs and little weed growth

OLIGOTROPHIC LAKE

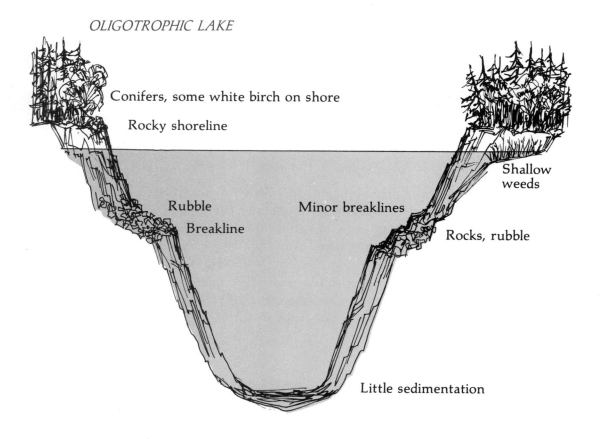

Conifers, some white birch on shore

Rocky shoreline

Shallow weeds

Rubble

Breakline

Minor breaklines

Rocks, rubble

Little sedimentation

The shoreline of a typical oligorophic lake is steep and rocky, with a scattering of everygreens and birch. These lakes are deep and contain few weedbeds.

except in shallow, protected bays. Most oligotrophic lakes are deep. Some lakes reach depths of 100 feet or more. Rocky reefs are fairly common and seem to jut from the lake floor without any pattern.

Food supplies for gamefish are scarce. Many lakes of this type are found along the Canadian border, where lake trout, whitefish, northern pike, smallmouth bass, or walleyes are found.

Mesotrophic (Middle-Aged) Lakes

We'll switch locations now, to a lake in northern Michigan. The broken-rock shoreline shows a more gradual taper and is a mix of hardwoods and pine. Shallow coves may contain weeds in quiet areas, while heavy weed growth is often found along the first dropoff. This is a mesotrophic lake, and it is common throughout the United States.

A mesotrophic lake is a fertile body of water that can support large populations of trout, largemouth bass, smallmouth bass, panfish, walleyes, northern pike, muskies, and other gamefish. Such lakes can be deep or shallow. A thermocline often forms in deeper waters. Some lakes do not develop a thermocline, although another nearby meso lake will. It seems to be an unstable characteristic of this age-class of lakes.

The physical characteristics of a mesotrophic lake vary from one area to another. The lakes have typical rock outcroppings in some areas, although these tend not to be as sharp-featured as they are in oligotrophic lakes.

The shoreline of a mesotrophic lake is often bordered by rocks. The nearby forest consists of hardwoods predominantly, although pines exist in some areas. Weed growth is usually found in shallow water,

MESOTROPHIC LAKE

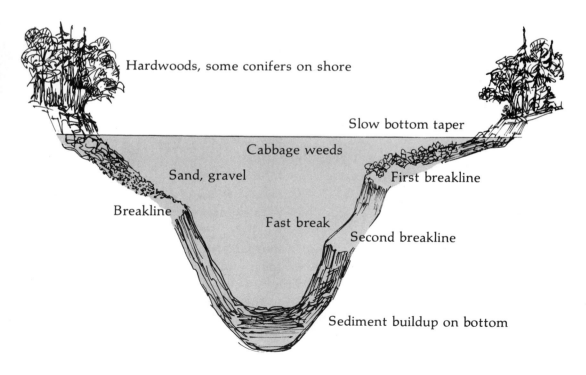

Hardwoods, some conifers on shore

Slow bottom taper

Cabbage weeds

Sand, gravel

First breakline

Breakline

Fast break

Second breakline

Sediment buildup on bottom

A typical mesotrophic lake with heavily forested shoreline containing some rocky areas, dropoffs that taper gradually to deep water, and a certain amount of weed growth.

while cabbage weeds are often present in deeper water. The dropoff is usually a long, slow taper down to mid-depths. This is followed by a steep drop down to bottom. The floor of many lakes is often a build-up of sediment and decomposed materials.

Eutrophic (Old) Lakes

Let's take a speedy cross-country trip and look at a typical eutrophic lake. This one is in the South, but eutrophic lakes are found throughout the country. Location makes little difference in the aging process of a lake.

This Florida lake is shallow and weed-filled; the surrounding terrain is flat. Trees are often sparse along shore, and the water sits on a soft or mucky bottom. Thin reed beds may be found along the banks, and aquatic vegetation often grows from the lake floor to the surface.

Bass, pickerel, and some panfish are common. If the lake is really old and located in the North, it will support populations of carp or bullheads. If it's a southern lake, it will hold trash fish. Sediment has filled in spawning sites, and oxygen depletion has killed many species.

Such waters are usually rich in nutrients—either man-made or natural. Weed growth and algae, or "bloom," can cover much of the lake's surface and blot out most of the life-giving oxygen.

Early eutrophic lakes are capable of sustaining good fishing. Waters are often warm and contain weeds rooted to the bottom. This weed growth often extends from the shallows down to a depth of 18 or 20 feet. Eutrophic lakes are typified by shallow water and flat or semi-flat terrain. Lakeside hardwoods, such as oak and maple, are common in many sections of the country.

A deep eutrophic lake is capable of forming a thermocline, but as the lake continues to age and fills up with sediment, this fish-producing band of water ceases to exist.

EUTROPHIC LAKE

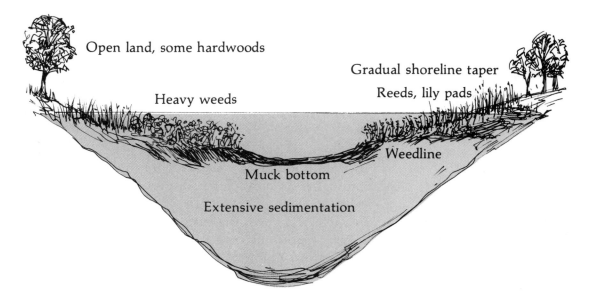

Open land, some hardwoods

Gradual shoreline taper

Heavy weeds

Reeds, lily pads

Weedline

Muck bottom

Extensive sedimentation

A shallow and weedy eutrophic lake. This type of lake is characterized by a soft and mucky bottom with thick aquatic vegetation and a reed-rimmed shoreline that tapers very gradually to deeper water.

Dropoffs, as stated before, are slow and gradual. Points are usually rounded and fairly shallow. Large flats are often covered with just a few feet of water. Most are muck-bottomed and devoid of fish life. Some lakes have sunken islands or above-water islands still rooted to bottom. These areas often produce fair-to-good fishing.

An angler should determine the type of lake he's fishing before he begins. The next step is to determine the types of structure present in the lake. For instance, does the lake have shallow or medium-depth weeds? These areas can be good early or late in the day, or after dark.

What do shallow-water flats offer? If some sand grass or weeds are available, they can be hotspots at night for largemouth bass or walleyes, although good fishing can be had during daylight hours in dark-colored water. Such areas are usually best during summer months.

At what depth are the deep weeds and the deep-water weedlines located? What type of weeds are present? These questions, when answered, will determine where you find fish on dark or sunny days. A bright day usually will attract largemouth bass, northern pike, or walleyes to the deep-water edge of weeds, often in 15 to 20 feet of water. They usually show little interest in lures, and many will be half-buried in weeds. Overcast skies or periods of darkness may spur these fish to visit the shallow-water edge of the weedbeds. A good movement will find fish moving up onto the flats, and into the shallows to feed.

Analyze whether the lake has a lip of clean bottom, and the length of this lip. This stretch can be any length and is a continuation of the gradual taper of the bottom contours. It extends normally from the deepest point of the weedline down to the first major breakline or dropoff into deep water. It's common for walleyes to travel and feed heavily along this lip if forage fish are present.

At what depth does the first major dropoff occur? This dropoff can show a bottom of muck, sand, gravel, rocks, boulders, or any combination of these materials. Gamefish often hold along this first dropoff if a thermocline is present. Such areas offer cooler water and abundant forage. The steepness of the breakline may determine the species of fish present, but don't count on it. I've seen walleyes and smallmouth bass using such a breakline. Then, ten casts later, I'll catch a cruising northern pike. (It doesn't take a big stick with a lot of knots in it to pound some sense into my head.) If you pick up one species of fish, and then catch another species that is uncommon to that particular stretch of water, it's just possible that a very good fish movement is under way. Stick with it and count your blessings.

Is there a secondary dropoff or breakline? If so, at what depth is it found? One spot where I take big walleyes often is along a secondary breakline. This location seems to attract the really large fish during hot summer months in mesotrophic lakes. Such dropoffs may have an inward or outward break, and gamefish are attracted to both. I've seen several cases where small schools of big walleyes will suspend just off the secondary breakline. These fish can be taken regularly by using a floating jig-head and worm or leech. A Lindy rig, or a Baitwalker with a long leader, works well here.

What is the bottom content? We've just learned that mucky bottoms are found on eutrophic lakes, combination bottoms on mesotrophic lakes, and hard, rocky bottoms on oligotrophic lakes. The character preferences of various gamefish will determine whether they are strict bottom dwellers or not. Most species will spend some time near the floor of a lake, but will more often associate themselves with some type of structure along breaklines. Finding fish on breaklines may be more difficult, but once found, they are usually easier to catch.

These simple keys should help you learn the potential of any given lake. Practice will enable you to spot character differences between lakes just by driving past them. It's not necessary to fish a body of water to recognize which of the three categories it fits into.

Shield Lakes

The border waters between the United States and midwestern Canada offer a different breed of natural lake. A "shield" lake is a fragile body of water located on or along the Canadian or Precambrian Shield, a band of rocky terrain stretching across northern North America. These waters are located in areas where nutrient-producing sediment or rock layers have eroded away in the lake basin and in nearby terrain. These lakes support coldwater gamefish such as smallmouth bass, lake trout, whitefish, walleyes, and some northern pike. Shield lakes are excellent fish habitats. Many are found in wilderness areas.

The Canadian Shield contains the rock formations common to shield lakes. This shield area encompasses most of Ontario, all of Quebec, parts of Manitoba and Saskatchewan, the eastern two-thirds of the Northwest Territories, all of Labrador, and small portions of northern Michigan, Wisconsin, Minnesota, and North Dakota. Lakes found within this region are wilderness gems—rough-cut diamonds amid a sea of spruce. Clean waters sparkle, and fishing is generally good.

There are two types of shield lakes: a large lake with little deep water over 40 feet, or a lake with much deeper water. The former is typically a walleye haven.

These shield lakes are usually oligotrophic waters. Shorelines are made up of boulders, ledgerock, gravel, and rubble. Sand is not common in this area, nor are muck-bottomed lakes or mucky land. If muck is located nearby, even within this particular shield area, it isn't a shield lake. The water qualities are soft, contain few minerals, and lakes are infertile and support little vegetation.

Shield lakes usually remain cool during the summer while other nearby oligotrophic lakes warm up. Cool water prevents the growth of algae, which in turn retards the minnow population in a lake, increasing the competition for food among adult gamefish in shallow water. When gamefish have to compete for food, they often tend to concentrate in certain areas of a lake.

Many shield lakes are rich in dissolved oxygen, which enables deep-water species such as whitefish or lake trout to live in the depths all summer. These gamefish can either suspend over deep water or hold on or near bottom.

Gamefish found within shield lakes are often easier to catch than the same species found in more southern waters. Northern waters are relatively infertile, and food competition is keen. Crayfish, small minnows, and insects are the basic forage material for smallmouth bass and walleyes in shield lakes. Lake trout often feed on cisco. Growth is slow among gamefish, and it may take a smallmouth bass eight years to reach a 15-inch length.

Walleyes and smallmouth bass often use fairly shallow water (6- to 8-foot depths) to travel from one area to another. They seldom travel far just to locate food, however. Shield-lake gamefish move very little for food-gathering purposes due to the shortage of available munchies. Good spots to look for these gamefish include boulder-covered bottom areas in water less than 20 feet deep (although shield smallies will hold in deeper water); any section of the lake that has a creek-fed cove or bay with several underwater structures nearby (like rock piles, boulders, gravel, islands, and lip areas); or submerged logs and boulders close to shore. Look for islands that are rimmed with boulders instead of ledgerock. Sunken islands are a good choice, as are long, broad points that extend out into the lake from an island.

Some structure locations in shield lakes are more important during one period than during others. Much depends on whether the angler is fishing during the prespawn, spawn, or postspawn period. Habitat preferences can differ from one gamefish to another. The locations listed above generally attract smallmouth bass, and to a lesser extent, walleyes, during all periods of open water.

Two years ago, I fished in Ontario's Rainy Lake for smallmouths. It was late in July, and clear skies had settled into the area for several days. The weather was mild—just right for a full day of fishing.

We tried several supposedly hot areas for smallies, but fishing seemed unseasonably poor. It took two full days before we found good concentrations of fish. One rocky face we discovered had a lip of submerged rocks, boulders, and rubble that jutted from shore out to the first dropoff, where the water fell out into 25-foot depths. We found our fish here.

Several large boulders were visible in 8 feet of water near the edge of the lip, where the water increased its depth before falling over the dropoff. I was casting from the stern, my wife Kay from the bow. We slanted casts on either side of the boulder. I allowed my Little George to sink and brought it back to the boat. As the lure fluttered past the dark side of the boulder I felt a wrenching strike. The hook was set, and a good-size smallie scrambled into the air. Kay's Jig-a-Do streamer produced similar results. We waltzed around the boat, passed rods over each other's heads, and finally subdued the pair. These fish came to the boat red-eyed and still fighting. They weighed about 3 pounds each.

We would fish that rock-studded lip for an hour, move away for another hour and backtroll for walleyes near an inflowing stream, and then head back for a return bout with bronzebacks. Each time we fished that lip we scored well on smallmouths. But one small area like that can't withstand constant fishing pressure. We had learned how to catch those shield-lake smallmouths. Further exploration produced several other hot areas.

Impoundments Are Fertile Fish Factories

An impounded body of water can be divided into six major types: lowland, flatland, hill-land, highland, canyon, and plateau (depending on the nature of surrounding environment). Each has one common denominator: all are dammed at the lower end of a stream, river, or connecting waterway. The waters back up, flood the old stream channel, overflow into surrounding countryside, and create a fertile body of water with fast fish growth and good forage possibilities.

It's entirely possible for an angler to learn the characteristics of one impoundment, travel a short distance, and discover a new, different type of water. Bottom configurations differ, species of fish may differ, and fishing techniques can vary widely. An angler who is a "one-method fisherman" will pull his hair, rant and rave, and go fishless when trying new waters. Impoundments can be so different that methods that work in one place may be totally useless in another area.

47

To be successful, an angler must understand the differences among the six basic types of impoundments. Surrounding terrain gives the first clue to impoundment type. If flatland surrounds the impoundment, then it's probably a "flatland" impoundment. If mountain ranges tower overhead and the impoundment is in a canyon, it's a canyon-type impoundment. The other classifications are almost as easy to categorize. Shape of the impoundment, and surrounding countryside, are the keys to easy identification.

Impoundments, regardless of type, can be deep, semi-deep, or shallow bodies of water. The depths of hill-land impoundments can fluctuate greatly.

The majority of impoundments discussed in this chapter will be fairly large bodies of water with at least 1000 surface acres at pool stage. Many waters of this size already exist, and more are being built yearly. Large areas such as this enable forage fish to reproduce. This, in turn, allows gamefish to grow fat and sassy on abundant feed. Most impoundments are fertile fish factories during the first ten years of life. Thereafter they maintain a steady level of fish productivity, although at a pace somewhat slower than during the formative years. Let's take an in-depth look at characteristics that prevail in the six types of impoundments.

Hill-Land Impoundments

This type of impoundment is very widespread. It's also one of the toughest to read. My experiences with hill-land impoundments date back to 1968, when I first fished Lake Sam Rayburn in Texas. Then, and through the early 1970s, Lake Sam was hot. Limit catches of bass were common. Big fish didn't appear until the early '70s, when I fished it again and caught 6- to 8-pound fish instead of schoolies. This lake contains diverse types of structure. It offers bassin' water ranging from skinny, weed-filled shallows to depths of 60 feet or more. Some hill-land impoundments can be more than 150 feet deep. Depths are determined by surrounding terrain.

Lake Sam Rayburn has weedbeds, submerged and emergent timber, humps, flats, sharp breaklines, a river channel with numerous feeder

Impoundments offer a wide variety of shoreline and underwater structure.

streams, old roads, points, cemeteries, coves, and other structure elements. A hill-land impoundment normally has all these features, although some may possess only a few.

The upper end of the lake is usually shallow, with a flat bottom contour. The lower portion of the impoundment is deeper, and possesses a sharper shoreline.

River channels are normally located somewhere in the center portion of the lake. The old riverbed is straight. The edges of river channels usually have steep sides that provide good cover and dark areas for resting fish.

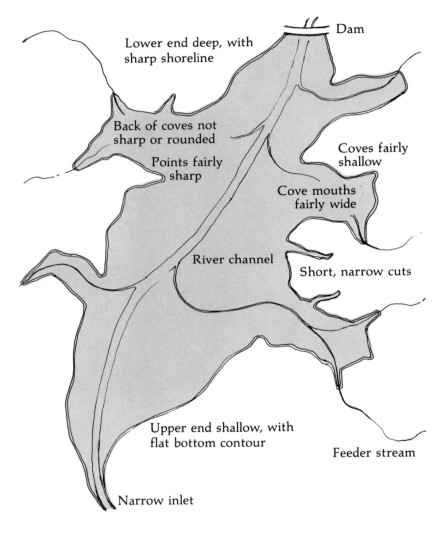

HILL-LAND IMPOUNDMENT

Points are favorite locations for anglers. Hill-land impoundments have rounded points that can be quite steep in mid-depth or in deep parts of lake. Even shallow hill-land lakes have rounded points, although I've had little success taking fish from these areas, except in deep water nearby.

Coves located in the upper portion of a hill-land impoundment are usually moderately deep, while coves in the downstream portion are generally deeper. Dropoffs are more rapid in this lake-type than in a flatland reservoir. The water usually drops off rapidly from shore into about 10 or 12 feet of water before the depth-decline tapers off. In other words, look for water that drops off fast, and then levels out to a fairly smooth lake floor.

Hill-land impoundments are generally weedy lakes, especially in southern regions. Heavy weed growth provides abundant cover for forage fish and hiding places for bigger species. It also helps cool the water in hot-weather months. I've taken any number of "school bass" from beneath floating weed mats on Toledo Bend and Lake Sam Rayburn during the summer. Southern impoundments usually feature stick-ups—cypress or pin-oak trees that emerge through the surface. Root sections or submerged branches are good spots to fish.

The one factor indicative of hill-land reservoirs is lots of structure. An angler may be fishing the old river channel for bass during a cold front or he might fish shallow covers during the prespawn or spawning period. Submerged timber provides attractive cover for gamefish, as does an abundance of other structure types.

Flatland Impoundments

Flatland impoundments are fairly common in the eastern two-thirds of the nation. These reservoirs are often surrounded by farmlands. They are usually shallow, and 25-foot depths are average.

Such impoundments are primarily water-flooded farmland. Long flats are common, but steep dropoffs and underwater humps are unusual. Small islands can exist in these lakes, although some islands are more like medium-height hills or humps that rise from the middle of the lake.

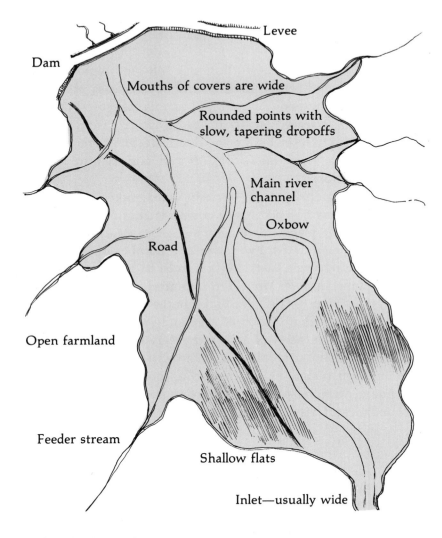

Levee

Dam

Mouths of covers are wide

Rounded points with
slow, tapering dropoffs

Main river
channel

Oxbow

Road

Open farmland

Feeder stream

Shallow flats

Inlet—usually wide

FLATLAND IMPOUNDMENT

Flood control was a major concern of the builders of flatland impoundments. Levees and dikes were common long before the lake filled, and these areas, along with the river and its feeder streams or oxbows, form the largest percentage of structure in any flatland reservoir.

River channels can be straight or crooked. Some channel straightening is evident in many reservoirs. Ditches once used for rainwater runoff are common. If these connect with an old riverbed, an angler can often enjoy some great action.

Oxbows are relatively new channels cut by a meandering current, or by a flooding river. These locations are often found in otherwise flat ground. They can deliver a spectacular brand of action. Gamefish that spread out after the reservoir reaches pool stage can often find sanctuary in deep cuts in an oxbow. Good vegetation is usually found near oxbows, or the levees directly above them. A dike that parallels the oxbow can represent a breakline for fish migrating into the shallows to feed. Many levees were planted with shrubs to hold the soil in place long before the lake was filled. Willows are common in many areas. The deep-water edge of these shrubs represents good fish cover in a flatland reservoir.

The points on flatland reservoirs are usually rounded, and can extend a good distance out into the lake. Some points are brush-covered but contain few trees. Many such points are fairly shallow in nature and provide good fishing only if located near the old river channel, a dike or levee, or an oxbow with slightly deeper water and some structure cover nearby.

Flatland impoundments have shallow coves. Some coves have small streams flowing into them. Weedbeds are quite common. The cove configuration depends on what the land looked like before it was covered with water. Coves with feeder streams can be hotspots for fishing provided that the angler can locate structure leading from the deeper creek channel to the main riverbed or up onto other structure.

One type of structure common in many flatland reservoirs is an old road or causeway used by the state or landowners before flooding. Most roadways were slightly elevated, with a ditch on either side. Trees often lined these highways. The ditch, brush, and trees along old roads are excellent fish producers.

Causeways were built across flatland impoundments to carry the load of vehicular or railroad traffic. Surrounding water near a causeway is usually shallow except in that portion where the old river channel passes beneath the bridge. Concrete bridge or causeway abutments located near deep water often attract lots of fish.

Other good structure on flatland lakes includes old buildings, basements where farmhouses were razed, small ponds that once were connected to the river, and riprap. The latter is often made out of concrete chunks, placed years ago to help contain high waters during river flooding periods. Gamefish often feed near riprap. It is overlooked by some lake fishermen.

Lowland Impoundments

It's a common misconception among anglers that lowland impoundments are found only in the South. Some of the top Wisconsin muskie waters, known locally as flowages, are really lowland impoundments. Many lowland reservoirs are found in the South, but they are also common in the Midwest. Some fishermen have just never learned how to categorize these waters properly.

A lowland reservoir receives its name from the surrounding countryside. Such impoundments are located adjacent to low, swampy terrain. In Michigan or Wisconsin, it might be a tamarack swamp dammed to supply electricity through a local power company. Bond Falls Flowage, in northwestern Upper Michigan, is a classic example. The lake contains northern pike, muskellunge, walleyes, smallmouth bass, and other species. A drawdown of the lake's surface during periods of high energy use or little rain can reveal huge quicksand or marl beds. I sank to my neck ten years ago in a quicksand bed at Bond Falls. But that's another story.

A southern lowland impoundment is often nothing more than a dammed swamp that allows water to spread over a large area. Many

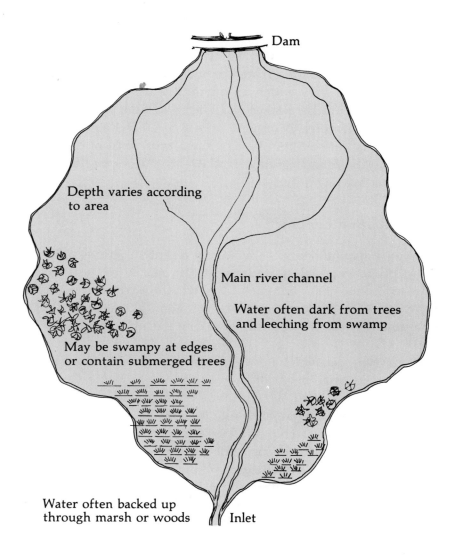

Dam

Depth varies according
to area

Main river channel

Water often dark from trees
and leeching from swamp

May be swampy at edges
or contain submerged trees

Water often backed up
through marsh or woods   Inlet

LOWLAND IMPOUNDMENT

lowland reservoirs are shallow and filled with trees. They can be half-submerged tamarack, or cypress, depending upon the area. Fish inhabit the timbered edges, the old river channel (if present), or small tributary feeders that drain a marsh or swamp.

Lowland waters vary widely in depth. I've fished some 25- to 50-foot depths on northern lakes and longed to find 10-foot depths on some southern reservoirs. A dropoff from 8 to 10 feet can provide needed sanctuary for southern bass, while a muskie from northern Wisconsin may be found moving from 25- to 10-foot depths during a shoreward feeding migration.

Canyon Impoundments

Canyon impoundments are relatively recent structures built for a variety of purposes. Anglers are interested primarily in the ability of a reservoir to produce fish, but such lakes were not constructed solely for fishing. Many were built to provide an economical source of electricity or to harness the runaway powers of raging streams during spring floods.

Canyon-type reservoirs are the deepest impoundments. They often provide the majestic scenery common to the West, where most canyon impoundments are located. Most canyon lakes provide a two-story fishery, with warmwater gamefish like bass in the surface waters, and trout in the lower levels. This type of lake appeals to many fishermen because of its stark, rocky beauty and good fishing. Good forage is available, and rapid fish growth is common.

These lakes are always stopped up by huge concrete dams that are usually located in narrow gorges. Towering walls and steep dropoffs are common. Such lakes contain very little vegetation except in some shallow coves. Most have clear water and good visibility, an asset for both angler and fish.

Deep water is common to canyon lakes. It's not uncommon to find 100-foot dropoffs near shore, and depths of 500 feet or more. Much of this water isn't fully utilized by gamefish, although I have met anglers

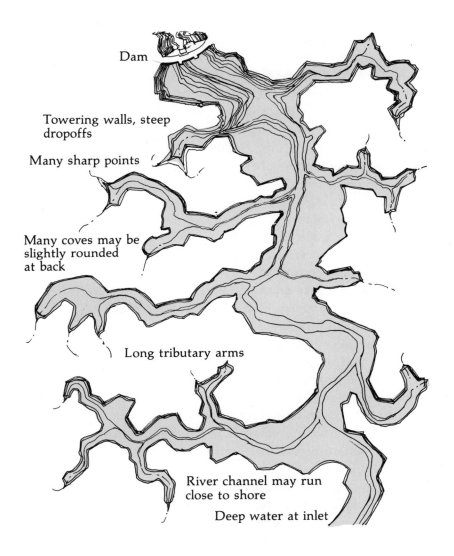

Dam

Towering walls, steep dropoffs

Many sharp points

Many coves may be slightly rounded at back

Long tributary arms

River channel may run close to shore

Deep water at inlet

CANYON IMPOUNDMENT

who say they have caught trout and bass at 100-foot depths. Straining water this deep for gamefish can be trying. Fortunately, anglers can usually find better action in much shallower water.

Canyon lakes are often found in some of the most spectacular scenic areas in North America. Lake Powell in Arizona and Utah is stark, but its rugged beauty belies the fact that fantastic fishing can be had amid its sheer rock walls and deep side canyons. My first trip to that area six years ago was mind-boggling; my partner and I nailed trout one day and bass the next. I count the experience of fishing such a canyon reservoir as one of life's great pleasures.

The shoreline of most canyon reservoirs is comprised of steep cliffs, some over 1000 feet high. Overhanging ledges can block the sun and provide cool, shaded places to fish. Such areas can also attract gamefish trying to avoid direct sun rays. Broken rock faces that tumble down steep cliffs can form an erratic shoreline of boulders, rock slides, and ledges. Boulders that bounce off rock walls and crash into the water can form breaklines or breaks on structure leading from deep to shallow-water feeding zones. Fish use such areas regularly.

Upper portions of a canyon reservoir may be less steep along the shoreline. Some lakes have mesas formed by a tapering rock wall face that is smooth and rounded—a steady attraction for trout.

Canyon reservoirs are often narrow. Some are more than 100 miles long and contain many long, narrow coves. Numerous turns, bends, and arms feed into the main lake. Tributary streams often enter these feeder arms and some may have several creeks draining into the lake. Most coves are narrow and pointed, although a few may be flat.

Vegetation is sparse in most canyon impoundments. Weeds can't grow, although sagebrush may be found in these lakes for a year or two after reaching pool stage. Cottonwood or mountain cedars are fairly common in the extreme ends of coves. There is little out-of-water structure or vegetation to block sunlight, except for the sheer rock cliffs. The water is often clear, with good visibility down to 50 feet.

An angler tasting the pleasures of a canyon-type lake can be awed by the beauty but overwhelmed by where he should fish. It all looks good. Structure other than riverbeds, feeder channels, broken rock formation, and sheer rock cliffs are seldom present. One of the secrets to fishing this type of water is to locate areas *out of the sun.* I've taken bass and trout from tiny crevices between great boulders. Some fish have been caught by jigging along steep rock faces that fall into 100 feet of water. A jumble of fallen rock that would be called riprap in other reservoirs often provides top fishing. Shadowed areas in early morning or late afternoon can produce fast action, provided that the angler is in the right place at the right time. Many hotspot areas on a lake can be 10 or 15 miles up or down the canyon. Running time cuts down on fishing time and success. Plan your most productive fishing hours to coincide with your arrival in a good fish-producing location.

Many western anglers have this shadow business down pat. They fish the eastern portion of canyon walls in the morning, the western portion in the afternoon, and take it easy during midday. What a life!

Plateau Impoundments

Plateau impoundments are usually found in midwestern North America, but can be located right up to the fringes of the Rocky Mountains. Irrigation of farm crops was the major reason for building most of these lakes. Such reservoirs receive a large volume of water daily. Much of it is backed up by dams and released. The water levels of large reservoirs can go up and down. This affects gamefish.

Plateau reservoirs are large. Depths can range from 50 to 200 feet. The surrounding terrain is basically flat. All waters seem to drain naturally from the up-lake areas down to the dam. Spring runoff can create heavy siltation in many areas; sediment settles to bottom and ruins previously good areas.

The plateau basin maintains a steady gradient from headwaters down to the dam. Sharp dropoffs, and rapid underwater structure changes, are uncommon. The river channel is usually straight, and follows the center of the reservoir. Riverbeds are normally flat, although the tops of the channel edges are distinctly rounded. Vegetation is sparse, and generally limited to small trees and some brush left behind by rising waters. A drawdown of these lakes often reveals some brush near creek channels. Such areas can be productive.

Coves are flat and wide-mouthed where they enter the main lake.

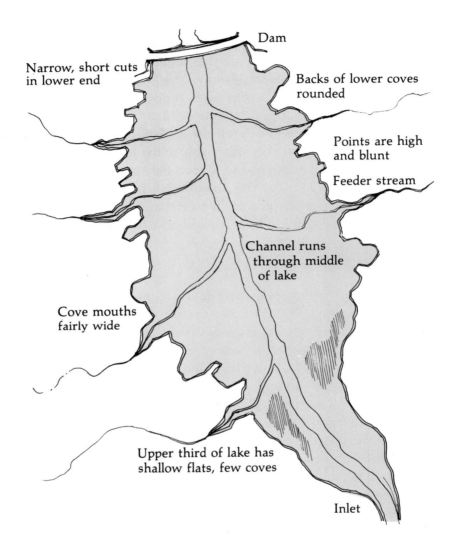

Dam

Narrow, short cuts
in lower end

Backs of lower coves
rounded

Points are high
and blunt

Feeder stream

Channel runs
through middle
of lake

Cove mouths
fairly wide

Upper third of lake has
shallow flats, few coves

Inlet

PLATEAU IMPOUNDMENT

Some coves will contain one or more feeder streams. Anglers can learn to read these coves by the shoreline. A steep-edged cove normally contains some deep water, while a flat-sided cove is normally flat on the bottom and relatively shallow. Both can be good spots to fish, depending on the season and the species of gamefish involved.

Erosion is fairly common in plateau reservoirs. The forces of water eroding down a sloping bank can provide shallow grooves near shore that can offer good fishing early in the season. These grooves often extend down into deep water because most of the erosion occurs when the lake is at low pool. Once the lake fills again these grooves will hold fish. Above-water terrain will often show signs of erosion, and will indicate that such structure is found underwater.

Moderately steep banks are found along the shorelines of some plateau impoundments. Such areas can produce good fishing occasionally and are worth exploring. They can be spotted by steep-sided hills falling away to the shoreline of the lake.

Highland Impoundments

Highland reservoirs are common in the eastern sector of this continent. A few examples of such areas would include Dale Hollow or Percy Priest reservoirs in Tennessee, Lake Ouachita in Arkansas, Lake Sidney Lanier in Georgia, and Table Rock on the Missouri-Arkansas border. All are lakes I've fished several times.

These lakes are the result of a foothill stream being dammed up. Such low-mountain areas are common in Kentucky, Tennessee, Georgia, South Carolina, Arkansas, Missouri, and California. Impoundments such as these are found in the foothills of southeastern mountain ranges and are characterized by steep banks, clear water, and many rocky outcroppings. Dale Hollow Reservoir on the Tennessee-Kentucky border is a typical highland impoundment.

The underwater structure typical in such lakes includes sharp dropoffs and sloping shoreline banks covered with timber. I once combined a late-fall fishing trip and squirrel hunt along oak ridges adjoining Dale Hollow. The fishing was superb and so was the squirrel hunting.

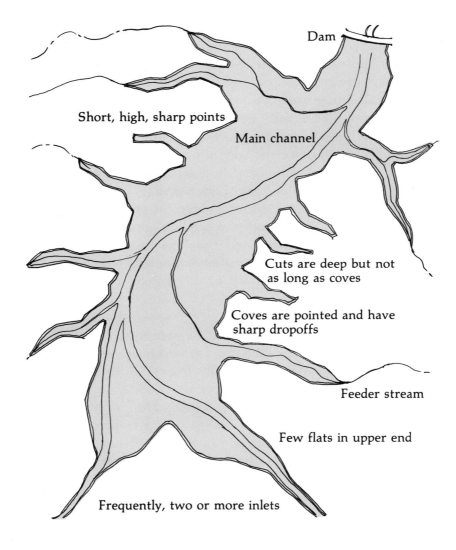

Dam

Short, high, sharp points

Main channel

Cuts are deep but not
as long as coves

Coves are pointed and have
sharp dropoffs

Feeder stream

Few flats in upper end

Frequently, two or more inlets

HIGHLAND IMPOUNDMENT

Highland reservoirs are often "two-story" lakes with trout in the cool depths and striped bass, smallmouth bass, largemouth bass, and muskies or walleyes in slightly warmer waters. These lakes are picturesque, although not in the rugged manner of a canyon impoundment. Most highland lakes have several marinas along their shores but little other habitation. Most mountain people were removed (some, unfortunately, by force) when the Tennessee Valley Authority began their systematic construction of dams.

Steep, rocky points are common on highland lakes. They often taper well out into the lake, with sharp dropoffs near the tip. Many coves are long and pointed. Many have one or more streams flowing into the main lake. Steep-sided walls can be found in the inlet areas, although some lakes have sharp cliffs (mostly wooded) that fall away into the water where rocks and small boulders provide cover for gamefish. Rocky ledges are common near shore. Stair-stepping ledges often drop-off within casting distance of the beach.

Mossy or weedy areas are not common, except in the back portions of some coves. Many narrow coves will open-up on the back side. Deep water near shore is common, except in those spots where shoreline areas are flat and trees are able to grow. Such locations often have weed masses that attract largemouth bass and other species. Flooded brushpiles are common in more hilly terrain.

Good spots to try during hot weather are deep channels that run from feeder arms out into the main lake. Such areas, especially near long points or around islands, are home to both species of bass as well as muskies and walleyes.

Impounded waters aren't new. But few lake fishermen realize that impoundments can be very different, both above and below water. Structures are different. Gamefish react differently in some impoundments than in others (although all still have the same needs and preferences).

Techniques that work in one type of impoundment will probably work in another, provided that the angler realizes the differences in structure, where fish hold and feed, and why they do so. Everything in lake fishing is related to structure. Learn the structure differences in each lake, and you'll be on the road to becoming a fishing star.

CHAPTER

Strip-Mine Pits Hold Fish

My first peek at a strip-mine pit was a disappointment. The surrounding earth looked like it had suffered the wrath of God. The ground was tortured beyond belief, huge spoil banks littered the terrain, and the water looked as appetizing as an open sewer. But first impressions are not always correct, as time later proved.

My host was apparently reading my mind. "I'll grant you it's not long on looks right now, but come back in two or three years and you'll not recognize this pit. We'll have cover crops planted nearby, trees lining the lake, and the fishing should be superb." He might be right, but then I felt sick to my stomach at the rape of some fine terrain. I figured my obligation included taking a few casts; perhaps it would soothe my soul. Anything was better than looking at what I felt to be a tragic, man-made mess.

I snapped on a surface darter and tossed it near a few cattails that had somehow gained a foothold in the slightly acidic water. Force of habit made me jerk the rod tip to add life to the lure. One jerk, a slight pause, and I was just cranking up to jerk again when the water erupted and a largemouth bass jerked back. It reminded me of the old saw defining a fisherman—a jerk on one end of the rod waiting for a jerk on the other end. As the fish jumped the second time I was beginning to feel like a fool. Like many fishermen, I had tossed bones of hatred toward all strip-mine companies. I started to change my mind as I played that 3-pound bass. I lipped him from the water, critically examined him for any obvious malformities, found none, and released him unharmed.

Ten consecutive casts produced six strikes and four hooked and landed bass—all largemouths. "We've got another strip pit nearby that delivers better action than this. It has bluegills, bass, and catfish," my host told me. This I had to see, purely in the interest of science, mind you.

I saw, I fished, and came away a believer in the reclamation of strip-mine lands. It's been hard to convince outdoorsmen that strip pits offer superb fishing. Since that first trip to southern Illinois I've fished strip pits in Ohio, Indiana, Missouri, and other states. The reclaimed lands are eye-appealing, and the lakes are generally full of fish.

The key to fishing strip pits is to first gain some insight into how the coal was removed. Many different techniques have been used for coal removal. Most pits had one, two, or a series of several tote roads winding along the bottom and then up along the edges every 10 or 15 feet. These roads, once submerged, offer attractive structure for gamefish. The stair-stepping ledges are vertical-sided, with abrupt dropoffs. Enough rubble is left behind by mining operations to litter the floor of the pit and the tote roads with lots of break-type structure. Fish prefer using the roads, rubble, and vertical cliffs as they migrate from deep-water sanctuaries to shallow feeding areas.

Most strip pits have a fast-breaking shoreline with several points or fingers that jut out into the water. These points taper off fast, drop quickly into deep water, and provide avenues of travel for migrating

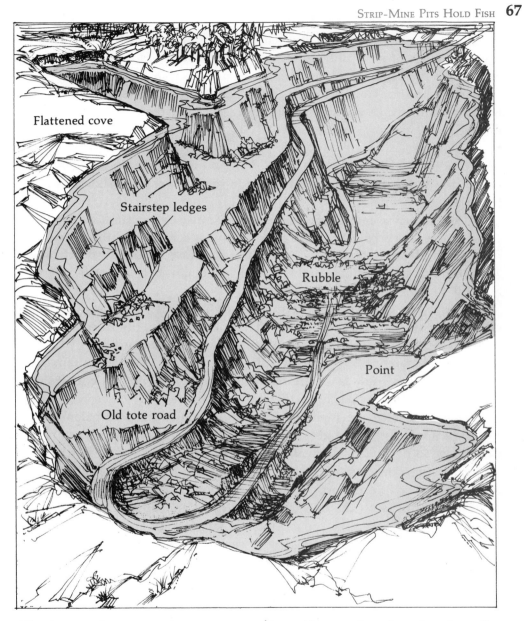

Flattened cove

Stairstep ledges

Rubble

Point

Old tote road

This drawing shows a typical strip-mine pit with an old tote road winding along the walls. The walls are steep and cut by ledges. Many pits have coves at one end. Early or late in the season, fish are usually found around points, ledges or the lip of the tote road. In warm weather they hug bottom.

gamefish. The bottom is usually marked by humps and deep ridges.

The walls of strip pits are steep. A ridge usually is found 6 to 10 feet above the high-water mark. Such visual clues show rapidly decreasing bottom contours near shore. Brush often litters the banks. Many reclaimed pits are surrounded by vegetation that prevents erosion during heavy rains.

Most strip lakes are devoid of cover. The only cover for fish is deep water, and many pits are more than 100 feet deep. Sometimes brush or a wind-toppled tree can provide some cover in shallow water, but don't bet on it.

Clear water is another problem anglers must overcome. I've fished some pits where a coin dropped overboard could be seen falling for 20 feet. The waters of reclaimed pits are usually close to a neutral pH of 7.0, although some remain slightly acidic. This gin-clear water is difficult to fish.

A strip pit, when reclaimed and filled with water, is constantly checked by state or federal officials. These pits are usually filled by natural seepages—from runoff water from high ground or from rainwater. A newly filled pit is usually highly acidic from acid drainage or buildup. These new lakes are referred to as being "hot," a condition that prohibits any fishing until they've been treated.

Many hot lakes are treated with lime to reduce the acid balance toward a neutral pH. A highly acidic lake may require several treatments to neutralize the waters, but this is done as just one step in the reclamation process. Peabody Coal Company has been a leader in the field of strip-pit and strip-land reclamation. I've fished some of their pits, hunted ducks on the lakes, and shot quail and doves along Peabody lands. Every case proved to me that after an area has been mined for coal, it can be restored with scenic fishing lakes and superb upland cover. Mining and outdoor sports can co-exist, to everyone's benefit.

Few strip pits are fed by any stream. In fact, laws exist that prevent mining operations from using lands located near streams or natural lakes. These pit lakes are often infertile, and little vegetation grows in the water. Cattails often take hold near shore, but shallow or deep-water weeds are uncommon.

When some strip-pit lakes were formed, trees were submerged when the water table rose. A group of trees left standing in a lake can often offer thrilling sport. I fished one strip pit in southern Illinois where a tree emerged from the lake. It was small, but the lower branches and submerged roots provided cover for largemouth bass. I've fished that tree several times, and have taken bass from the area on every occasion. The bass work up from the depths, encounter a breakline formed by an old tote road, cross that, and then go to the tree's roots and lower branches. They form the cover the bass need to move into shallow feeding areas. Learn to look for such areas in all strip pits.

The bottom composition of most pits is of coal chunks, sand, shale, rubble, clay, or a combination of such material. Inshore areas may be hard-bottomed, or the bottom can be a soft, oozy muck. The latter is fairly common in some pits, and presents tricky wading. Many companies with fishing access on strip pits advise anglers to use a boat or to fish from shore. Wading is not advised because of the soft bottom and steep dropoffs.

Fishing strip pits calls for patience, a knowledge of the water and its structure, light line and small lures. Fishermen who score consistently seldom use mono heavier than 6-pound test. When the water is as clear as alcohol, lighter line is needed.

An outdoorsman who lives in the vicinity of a working strip pit has the edge on other anglers. He can study tote roads, vertical cliffs, and spot fish-holding structure as they are formed. Local newspapers often publicize the filling of a new pit. Two good bass fishermen that I know head for a pit just before it fills with water, and take photos. These photos are of little value until the lake is fully formed, the water has been tested, and fish plants made. The old photos are taken out of storage and studied at great length. It may often be four or five years between mining and filling, but these old-timers bide their time and wait. Other locals have decided that these fishermen use a secret lure, or spit on their hooks. They don't realize that these two fishermen have learned the structure of a lake and have mapped their strategy years in advance.

The banks of some strip-mine lakes in southern Illinois are so heavily wooded that the lake, at first glance, resembles a typical natural lake. Shaded coves are found around every point. Bass and other gamefish feed with abandon in the dark, cool waters. One pit I'd fished there had been mined originally by Peabody Coal Company. A good ramp allowed easy utilization of the lake. We pushed off and spread out, two men each in three boats. Our objective was to fish various portions of the lake and report our success, or lack of it, during dinner.

We rowed slowly down the lake. I pegged cast after cast into deep water off sharp, tapering points. Thirty minutes passed without a hookup. Then my companion suggested that we fish the shaded shoreline on the far side. "Bass in this lake feed actively, even in bright sunlight. But they feed in shadowed water. Let's try a favorite spot of mine," he said.

His lunker hole would have pleased anyone. It had overhanging trees to shade the water. The shoreline dropped off in a series of sharp breaklines ranging from 3 to 10 feet. Another breakline occurred at 18 feet, and still another at 30 feet. A wind-blown tree lay half-submerged near shore with its crown resting on the second breakline. "Plenty of jumbo bass have been taken by fishing in those branches. Here, try this plastic worm rig." He handed over a purple 5-inch plastic worm with a ¼-ounce tunnel sinker. "Cast near shore, lift it off the branches, and feed slack line so it will tumble down the breakline among the branches," he told me. I noticed his rig was out and he planned to fish one side while I fished the other. Teamwork, I guess, was the rule in this location.

Bill had a fish gobble his first cast like a black bear devouring the nearest berry patch. That bass slammed the plastic worm, thrashed mightily underwater, and smashed up through the surface like it was learning to fly. He leaned on the fish as hard as his 6-pound mono would take and turned the fish out into deep water. His sly grin as much as said, "I told you so."

Meanwhile, my worm had tumbled from the first breakline down to the second. I was freespooling line when it switched sideways, and began moving off at a rapid pace. I locked the reel up, took up all the slack, and belted the hook home. Only one thing makes a sinking plastic worm go down faster, or move to one side, and that's a bundle of dynamite called a largemouth bass. My fish slammed to the top, turned one mouth-open cartwheel, and smashed down in the tree limbs near shore. I fretted about my light line, but the bass headed back the way it came and cleared the cobweb-thin mono on his next jump.

Bill was just netting his 4-pounder when I settled down to a rough-and-tumble struggle in deep water. The fish tried to sound as it tired, but the limber rod enabled me to keep his head turned toward the surface. After some water splashing, and a feeble belly roll, I had a 5-pound bass. Bill was chuckling as I admired my fish. "Some kind of hotdog fisherman you are to get turned on over a strip-pit bass," he muttered. He obviously enjoyed ribbing anglers who had once opposed fishing in such waters. What he didn't know was that I'd been converted like a born-again Baptist to strip-pit fishing years before. My silly grin is the same one I always wear when I boat a nice bass.

We met at lunch to discuss fishing with the other members of the party. One boat had found some fish suspended over deep water, a common occurrence in strip lakes. Bob Smith, a frequent partner of mine on fish-finding trips, told me that bass were holding *near* the vertical walls. "At first, I thought my sonar blips were rubble or large rocks sticking out from the vertical faces of the pit. We tried fishing the first breakline at 12 feet and bombed out. It was a lucky catch that revealed the secret of our success. I had sifted the water along the tote road at 12 feet without a strike and was convinced that the bass must be holding at the next breakline located 24 feet down. The sun was high overhead and reason told me the fish may be deep. My next cast landed on the top tote road and I crawled it to the edge and freespooled it down to the next level. A bass intercepted it on the way down, and a new pattern was born. We hit fish all morning once we learned that trick," he told me, his grin so wide it looked like his throat had been cut. He had ample reason for smiling; he caught four largemouths weighing more than 4 pounds each.

During hot summer months with intense sunlight, fishermen should use deep-water fishing methods. Fish will often hold in 18 to 25 feet of water during the day, and move onto shallower structure only after dark or during low-light levels. On a cloudy day, some straggler fish may be in the shallows, but chances of success increase if you fish the dark side of the lake or along the first breakline. Try a point that works down to the first breakline, with additional contour breaks found between the first and second breaks. Plastic-worm rigs, jig-eel combinations, deep-diving plugs, or leadhead jigs are top choices for fishing this water. An Ugly Bug Plus, a nasty-looking critter at best, has scored well for me on largemouth bass and some big bluegills. I would toss it out, allow it to sink to bottom with a fluttering spinner, and hippity-hop it back up the vertical underwater cliff. I would catch a fish every other cast.

One aspect of strip-pit fishing I haven't explored is night fishing. I'm a firm believer in after-dark fishing and several such methods were discussed in my book, *How to Catch Trophy Freshwater Gamefish.* I've just never had the opportunity to fish strip-pit lakes in the late evening. I have talked with several anglers who have made a practice of doing so. These guys take fish as regularly as an Alaskan brown bear scooping salmon from a stream.

They tell me that trophy bass usually make a shoreward migration from 10 P.M. to midnight. The men scull their canoes silently, and try to stay a long cast away from shore. One man uses a 5½-inch Rapala; the other uses a 5½-inch jointed Rebel. Both claim that size and color aren't important; what is deadly is the way they manipulate their lures. Each maintains that surface disturbance allows after-dark bass to home-in on anything in trouble, in this case the minnow-imitating lure. The arm movements they showed me reminded me of a bowler trying to will that tenth pin over. Upward rod-tip lifts, short jerks to either side, and sporadic short bursts of speed might describe their action-producing lure movements. Keep the lure moving, and make as much commotion as possible with it. A shallow-water bass will hear the noise, follow, and strike. Many strikes occur either as the lure plops down or just before it's lifted from the water.

One thing that amused me about these nighttime tactics is that both men have tipped canoes over while applying body English to their lures. They say that the tipovers occurred after a series of short strikes had disrupted their concentration. I guess so. . . .

Dan Gapen, a Minnesota lure manufacturer, says that his Baitwalker rig does wonders when trolled or backtrolled slowly along vertical cliffs. He baits the trailing hook with a leech or nightcrawler and motors slowly. Wind-drifting often works in certain deep areas. He releases line until he feels the rig make contact with the first ledge. He'll then work out into slightly deeper water, release more line, and allow it to fall midway down the second dropoff. "Many strikes occur either along the old submerged roads or as it drops off the ledge. Some fish pick up the bait as the wind pushes me down the lake. The Baitwalker should be making periodic contact with the face of the wall. Many times, this technique will clean up on suspended fish," he said.

I have a theory about strip-pit lakes that I haven't had time to test with enough documented on-the-water research. After most cold fronts, largemouth bass (and most other species) will hold deep in a sanctuary, especially after a storm. This is typical behavior in most cases, but I firmly believe that there are exceptions to this rule. I think that a driving rainstorm *may* wash worms and nightcrawlers into a strip-pit lake. As running water builds on spoil banks and begins heading for the lake, any earthworms caught in the runoff are washed into shallow water near shore.

I base this theory on one fact. Several years ago I fished a strip-pit lake in Missouri. A storm passed through, accompanied by heavy rains, and two hours later I saw largemouth bass feeding in shallow water. I *didn't* see the worms but couldn't imagine any other reason for the fish to be shallow at that particular time. Food had to be the reason.

Strip-pit anglers may be missing a good bet by not fishing live or plastic worms in shallow waters immediately after a front passes through. If cloudy skies prevail during this time, shallow-water fishing could be excellent. Give it a try.

The Great Lakes

There is something awe inspiring about the Great Lakes. These huge inland seas rank among the largest lakes in the world. Take one look across a barren stretch of any one of these lakes, and a feeling of insignificance sweeps over you. All of these great waters share one thing in common—they are home to many species of fish.

Lakes Superior, Michigan, Huron, Erie, and Ontario are coming back. I can remember how barren these lakes once were. Gamefish had long suffered at the hands of indiscriminate gill-netters, the ravages of sea lampreys, and the man-made horrors of industrial and urban pollution. Just fifteen years ago Lake Michigan was considered barren of most gamefish. Since then, however, stockings of salmon, lake trout, rainbows, and brown trout have brought this and the other lakes back from the brink of disaster. They now represent some of the most highly productive fishing waters in North America.

75

A study of the five Great Lakes is best represented by a composite overview of all waters. These lakes often border industrial centers and large cities, but each has wild, rocky stretches where few anglers fish. All have been polluted at one time or another. Each lake has fought its individual battles with DDT, PCB, PBB, Mercury, Mirex, and/or a host of other chemicals. Oil spills, inadvertent dumping of waste chemicals, and other deliberate pollution discharges have wreaked havoc on the water and gamefish. It's been only during the last few years that some species have recovered.

Many gamefish found in these lakes are migratory. They are often anadramous—species that are born in a stream, move downstream to the big water, spend varying lengths of time in the lake, and then return to spawn in the running water of streams or rivers. This trait is common to steelhead, brown trout, some lake trout, some brook trout, and coho or chinook salmon. Other species that inhabit the lakes include lake sturgeon, yellow perch, whitefish, chubs, northern pike, walleyes, muskellunge, smallmouth bass, largemouth bass, sauger, and some panfish species.

Most of the fishing that takes place on the Great Lakes is *usually* done within 15 miles of shore, and more often within 2 miles of the beach. Most gamefish in these inland seas are available only during certain periods. Coho salmon and chinook salmon have the most dependable habits, but even they can suddenly disappear without notice.

This sudden appearance or disappearence is a trait typical of most Great Lakes species. One area I fish in southern Lake Michigan attracts thousands of jumbo yellow perch during July. Try to find them any other time, and you might as well be looking for a No. 20 dry-fly hook in a box containing a million No. 4's. The fish are there when they are there; where they then go is a mystery. The trick is to catch them when they're available and concentrate on other species at other times.

The coho and chinook salmon migrations have been well documented in Lake Michigan, but not in the other lakes. These gamefish are available after spring ice-out in the southern portion of the lake. Then they move north, along both the Michigan and Wisconsin shorelines. It usually takes the fish about five months to arrive off northern spawning streams. The issue becomes somewhat confused

Aerial view of the Platte River mouth in northern Lake Michigan, where hundreds of fishing boats line the shore, suggests the vastness of the Great Lakes. Gamefish abound in these huge inland seas.

because not all salmon migrate; some stay in southern waters year-round and enter southerly streams to spawn during fall months. Successful Great Lakes fishermen are able to ferret out reliable information, and arrive at Point A when the fish do. It's often easier said than done, however.

In order to analyze the different types of Great Lakes waters, it's important to take an in-depth look at each one. In some ways they are much the same; in other ways, they are as different as cats and dogs. Each lake may feature different fish movements, and at radically different times of the year. The savvy angler learns these movements, and cashes in on good fishing.

Lake Superior

This lake is the largest freshwater lake in the world, and is the northwestern-most of the five Great Lakes. It serves as an international boundary between the United States and Canada. It covers 31,800 square miles. Superior's greatest length is east to west, where it stretches some 350 miles. It is 160 miles wide at its widest point. In some places the water is 1,333 feet deep.

The shoreline is rocky. Some vertical cliffs rise several hundred feet above the water along the northern coast. Some areas are fringed with sandstone cliffs, particularly along the Pictured Rocks National Lakeshore property in Michigan's Upper Peninsula.

Nearly 200 streams empty into Lake Superior around the shoreline; Michigan, Wisconsin, Minnesota, and Ontario border its waters. These waters are spawning grounds for trout and salmon and many other freshwater gamefish can be found in widely spaced bays or along wind-swept reefs.

Several islands break the wide expanse of Lake Superior. The largest is Michigan's Isle Royale. Ontario's St. Ignace and Michipicoten islands are rocky and big. Their offshore waters offer good fishing. Hundreds of other islands are used solely as nesting sites for gulls.

Cold water typifies Lake Superior. In many areas, the water temperature seldom gets above 40 degrees on the surface. Rocky reefs, steep ledge rock and dropoffs are found, and much of the water along the edges is a maze of giant boulders. Here, anglers can find trout and some salmon.

Some of Lake Superior's finest fishing can be found in shallow bays that indent the shoreline. These coves are often sheltered from strong winds, and some contain slightly warmer water (although few waters ever reach 50 degrees). Only a handful of areas will have any weed growth. If present, weeds usually grow at the extreme head of a cove, often where a stream enters. Windblown coves don't have any aquatic vegetation.

These bays often contain pike, perch, some walleyes (few in numbers), as well as trout. Lake trout were the native trout species in Lake Superior for many years, but plantings of brook, brown, and rainbow trout have bolstered this fishery. Lake trout live near the sharp edges of steep cliffs, underwater boulders, and along shoals during fall months. Other times they may be found almost anywhere, although seldom at depths over 200 feet.

Rainbows, browns, and brookies are commonly taken in spring and fall near in-flowing streams or in harbors. This latter location is one of the best, as fishing can be done off piers. Any stream mouth entering the lake has a better-than-average chance of holding trout at these times. Fish the edges of moving water, particularly along the edge of the first dropoff into deep water.

Perch, northern pike, and walleyes are often taken in some of the larger rivers entering Lake Superior. In Minnesota's St. Louis River at Duluth, tremendous numbers of large walleyes move upstream to spawn in April or early May. These fish can be caught in offshore waters. Shallow, sloping bays near rivermouths are good places to fish.

Lake Michigan

This lake, once known by Indians as *Michi-guma,* or big water, is the largest lake inside the United States and the third largest of the Great Lakes. Lake Michigan is about 300 miles long, with an average width of 75 miles. It covers approximately 22,400 square miles. It is a fish-rich lake, one of the richest in the world. It's deep—more than 900 feet in several places—and is about 21 feet lower than the surface of Lake Superior. Thousands of streams, creeks, and rivers empty into

Lake Michigan. Many are prime spawning waters for trout and salmon. Several large bays enter this big water, among the largest being Green Bay, Grand Traverse Bay, and Little Traverse Bay. Little Bay De Noc and Big Bay De Noc in Michigan's Upper Peninsula are also rich in fish life.

Excellent fishing can be enjoyed in Lake Michigan. Although it's fringed by Michigan, Indiana, Illinois, and Wisconsin, and such large cities as Chicago and Milwaukee, Lake Michigan is one of the finest fishing waters in the country for salmon, trout, perch, and other species.

This lake offers a panoramic change of scenery from one area to another. Some sections, like Wisconsin's Door Peninsula, are extremely rocky along the shoreline. Ledge rock and large boulders provide a look at a lake shoreline similar to the oligotrophic lakes in Canada. This section is relatively new, but it's not new in comparison to more northerly waters. Trout, salmon, and smallmouth bass call these rocky areas home. It's not uncommon to find sharp points, fast dropoffs, and

A lonely fisherman (left) works the surf for trout along the shore of Lake Michigan.

This is what the lower Manistee River looks like when anglers head offshore into Lake Michigan for a run on salmon or trout (right).

ledges that drop off into deep water. Structure such as this is common along Door County.

Cross the lake east of Door County, or head farther south along Lake Michigan, and the shoreline changes its shape. Michigan has steep sand dunes that extend from the shoreline inland for several miles. Many of these dunes are high and drop off into 30 or 40 feet of water near shore. The inshore waters are often gravel, boulder, or rocky reefs. Much the same is true along Wisconsin, except for an absence of dune-like terrain.

The basic shoreline structure of Lake Michigan will show stretches of shallow water near shore in some areas. In some places, the bottom may be comprised of a series of sandy stair-stepping ledges that drop off into 20 feet of water within a stone's throw of shore. Most gamefish, particularly trout, tend to follow these deep-water areas where they swing in close to shore. Rivermouths attract fish, too.

Southern Lake Michigan offers another personality. This area is

Rivermouth fishing can be exciting sport in the Great Lakes. This angler has just landed another rainbow on spawnbags.

characterized by long, sloping bars that jut far out into the lake. It's often possible to travel 6 or 8 miles out into Lake Michigan before you'll find 40-foot water.

The entire lake has reefs and submerged sandbars surrounded by deep water. These areas, wherever they're found, often offer an exciting brand of fishing.

Rivermouth areas, or hot-water discharges, can be sites of productive fishing in spring and fall; and even summer can be good in these areas if an offshore wind blows cooler water into the rivermouth. I've made many limit catches of trout in July off rivermouths. Trolling is often the best way to catch lots of trout during summer if you're fishing near a rivermouth or a nearby sandbar surrounded by deep water.

Salmon, both coho and chinook, have been responsible for the rebirth of Lake Michigan fishing. This formerly barren lake is now alive with large salmon, some weighing 40 pounds. Big steelhead (lake-going rainbow trout) often reach weights of 15 pounds. The largest brown trout taken weighed 33½ pounds. Spring and fall are the best times to go after these gamefish.

Smallmouth bass are common in many areas. Waugoshance Point at the northwest tip of Lower Michigan is famous for the smallmouth bass fishing done amid the rocks and boulders. Other good spots are Green Bay, Little Bay De Noc, and portions of Grand Traverse Bay. June, July, and early August are the best fishing months.

Yellow perch action usually peaks during July or early August, depending on the weather. Look for these gamefish around rocky areas, where they feed heavily on crayfish.

Lake Huron

Lake Huron is 250 miles long and up to 155 miles wide. It has a drainage of 50,000 square miles. It's the second largest Great Lake.

Huron is about 22 feet lower than Lake Superior, which drains into Huron via the St. Mary's River. It is as much as 750 feet deep, and contains two major bays—Georgian Bay on the Ontario side and Saginaw Bay on the Michigan shore. The lake is dotted with islands. Some of the larger rocky islands include Michigan's Drummond and Mackinac, and Ontario's Manitoulin.

Clear waters are common in Lake Huron with the exception of some portions of Saginaw Bay, where shallow weedbeds and muckbeds are found. This lake holds almost all species of freshwater gamefish found in Michigan or Ontario, including trout, salmon, perch, largemouth and smallmouth bass, northern pike, walleyes, muskies, and others. Warmwater areas such as Saginaw Bay teem with rough fish like carp, garpike, goldfish, and suckers or dogfish.

The upper portions of Lake Huron are comprised of clean waters, with long tapering beaches that extend out for several miles before coming to deep water. Some areas do have dropoffs close to shore, but this is the exception rather than the rule. Much of this lake is boulder-studded. The upper portions are surrounded by spruce or pine forests. Rocky shoals are common, particularly in Georgian Bay. A group of small, rocky islands are found along the south shore of Michigan's Upper Peninsula. The Les Cheneaux Islands offer a bonanza of pike, perch, and trout fishing, in season.

The waters surrounding Drummond Island are rocky, marked by several small bays. Potagannissing Bay is best known for its pike and bass fishing, although anglers take an occasional muskie or walleye. These waters are best fished in the manner described in the chapter on natural lakes.

The southern portion of Lake Huron is as different from the upper lake as night and day. It, too, offers good fishing, but there are fewer shoals or fish-holding structure. Many fish, especially trout and salmon, suspend over deep water, many times along shipping channels. Inshore waters near the tip of Michigan's "Thumb" offers excellent trout, salmon, perch, and smallmouth bass action near reefs and piers. Offshore reefs near Grindstone City have been steady hotspots for many years.

Saginaw Bay is a strange breed of cat. The bottom portion of the bay near Bay City is shallow, muddy, and full of aquatic vegetation. Anglers here find sporadic largemouth bass action, some catfish, and the occasional northern pike during spring months. The upper portion of Saginaw Bay near Port Austin and Grindstone City is clean water, with plenty of small, rocky islands and shoals. Coldwater species are common in this upper section.

Lake Erie

This lake was once known as a "dead" lake, supposedly incapable of sustaining any fish life. It was heavily polluted and served as a settling basin for the waters of the upper three Great Lakes. The fact that Lake Erie is now world famous for its walleye fishery says a lot for man's ability to clean up his act.

It is shallow in comparison with the other Great Lakes. Its maximum depth is only 210 feet. Erie is 240 miles long, and between 38 and 57 miles wide. Its overall area is 9,930 square miles.

Kim Richey, the author's daughter, holds a huge brown trout her father landed while fishing on Lake Huron.

This shallowness makes the lake prone to tremendous, sudden waves. It also has lots of small bays that indent the shoreline and offer anglers a crack at warmwater gamefish.

Walleye and smallmouth bass anglers are now flocking to Erie. The walleye fishery, according to a fisheries biologist I spoke with during preparation of this book, is possibly the best in the world at this time. Plenty of 6- to 10-pound walleyes are being taken around the offshore islands near Sandusky. These fish are often suspended during summer, but they lurk near rocky shoals during spring and fall migrations of shad and other forage fish. The principal method of taking fish is with a weight-forward spinner like the Erie Dearie. It is cast parallel to a shoal, allowed to flutter down near bottom, and retrieved with enough speed to bring out the spinner action. Many fishermen add a worm to the trailing hook as an appetizer.

Smallmouth action is also torrid among the same islands in the western basin of Lake Erie. In the spring, limit catches consisting of 3- to 5-pounders are often made. The same basic techniques work on bronzebacks as well as walleyes.

Trout and salmon fishing hasn't really caught on in Lake Erie. Sporadic catches of these species are made, but it's simply nothing to build a fishing trip around.

Good winter perch and walleye action is done around the offshore islands in the western basin. Some private airlines charter flights to and from these areas. The planes land on the ice within fishing distance of the best spots.

Lake Ontario

This smallest of the five Great Lakes is also a red-hot fishing lake. With a length of 193 miles, and a width of 53 miles, Ontario has a total area of 7,520 square miles. Lake Ontario is deep, with some depths ranging from 500 to 778 feet.

Ontario doesn't freeze during winter, except in the shallows. This eastern-most lake has innumerable rocky islands along the north shore, in Ontario waters. These areas contain some tremendous muskies, largemouth bass, and walleyes. Northern pike are common in shallow bays, while muskies are often found off deep-water points. Some excellent smallmouth bass action can be had in and around the islands. Much of this north shore is rocky. Boulders and shoals give gamefish avenues to follow from deep to shallow water.

In the southern portion of Lake Ontario, more trout and salmon have been stocked recently. Huge runs of coho and chinook salmon, as well as rainbow and brown trout, are being taken in several rivers and off harbors around Rochester and Oswego, New York.

Superb sport can be had by casting off rivermouths, either by wading or from a boat. Spring is the best time for trout; fall for salmon.

The Great Lakes are unique bodies of water. It would be easy to devote a full chapter to each due to their varying types of structure and shoreline terrain.

Fishing any inland lake is a challenge, but the ever-changing structure of the Great Lakes can present challenges that are seldom encountered in other waters. These waters are among the finest fishing lakes found in North America today.

Farmponds Are Fun

Many years ago I was investigating a series of farmponds located near Kankakee, Illinois. I was doing research for a magazine article about fishing such waters. Naturally, I hoped to catch fish. My host assured me I would.

Leo Pachner, my host on this trip, was a farmpond fishing addict. He had a handle on all ponds in his area and knew what species of gamefish were found in each one. Landowners were drawn to his charming unselfish manner.

A small, 10-acre pond was his first choice when I told him I'd like to catch bluegills. "I've got a pond that delivers some trophy gills, many in the 10- to 11-inch class. We can fish with bait or flies, as you choose," he said. I chose flies, hoping for some surface or subsurface action. The thought of landing trophy bluegills on fly tackle had me as charged as a lit dynamite fuse.

"Bluegills are spooky in farmponds," Leo told me. He advised me to sneak down the shoreline in a crouched position, take advantage of small shrubs near the bank, and cast as delicately as possible. I felt like a fool, adopting an infantryman's position to fish a pond in central Illinois.

I followed his advice and made an effortless delivery with a No. 14 Adams dry fly. This trout fly has lured lots of big bluegills in the past for me, and I often resort to it in strange waters. The delicate 5X tippet rolled out and the fly danced saucily on top. I allowed it to remain motionless, kept my silhouette low, and shivered the fly with faint, rod-tip motions. A husky bluegill sliced up under the fly, rolled sideways, and plucked it from the surface like a hawk nailing a hapless meadow mouse.

I saluted the fish with a soft raise of my rod tip, and again felt the pleasurable sensation of a saucer-shaped gill pulling at right angles to the line. He splashed, darted first in one direction and then another, and soon I led him to the bank. The bluegill was a male, decked out in his spawning finery, and a superb prize.

I nailed other bluegills that day, but none any larger than that first 11-incher. That fish, and that day, reaffirmed my conviction that farmponds are usually underfished. Many gamefish in them die of old age and crowded conditions. Only a handful of such ponds are managed properly for an optimum yield of food fish and fine sport.

Several years ago, I conducted a survey of farmponds in Michigan, my home state. I spoke with field agents of the Soil Conservation Service, and learned that farmponds exist in nearly every area. Most are on private lands, but access is available with a courteous request. A shared catch with a landowner is just one way to be invited back again. Respect of another's property is a mandatory obligation in all cases.

Thousands of farmponds are located across the country. The word "farmpond" denotes a pond on a farm, where many are found. In the West, though, some livestock tanks contain fish. Such areas are rarer than ponds found in farming country. Some farming spots often contain 1000 ponds per county. Most are stocked yearly with gamefish.

Largemouth bass, crappies, bluegills, sunfish, channel and blue catfish, and trout are found in these farmponds. A pond with cold underwater springs seeping in may contain an excellent trout population. Many ponds are filled with warm water, and can't support a trout fishery. Bass, panfish, and catfish are the dominant species in these waters.

Farmponds are created in two basic ways: by damming a stream or by an underground spring. Both types of ponds offer good fishing, but they usually require different fishing techniques.

Farmpond anglers team up to land a trophy trout. When a pond is fed by an underground spring, the water is cold enough to support fish of this size.

Farmponds are generally small. A 5- to 10-acre pond is a large one. Many are less than one acre in area. Size is often irrelevant to fish productivity; small ponds tend to concentrate gamefish in spots easily reached from the shore. I've fished only a few ponds where a pram or canoe was needed to reach the middle portions. Wading is a good way to fish some ponds. My luck has been far better on small waters than on large ones.

Shoreline cover varies from one pond to another, although most will have a fairly steep bank on one or more sides where the dragline or backhoe was used to create the original hole. These ponds often have grass, weeds, shrubs, or small trees planted to secure the soil against erosion. Farmponds that have been created by damming a stream are usually no more than 10 feet deep. The deepest part is usually found near the dam. Upper portions of the pond may contain only a foot or two of water.

Many farmponds are bowl-shaped, with gently sloping banks. The gradual taper of pond banks provides little structure or cover for gamefish. Some ponds, however, may have one bank that is steeper than the others. The steep-edged side is a good place to fish.

One valuable information source for anglers is the landowner. He will probably remember what the pond looked like before it filled with water. He'll know the locations of any deep areas or furrows. He'll also know the depths of submerged weedbeds, old stumps, or other debris. Owners are usually eager to give solid information because many realize their pond is underfished.

The one major problem with most ponds is that they *are* underfished. Many species are stunted due to overcrowding, too little food, and a lack of spawning sites. A fisherman can do a pond owner a big favor by fishing periodically and removing any hooked fish. Returning fish to a pond doesn't help the fish population. It simply increases the competition for food and stunts the growth of all species.

Cover, whether shoreline or submerged, can determine whether you catch farmpond fish or throw your hands into the air in exasperation. Many ponds are fringed with a smattering of reeds. Shallow-water areas are often weed-filled. Weed growth in a pond is crucial to the security of gamefish, and it provides some comfort and food. This condition often angers fishermen because lures must be cleaned after every cast. Yet such weedy conditions can provide the very cover that gamefish require. Too many weeds can warm a pond and choke the available fishery resource, though.

Some ponds contain lightly colored water. Many farmponds are utilized in two ways: as a means of outdoor recreation for the landowner, family and friends; and as a watering area for livestock. Cattle or horses feeding near the pond will tramp down the banks and dirty the water. Such conditions can create the "edge" anglers need to catch bass. The dark water filters out light rays and enables largemouth bass to feed near shore.

Types of Structure

There are many locations in farmponds where gamefish can be found. Some ponds will have all the features listed below, while other ponds may contain only a few. These are the areas you should consider when fishing any farmpond . . .

Tributary inlets. Any in-flowing stream can mean good farmpond fishing. These locations are often good year-round, but especially in spring. The water flowing into the pond often carries with it food and oxygen-rich water. A stream may be muddy, and this can be an asset in a clearwater pond. The reverse is also true in dark-colored ponds where clean water flows in. Gamefish are often attracted to such structural features. Any type of cover at the inlet, such as a dropoff or weed growth, will increase your catches in this location.

Thick reeds or bulrushes. These areas are good in spring, if the water there is at least 2 feet deep. They can be steady hotspots anytime if the water is deeper. Fish both sides of the reeds if water is found in front of the cover, or between it and shore. Bass and bluegills often spawn here during spring months. This structure will attract small minnows or forage fish that act as a food source for larger gamefish. Try casting near reeds or rushes after dark. Largemouths frequent these spots once the sun goes down.

Lily pads.   This type of structure is found in many ponds. In some it may be the only cover available. Fish the outside edges, the inside edges, and any openings between the lily pads. I once caught a 5-pound bass by casting a Jitterbug into an opening, allowing it to lie motionless for several seconds, and then easing it out into the open. That fish was all over my plug. We conducted a midnight dance across the pond before he waltzed himself into submission.

Islands.   Many ponds are constructed so that a small island exists in the center portion. These areas can be fruitful if deep water is found off the point. Shallow-water island points are seldom good fishing spots, except under a darkened sky, or whenever other cover such as reeds is located nearby. Bare island points have little cover, and gamefish have no reason to visit them except under cover of darkness.

Points.   A farmpond may be constructed so that points jut out into the water. This type of structure is especially productive if some of the deepest water is found off the tip of the point. Many points actually contain aquatic weeds or grasses. If this vegetation is deep, the fishing should be excellent. Any brushpiles or debris found on the tip of the point will increase your chances of taking fish.

Submerged trees.   Any submerged tree in a farmpond is a potential piece of good fish-producing structure. The shaded side of a still-standing tree that was submerged when the pond filled can be a good place to fish. An upright tree with branches is better yet, because most fish will take cover under the limbs. A tree that has fallen into the pond is a haven for gamefish because it generates more cover and often attracts forage fish. If a horizontally submerged tree is in deep water, so much the better.

Channel edges. A channel edge on a farmpond is usually found where a small stream has been dammed up. The creek channel is seldom deep, but often has a clearly defined bed and higher sides and often forms the deepest water in a pond. This is a good place to fish, especially during summer months. Some creekbeds will have brushpiles situated along the tops of the banks. Old logjams are often found wherever the channel makes a sharp turn. Bass and catfish favor such locations.

Sloughs. The construction of some ponds causes water to flood into very shallow, grassy depressions. These may be dry part of the year, but contain water during spring months. Panfish, bass, and even catfish will move from deeper water into such sloughs if sufficient water is available to cover their backs and if food is present. The terrain around many ponds is rich in earthworms, and gamefish will forage into these areas for food during the spring. Good fishing can be had in these locations immediately after a heavy rain.

Weedbeds. Few gamefish can pass up the opportunity to feed and rest near a weedbed. Newly emerging weeds during spring months will attract spawning and feeding fish. A weedless bait can be slithered over the tops of weedbeds once they reach full summer growth. This can be an excellent area to fish during hot summer months.

Rocky areas. Some ponds contain no rocky areas, but others do. The productivity of these rock structures depends upon their proximity to deep water. A smattering of pebbles or gravel in shallow water *may* attract spawning fish, but it's not a solid bet. If the pond has deep water nearby, and if the rocky areas contain some bulrushes, it can be a winner. The only way to know for sure if rock structures attract fish is to try them at various times of day, in different seasons. Most ponds are small enough so that in one hour of fishing you can complete a circle. You might find, as I did on one pond, that gamefish moved to rocky areas late in the year or very early in the season, just after ice-out. For the balance of the year, this spot failed to produce a strike.

Dick Kotis works a Jitterbug over a farmpond in southern Ohio. He knows that in spring bass are often found in shallow water.

Flats.   Flat areas of shallow water will hold bluegills all year long, although they are usually best early and late in the day. Flats can hold spawning fish in spring months. They often attract species such as largemouth bass during the evening, or on overcast days. These spots are best if a dropoff exists along the deep-water edge, or if some other cover extends from the flats to deep water. A sharp dropoff will offer better fishing than will a sloping bottom contour leading away from the flats. It's possible to wade and fish some flats if the bottom is hard, although you should first check to see whether the area has a mucky bottom or not. It's just as much fun getting smacked in the nose as it is to struggle through a muckbed. I made that mistake only once, and it cost me nearly thirty minutes of prime fishing time (plus a wet backside) before I got out.

While doing research for this book, I learned something exciting. Some states have thousands of ponds available for fishing. Tennessee has more than 75,000 such waters; neighboring Kentucky has more than 50,000. Illinois, Indiana, Ohio, Michigan, Wisconsin, and others are represented equally well.

Farmponds are easy to fish, but are they easy to find? That question is best answered by the amount of energy expended by the fisherman. Ponds are so plentiful that many anglers drive by them and don't realize that a bonanza of fishing exists close to home. This is important, especially with the soaring cost of gasoline. I'd rather spend two hours fishing a farmpond near home than spend a similar amount of time in some goofy gas lineup. Why obtain overpriced fuel for a trip to a name lake that may or may not produce as well as the pond near home?

I've called on the Soil Conservation Service (SCS) agents for help often. They are usually more than willing to help me find a good fishing spot. These people work for the Department of Agriculture; a listing is usually found in the phone book. Most SCS offices are located in the county seat. These men often have a detailed listing of ponds in their county and know which waters contain certain species of gamefish.

Another trick I use is to keep my eyes open while driving down the road. Sunlight glimmering off a pond has prompted me to stop at many farmhouses to ask an owner's permission to fish a pond. I've been refused only twice in many years. I think I've knocked on more doors than an encyclopedia salesman, and my luck is better, I assure you.

How to
Read a Lake

In the preceding chapters, I've described the make-up of different types of North American lakes. Fishermen who want to learn how to fish a lake will study this information and file it away in their memory. Sooner or later, a situation will arise when it can be used.

Those fishermen who glance at a contour chart of a lake, scratch their heads a couple times before heading for a boat, and then proceed to catch fish are the envy of everyone. Some guides can do it, although it's usually on their "home" lake. The chaps I really admire, however, are those tournament bass fishermen who study a lake and then catch fish, almost every time. Sure, they're fishing for dollars, and few of us do that. But we can use their tricks to gain an insight into where fish are located. Here's how these pros find out.

The goal of most fishermen is to catch fish. They may enjoy jawboning with a buddy, watching a purple sunset, or seeing wildlife along a lakeshore; but the one force that drives anglers on the water is the desire to catch fish. The average fisherman wants the thrill of a fish tugging against a bowed rod, and he wants to eat freshly fried fillets for dinner.

The trick to catching more fish on any lake is to be able to read the lake. This doesn't require mystical powers or a pointed hat worn by a palm reader. It just requires common sense, some knowledge of what to look for, and the ability to understand what it is you've seen.

One of the first steps in becoming a skilled lake fisherman is to purchase a bottom contour, or hydrographic, map of a lake you want to fish. Hydrographic maps are available from many sources. Try Lake Survey Center, 630 Federal Office Building, Detroit, MI 48226 for Great Lakes waters; U.S. Army Engineers District Office, 906 Olive Street, St. Louis, MO 63101 for the Mississippi River and its tributaries (charts show some lakes); U. S. Geological Survey, Map Information Office, National Center, Reston, VA 22092; and Geological Survey, Department of Energy, Mines and Resources, 601 Booth Street, Ottawa, Ontario, Canada K1A OE9. Fishermen can often find maps in limited quantities by writing to the Waterways or Fisheries Division of the Department of Natural Resources of the state, province or Canadian territory they want to fish.

Study your map and locate those areas where fish migrations are likely. These migration routes are the avenues gamefish follow from a deep-water sanctuary to the shallow feeding zones. Pinpoint sharp or rounded points that dead-end in deep water. Note the close-together contour breaks, learn the locations of sunken islands or heavy weedbeds, determine where the deep-water weedline is located, and observe the exact depth of gravel areas or sunken stumps or boats. Any fish-bearing piece of structure found on these maps will put you one step ahead of other anglers.

Vernon Fowlkes, a fishing buddy of mine and former owner of Fo-Mac, Inc.—one of the first producers of electronic water thermometers—gave me a lesson on map reading many years ago on an

One of the best ways of determining the locations of underwater structure is to study a contour map of the lake. Here Vernon Fowlkes marks promising areas on his map before a fishing trip.

Oklahoma lake. "You Yankees are behind the times in learning how to read a lake. You've got to spend some time checking charts in order to spend time catching fish," he said. He chewed on me for an hour before outlining our tactics for the following day. He pinpointed a submerged timbered ridge that ended at the old river channel. He spotted a deep-water depression surrounded by 12 feet of water. Here we would find largemouth bass in 18 feet of water, he said. The area looked like a fly speck in a bowl of soup to me, and I said so. He shook his head at my Yankee ignorance and then launched into another friendly tirade about my lack of lake knowledge.

We went fishing the next day. The sun was a butter-yellow ball of fire in the eastern sky, a prelude to a blistering day on the water. "We'll find them! My spot is going to produce at least one 5-pounder and maybe some bigger fish." He chuckled in glee; I clutched the pedestal seat-arms in the bow and tried not to be terrified as stick-ups flashed past like a picket fence being blown by the frontal edge of a tornado.

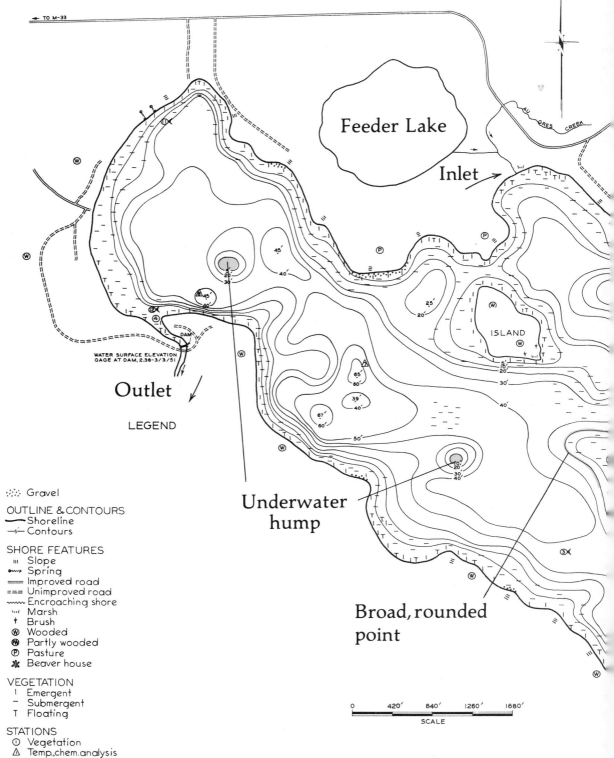

← TO M-33

Feeder Lake

AU GRES CREEK

Inlet →

Outlet

45'
40'
20'
30'

45'
40'

25'
20'

65'
60'

39'
40'

67'
60'

50'

40'

30'

20'

10'
30'
40'

ISLAND

DAM

WATER SURFACE ELEVATION
GAGE AT DAM, 2.36-3/3/51

Underwater
hump

Broad, rounded
point

LEGEND

.⋅.⋅. Gravel

OUTLINE & CONTOURS
—— Shoreline
—₅— Contours

SHORE FEATURES
⫴ Slope
∿ Spring
═ Improved road
=== Unimproved road
∿∿ Encroaching shore
⩊ Marsh
⸸ Brush
Ⓦ Wooded
Ⓦ Partly wooded
Ⓟ Pasture
⚹ Beaver house

VEGETATION
⏐ Emergent
— Submergent
⊤ Floating

STATIONS
① Vegetation
△ Temp, chem. analysis
⊡ Bottom sample
⨯ Fish sample

0   420'   840'   1260'   1680'
SCALE

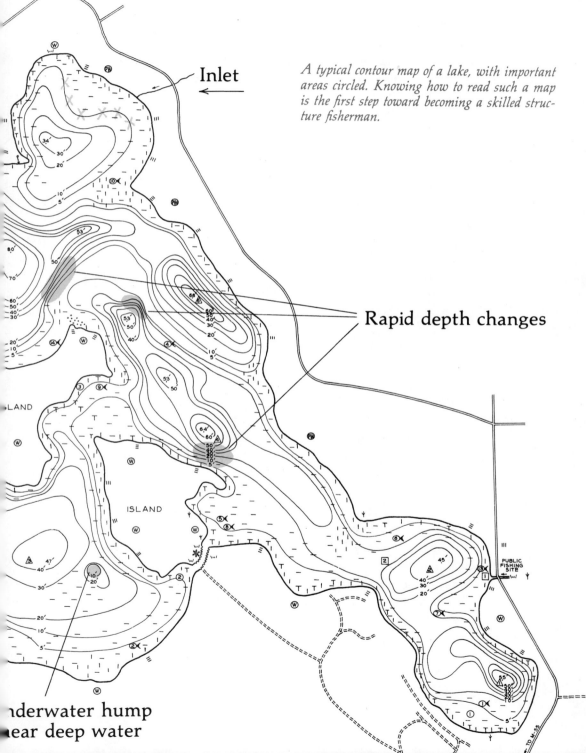

Inlet

A typical contour map of a lake, with important areas circled. Knowing how to read such a map is the first step toward becoming a skilled structure fisherman.

Rapid depth changes

Underwater hump near deep water

Vernon found the spot, and I tied the bow to a stick-up while he did the same with the stern. Firmly tethered, we began slithering purple, plastic worms along bottom, feeding slack into the line, and dropping them into the deep hole. I caught Vernon's dog-on-point motion as he leaned forward to give more slack line to a fish picking up the artificial. His line came tight, and he nearly threw himself out of the boat setting the hook. His rod bent into a dangerous curve as he chuckled to himself. "Hog bass need some persuasion, just like tapping a stubborn mule's head to get his attention. Give these hawgs a chance and they'll wrap you around a limb faster than you can say . . . There he goes again," he muttered, as the fish responded in anger to his being compared to a mule. The largemouth scrambled the water into a thick soup of frothy bubbles, arched his back and sailed into the air, and Vernon was doing his best to cope with the situation. I was enjoying myself watching the explosive interplay between angler and fish.

He landed the bass, as I knew he would. It weighed about 6 pounds. Vernon had made his point. I caught the next bass; it scaled 5 pounds. We landed two other fish from that spot before it turned sour. Our smallest was a chunky 3-pounder that jumped several times.

This anecdote emphasizes the point that good fishing areas on any lake can be found before the boat is launched. Weather conditions are a factor, but given good weather a fisherman can vastly increase his chances of an evening fish-fry by checking a contour map and then looking at the lake. Many contour maps are outdated, however, due to physical changes in a lake's surface or subsurface structure. Always try to obtain the newest possible contour chart available for any lake.

The task of studying a lake visually and determining what treasures lie below isn't difficult, but it takes work. A shimmering expanse of water captures the eye, and most people just mutter, "It looks like a good fishing lake." The lake may hold plenty of fish or it may not; much depends on underwater structure. Most, but not all, underwater structure can be clearly seen by looking at the surrounding shoreline. Learn shoreline structure, and the underwater areas will take care of themselves. Everything will then fall into place, just like pieces of a jigsaw puzzle.

The mouth of an inflowing stream is always a good place to fish on any lake. There is usually a deep hole in the area and often rocks nearby for cover.

Reading a lake from above water is not difficult. Just keep in mind that roughly 90 percent of any lake contains no fish. The next fact should be obvious: *only 10 percent of any lake has good fish-bearing structure.* This means that regardless of how inviting a lakeshore appears, only a very small percentage of the available water contains fish. Anglers should learn to differentiate between scenic areas, and those that actually produce fish. There is a difference, as we shall soon see.

All gamefish need three basic factors in their everyday life: food, shelter, and protection or comfort. A brief look at each should point us toward an easier analysis of fish-bearing structures, both above and below water.

Food

Gamefish feed upon insects, plankton, minnows, small forage fish, crayfish, mollusks, or whatever else is available in a particular lake. Gamefish can go for several days, often following a cold front, without food. This is a logical explanation for why we often encounter poor fishing.

Food must be immediately accessible to sportfish. Food is of little value to gamefish if they must spend the energy to swim 1 or 2 miles down the lake to an area where forage is present. A general rule, then, is that *gamefish are found in areas where their food is located.* An example would be a lake where crayfish are the primary food for smallmouth bass. We all know that smallies eat crayfish, and we also understand that crayfish are not found everywhere in a lake. Good structure located near a crayfish habitat should be a prime fishing area.

Shelter

Gamefish "shelter" refers to different things for different species. For example, crappies will use a brushpile as shelter to hide from other predatory species. Shelter could also be a stump field, a maze of stickups, logjams, weedbeds, islands close to deep water, a swimming raft anchored in deep water, or anything else that offers shelter to fish.

Overhanging ledges usually denote similar structure below the surface of the water. This angler is fishing a lure close to a likely hiding place.

Note the patch of lily pads in the back of this cove. Such spots attract big northern pike in spring. These anglers are covering all the water in the cove, working back toward the pads.

It could be a point extending from the shallows into deep water, a jumble of boulders or ledgerock, or a spruce toppled into the water on a northern lake.

Comfort or protection

Comfort can mean many things when referring to gamefish. It might be oxygen-rich waters, or a water temperature that keeps forage fish and gamefish actively moving. It also refers to those lake areas where fish can find protection.

Deep water is the sanctuary for many gamefish. Deep water usually offers the concealment larger members of a species need to protect themselves from overhead predation, the bright rays of the sun, and other factors, including fishermen. Many lake fishermen are shoreline-oriented anglers. They work the shallows, cast to lily-pad fields, and seldom heave their lures into deep water. They remind me of a stream steelhead fisherman afraid to fish near bottom for fear of getting snagged and losing his terminal rigging. Successful lake fishermen realize that bigger fish are usually found in deeper water. It's worth losing a few rigs to tangle with a possible trophy.

Fish those areas where fish have *direct* access to deep water. This doesn't mean fishing 100 or 200 yards away; position yourself no more than 10 or 20 feet from deep water. A frightened gamefish's first response to danger is to go deep. We've all caught and released a fish. What does it do? It often swims in a dazed circle, gets straightened out, and heads for deep water. It's heading for comfort and protection.

What to Look For

One of the biggest tip-offs to gamefish activity on any lake is the appearance of minnow life. Any area that supports good minnow populations near shoreline weeds or in offshore waters should offer first-rate action on gamefish.

Narrow, rock-lined coves with a tiny outlet are magnets for walleys and northern pike during spring. Reeds often grow along shore.

Kay Richey and Les Sandy of Sandy's Monument Bay Resort on Ontario's Lake of the Woods cast for muskellunge in a shallow, weed-filled bay. This is a good spot for muskies after the spring spawn.

What else would a lake fisherman look for when trying to pinpoint hot fishing areas? The first thing I look at on any lake is the shoreline. Is it flat, without a tapering shoreline leading into the water? If so, the lake probably is an old lake with a slow break into deep water. Fish will probably be in deep water much of the time, except during overcast days or at night.

Is the shoreline sharp, with many points or islands? If so, the water usually drops off rapidly from the first breakline. Good fishing can often be done near the islands or off points.

Is the shoreline extremely rocky, with sharp cliffs and vertical rock faces? Such waters usually are found on young lakes and indicate a rapid dropoff, often near shore. These kinds of lakes are often tough to fish, but not impossible to read. Gamefish are often found in some shallow bays with good underwater structure nearby, near in-flowing streams, or in pools cut by small waterfalls.

This is the first step to reading a lake. Learn to look at shoreline features. Common sense will tell you what bottom contours can be found away from shore.

The next step is to look carefully for fish-holding areas such as standing timber in impounded waters, small islands, rocky reefs that kick up waves when water washes over them during a stiff wind, sandbars, weedbeds, or underwater humps. These can be located on a contour chart, or by actual observation. The most difficult thing to observe from shore is an underwater hump. A baitshop owner can often pinpoint locations of humps, or they might appear on a chart. The other types of structure can often be seen by looking for them. You must train your eyes and mind to find them, however.

Watch for shoreline features that could hold fish, such as docks leading out into the lake. Are there boats anchored in deep water, or swimming rafts? Is the shoreline indented with numerous coves, cuts, or small bayous, or is the shore straight and without visual structure? Good fishing can often be had in small coves, especially in the spring. Use your nose to locate fish. I can't sniff out gamefish like some anglers, but I can detect a fishy odor in these locations. Some anglers incorrectly associate this fishy smell with shallow water and decaying plant life. I

Pete Czura battles a nice smallmouth amidst a maze of tangled tree stumps and roots.

Waterfalls usually attract walleyes and northern pike which feed heavily on food washed into the pool below.

The author lands a stunning brook trout near a dropoff. This is always a hotspot for trout in any lake.

used to feel the same way, until a buddy told me that my long nose was smelling fish life. We caught many bluegills and some 3-pound largemouth bass that day. I've since learned to fish in areas where such strong odors are found.

Impoundments often have concrete piers, bridges, or causeways along or over the water. Small currents often form beneath such objects. This moving water can be a source of top-notch action. Never pass up areas with concrete abutments. They are prime covers for most gamefish.

Does your favorite lake have an old creekbed in it, or does it have an inlet, outlet, or both? All of them attract fish. Marshy waters near an inlet, or a delta near the outlet, may offer the finest fishing of the year, particularly in spring or fall if migratory species are found in the lake at that time. I've seen bass, pike, walleyes, muskies, and even yellow perch make spawning runs there. The fishing, if seasons are open at the time, can be terrific.

Does your favorite bass lake have sandy beaches, or a swimming area? These places are seldom productive during daylight hours but can deliver some fast action after sundown. They can be seen easily with the naked eye. I've caught some big largemouth bass by fishing sinking lures at night, even where people were swimming. The turbulence swimmers create loosens plant life or plankton. This attracts forage fish. Bass are usually close to an available food supply. Such areas are often overlooked by many fishermen.

How far must a bass, or any other species, swim from deep water before hitting the shallows of a beach, where food is available? A swimming beach usually has deep water within 50 yards, often much less, of shallow water. The swimming raft, anchored in deep water, is held in place with cement blocks or other heavy material to prevent it from drifting away in high winds.

A bass moving into the shallows will often hold at the first break on structure. In this case it's probably the raft's cement blocks on bottom. The next step is for the fish to move up to the lip of the dropoff and then into shallow water. I used to wonder why such swimming rafts often produced good bass fishing.

Now I know.

The S-T-S-T Method

Not too long ago, I was an elite member of the "chuck it and hope" group of fishermen. I'd motor up to a likely location, cut the engine, and begin flailing hell out of the water. I'd spot my casts in a regular pattern, allow some casts to overlap, fish high and low . . . and sometimes I would catch a fish.

All too often, I would spend more time casting, pulling weeds from my lures, and looking enviously at stringers of fish taken by anglers working deeper water. It was easy to chalk it up to luck on the other guy's part, but a chance encounter with an old-timer set me straight about luck. "There's little in fishing that can be attributed to luck. Oh, you might consider it luck when you nail a 10-pound largemouth instead of a 7-pounder, but that's about as far as it goes," he said.

"Luck," he went on, with a knowing glint in his eye, "is more a matter of thoughtful presentation, a knowledge of lake contours, a tidbit of know-how about fish habits and preferred habitat. But mostly it's getting down to gamefish and offering them something they think is edible. The only way to consistently catch fish and come off the lake looking like a professional is to adopt a specialized trolling technique."

I begged, pleaded, and even promised to clean his fish if he'd only impart to me his lake-fishing wisdom, preferably in one easy lesson.

"Kid, you've got a power of learnin' ahead of you. Get the fundamentals and learn to adapt them to specialized conditions. I'll give you the basics, but you'll have to learn how to make the method work in any lake of your choosing. And," he paused, for effect, "I want all my fish filleted, and no bones either, hear?" I heard, I saw, and I came away from the one-day trip excited about the endless possibilities of his methods.

I cleaned his fish, and he probably felt that I had cleaned his brain by the time I finished with my questions. He paid me one of the highest compliments I've received by stating that I was a savvy kid, due in part to my never-ending string of questions. He'd answer one, I'd file it away, and pound another home before he could catch his breath. The secret in fishing, if one exists, is to seek the truth about the sport. The fastest way to reach this goal is to ask questions of any successful fisherman.

The old-timer's technique: trolling. But he didn't do the standard type of trolling that often produces poor results. His method was a systematic combing of underwater structure based on the use of a sonar unit, water temperature measurements, and time-honored trolling tactics.

I worked at learning this method, and ten years later, I'm still only at grade school level. The technique has helped me catch all species of freshwater gamefish. I've taken largemouth bass from Florida lakes, stripers from Arkansas' Lake Maumelle, trout from hundreds of midwestern and Canadian lakes, muskies in Wisconsin and Minnesota, and walleyes from North Dakota waters, just for starters.

I fished, using my mentor's technique, for several years. It deserved a name, but what? I analyzed the component parts of the tactic—sonar, temperature (water), structure, trolling—and decided that the easiest way to name the critter was simply to call it, "S-T-S-T."

The STST method is one of the best techniques I've encountered in thirty-five years of fishing. It comes close to winning my prize as the method closest to perfection of any I've tried. The method works on almost any type of lake, with the possible exception of farmponds. It has helped me catch largemouth bass on large ponds where an angler can troll from a canoe or cartop boat. I've taken trout in New Zealand, lakers in the Northwest Territories, and other gamefish at all points in between, using STST strategy. Here are the basics:

The Equipment

The ideal trolling boat should be about 16 feet long and powered by a 25 to 35 h.p. outboard engine. Anything smaller doesn't have sufficient power to motor long distances. An engine with more than 35 h.p. often develops plug fouling, which cuts down on your ability to troll at slow speeds. The boat should be equipped with splashboards for backtrolling. A wide-beam, deep-vee hull is good. Avoid dressing up your boat with useless, gimmick items that cost money but deliver few fish, and often get in the way when you're playing a trophy.

Buy the finest sonar unit or chart-recording graph you can afford. Follow this up with a dependable water thermometer, preferably one graduated in single-degree increments. These items, when combined with a knowledge of structure and trolling tricks, will put more fish in your boat.

Preceding chapters have emphasized the importance of reading a lake above water, and obtaining detailed contour maps of the lake in question. A preliminary in-depth check of both details will shortcut the time needed to catch fish on any lake. It's often possible to hit a lake, motor directly to a productive-looking structure, take the water temperature, and begin fishing.

Lawrence Richey, the author's father, uses a sonar unit to locate structure (left). Trolling at the proper depth—based on his reading of water temperature—he connects with a nice rainbow trout (right).

Water Temperature

Water temperature is one of the foundation blocks in the STST method. Gamefish are cold-blooded and can therefore adapt to almost any water temperature. However, they do seem to feed and strike best when the temperature is within a specified range. Some species prefer warmer water, while trout and other gamefish like it cooler.

Wind direction, velocity, depth and size of a lake, and other factors are instrumental in determining the best fishing spots and the location of the proper water temperature. STST success depends on knowing the species of fish found in the lake to be fished. You'll be spinning your wheels if you apply these techniques for trout when the lake contains only largemouth bass. Determine the lake's fish life, and everything else will click in place.

Electronic water thermometer can gauge a lake's temperature accurately with a push of the button. See the accompanying table for preferred temperature range of most gamefish.

Some years ago, I studied water temperature and its relationship to fish in lakes. I devised a rather loose set of tables. The chart that follows is very general in the respect that most species will learn to adapt to warmer or cooler waters than they normally prefer. Therefore, the tolerance range and preferred temperature range are flexible. Largemouth bass may feed best *in most cases* at 72 degrees, but a southern lake may have water of 75 degrees year-round. Fish in that lake will then adapt to the warmer water. The reverse is also true, as study and on-the-water research have proved on many occasions.

Species	Preferred Temperature	Tolerance Range
Bluegills, sunfish	72° F.	65–80° F.
Yellow perch	68	60–75
Crappies	68	60–75
Walleyes	60	55–70
Northern pike	65	60–80
Muskellunge (all subspecies)	65	60–80
Coho salmon	54	45–60
Chinook salmon	54	50–63
Smallmouth bass	67	60–70
Largemouth bass	72	65–70
Lake trout	42	40–55
Rainbow trout	60	48–68
Brown trout	61	48–68
Brook trout	58	50–60
Splake (brook-lake cross)	58	50–62

The Layers of Lakes

A large percentage of lake fishing is done during summer. Waters in large lakes often undergo a stratification in June, sometimes earlier. The warmest water will be on top of the lake; it's called the epilimnion. This area contains most warmwater gamefish such as perch, panfish, and largemouth bass. The next deepest layer is usually a narrow band known as the thermocline. It contains cool temperatures, plenty of dissolved oxygen, and forage fish. Coldwater species such as trout are found here. The bottom layer is the hypolimnion; it contains little oxygen, cold waters, and few gamefish.

Some inland lakes never stratify, while others always do during warm summer weather. Size of the lake often determines whether this natural phenomenon will occur. Most lakes with 1000 acres or more, and even some smaller waters, will stratify as weather warms.

Consider the type of gamefish you're seeking; is it a warmwater or coldwater species? Consult the above table and commit it to memory. The next step will be a critical one for lake-fishing success.

Let's suppose we're looking for brown trout in a lake of 1500 acres. We've glanced at a contour map, located some fishy-looking structures, made a mental note of the shoreline contours, and developed a good hunch about a certain point that juts out from shore in a narrow finger before dropping into 30 feet of water. We'll motor into the area, lower the temperature-sensitive probe of an electronic water thermometer (I use a Garcia OTP [Oxygen Temperature Probe]), and begin taking a temperature reading every foot or two.

If the lake is stratified, you'll probably find 70-degree water at the surface, and down to about 10 feet. At 12 feet, it may be 67 degrees; 18 feet might register 64 degrees; and you might hit 61-degree water at 24 feet. This tells you that any brown trout will probably be found from about 20 to 25 feet down. Surprising? It shouldn't be. Gamefish will be near a food supply, in a water temperature band to their liking, and in a place where deep water is located near some type of underwater structure. In this situation, trolling is the one sure-fire method of taking browns.

Let's take another example. You have observed that a submerged weedbed rises from an area 18 feet deep to within inches of the surface. Your map shows water dropping off to 24 feet along the outside edge. This might be a prime spot to locate feeding browns because they tend to follow cover, in this case a deep-water weedline. The weeds also provide hiding places for baitfish.

The map also may reveal a sharp, narrow underwater hump in deep water. This is another good spot for brown trout.

Another area may have sharp-breaking contour changes, where the water drops sharply from 10 to 25 feet, with a series of two or more close-together ledges. Browns can usually be found in such areas.

A sonar unit is a priceless piece of equipment for structure fishermen on any lake. Mine isn't used to pinpoint fish populations; it gives me a detailed look at the lake bottom and contour changes. These changes are the key to successful lake fishing.

As I troll, I'll keep one eye glued to the sonar unit and the other watching ahead and to the sides for other boat traffic. If we're trolling in 24 feet of water for brown trout, I'll want my lure within inches of bottom. A sudden change in bottom depth indicates a quick change in direction. If the water starts becoming shallow, I'll head slightly toward deeper water. If the water drops off suddenly, I'll swing in toward shore. The key here is to keep working the proper depth and *around any structure* that might be attractive to the gamefish in question, particularly if the water temperature is right.

Two trolling tactics can be used with the STST method. The one I prefer is slow trolling. The other was first outlined by Buck Perry. He called it Spoonplugging, and the name still sticks. Both techniques are designed to systematically cover productive fishing water from the shoreline out to any practical fishing depth.

Slow-troll Method

The STST slow-troll method usually works best with a fairly long line, and whatever weight-and-lure combination is needed to take the rig near bottom at a speed conducive to peak lure action. My choice for much of this fishing is a Rebel lure. If shallow depths are desired, I'll go with a floating model, but if the fish are big and deep I'll choose a deep-diving lure with a large lip. Some studies made in recent years indicate that a normal plug delivers as much underwater sound vibrations as does one with a built-in sound chamber.

Deep-water gamefish such as trout, especially in summer, are attracted by a series of Cowbells with a floating-diving plug trailing behind on an 18-inch leader. Determine which forage fish are present, and then select a lure that resembles the baitfish. If yellow perch, for instance, comprise the bulk of the food for a gamefish it would be wise to fish lures with a perch-scale finish. Many tackle companies produce their wares in every imaginable coloration, including shiner, shad, alewife, yellow perch, sunfish, bass, rainbow trout, etc. It becomes merely a matter of choosing a plug of the right color and size to fit the situation at hand. I've seen many cases where neutral density plugs have delivered fast action when allowed to sink to the desired level before trolling begins.

A typical STST slow-trolling situation would be handled like this: The angler has determined where on the lake he wishes to fish, and at what depth. He'll choose a lure, and a proper weight (if necessary). He'll begin trolling just fast enough to bring out the proper lure action. The lure *must* be near bottom, at the proper depth and water temperature. The angler will release line until he feels the lure or weight bumping bottom at the right depth. Once this is felt, he will reel in just enough line to keep the lure a foot or less off bottom. This will place the lure in the correct zone most of the time.

Trolling in a line as straight as an arrow will produce some fish, but fish catches often soar when an angler trolls in a zigzag manner. Sudden turns to port or starboard will cause the trolled lure to switch directions. Many gamefish will follow a slowly trolled lure for long distances before striking. A lure trolled in a straight line isn't nearly as attractive as one that swerves suddenly to one side or another. Such tricks can generate savage strikes.

Spinning or baitcasting tackle can be used, although I prefer the latter because it allows me to feed more line into the troll whenever necessary. I'll use 6- to 12-pound mono for this trolling technique. Heavier line is used for larger fish or in deep water where the angler must use weight to get down near bottom.

Deep-water trolling may involve the use of a 3-way swivel and bell sinkers to take lures into fish-holding zones. It requires from ½- to 3-ounce sinkers to take a Cowbell and lure down to 25 feet. The weight needed is determined by the resistance of the flashers and the diameter

The author helps his wife Kay land a 25-pound muskie. She hooked the fish by trolling a Bomber on Tennessee's Dale Hollow Reservoir.

of the trolling line. It's best to attach any weight ahead of a flasher, often as much as 18 inches forward. Light line and a floating-diving plug trolled on 6- or 8-pound mono in 8 feet of water seldom requires any weight. If weight is necessary, an angler can usually get by with a ½-ounce sinker.

Slow trollers who employ the STST method often carry only a handful of lures for each gamefish species, but they may pack along a choice of weights needed to take their lures down. I've had to change weights a dozen times during one fishing day in order to meet condition and depth changes.

This need for weight adjustment is clearly indicated on those days when a strong wind is blowing. It may be necessary to use more or less weight to get down, depending on how the wind affects boat speed.

Another problem often encountered is a change in the depth of the thermocline. Strong winds can cause this narrow band of water to shift upward or downward, depending on direction and velocity. I've seen several cases where the thermocline may raise or lower itself as much as 20 feet during one fishing day. The STST angler must continue to take periodic water-temperature checks throughout the day and adjust his tactics accordingly.

Spoonplugging Method

Buck Perry blew onto the fishing scene many years ago, and has left an indelible mark on the sport. His Spoonplugging theory proved itself on so many lakes that it is now used universally. In many respects, he follows the STST approach to fishing, although his Spoonplugs can be cast or trolled while the slow-troll technique outlined above is just a trolling tactic.

Whether you subscribe to slow trolling or Spoonplugging, the key factor is lure presentation and speed control. These two factors, when combined with the proper lure fished at the proper depth along good fish-holding structure, will increase your catches dramatically. Only a certain small percentage of any lake will contain fish, but the following Spoonplugging technique enables anglers to strain all waters in the swiftest possible manner.

There are several Spoonplug sizes and all are designed scientifically to *dive to certain depths with a certain controllable length of line released behind the boat.* These lures will reach the prescribed depths regardless of trolling speed. Speed trolling, a supposedly new technique, has been around for years. Buck Perry revolutionized the method with his lures.

Line diameter is the one factor that will affect lure depth. The larger the diameter, the increased line drag in the water. The lure will dive shallower. Perry recommends the use of marked line when Spoonplugging. His lines are marked every 30 feet with a different color. Some of his lures will reach the required depths with a short- to medium-line length; others work best with a medium to long line. Some (the larger sizes that dive deepest) require a medium- to extra-long line.

Spoonplugs are often used when you want to fish around good structure at a certain depth. If smallmouth bass are holding along a breakline in 15 feet of water, you'd need to use a Series 100 Spoonplug. This lure is designed to hold at 12- to 15-foot levels, with a medium to long line out. (Here we're talking about releasing 50 to 60 yards of line behind the boat.)

My normal tactic is to work shallow water with smaller Spoonplugs. If I find fish at a 15-foot depth, I'll make one pass through the area, with the 100-size lure, at a slow troll. If this doesn't work, I'll approach the area from the opposite direction at a faster speed. If that fails to deliver a strike I'll move through again at a fast troll. One or the other of these tactics should deliver a strike. The better structures should be approached from as many directions as possible. If the area fails to produce, I'll move on to another location and come back at a different time.

The use of a Spoonplug can be teamed with a thermometer and sonar unit, although I caution anglers to refrain from using sonar gear in shallow water because sound waves can spook gamefish at certain times. Use markers to slot your trolling pass along the outside edges of weedbeds, points, underwater humps, reefs, submerged islands, or other structure. If the trolling area is well-marked, or shoreline characteristics can be used to pinpoint the proper area, you'll do well to keep the sonar unit off, especially in water less than 10 feet deep.

Spoonplugs are designed to stop wiggling whenever they become fouled with weeds, dead leaves, or other debris. It's often possible to rip the lure hard through the water with the rod tip to free the hooks. Another trick to using this lure is to slow down the trolling speed when the lure starts plowing a furrow in the bottom. It should merely bounce along bottom and not dig in. Once the lure starts running free again you can increase the trolling speed, and thereby sift the water much faster and in a more thorough manner.

To make a thorough sifting of the lake near structure areas, start in shallow water with the smallest Spoonplug. Work the area thoroughly, and then switch to the next larger lure and try deeper water in the same area. I'll often start fishing in 2 to 4 feet of water, and then move out to 4 to 6 feet and work the same immediate area. Then I'll try from 6- to 9-foot depths, and continue out into deeper water with larger lures until fish contact has been made.

If the lure begins bumping bottom continuously, work out into slightly deeper water until it quits bumping. Then move back into shallower water until the lure begins tapping bottom again. This in-and-out method is similar to the slow-trolling technique, although faster speeds can be used without decreasing the effectiveness of the lure.

If the fisherman should notice any bar, reef, or point extending from the shallows into deep water, and contact hasn't been made with gamefish in shallower water, fish are probably holed up in deep water off the structure. A deeper running lure bounced directly along bottom should work well in these cases. Do not waste time trolling past the supposed hotspot. Instead, turn right around and go back through it again. This lure was made for such fast in-and-out fishing conditions.

I consider the slow-troll and Spoonplugging methods two of the finest fishing techniques available to any lake fisherman.

You must learn how to read a contour map, judge the shoreline to determine offshore structures, use a sonar unit and electronic water thermometer, and troll properly. Once you perfect these skills, you begin catching fish with regularity.

Largemouth Bass

Many years ago, I caught my first largemouth bass on a bog lake in southern Michigan. Lily pads dotted the surface, and heavy mats of weeds grew from top to bottom. Here and there, an open avenue of water wound between wavering strands of cabomba, coontail, and other weeds.

I knew nothing about lake fishing for bass. My fishing amounted to a cast that arched high in a graceful curve, only to jerk backward mightily as the baitcasting reel backlashed. The plug, either a Jitterbug or Hula Popper, would splash down like a space ship making a touchdown on the Pacific. I would sit still, biding the advice of the outdoor writers of that era, and allow the concentric circles to spread. A minute or two would pass before I would twitch the plug—just enough to make it appear alive. Again, the advice of magazine writers was governing my actions. Those circles would dissipate and another twitch would move the plug an inch or two. It was painfully slow fishing in those days as several minutes usually passed between casts. The fishing was even slower, about as much fun as watching a worm wrestle.

Several city blocks of bog-lake shoreline had been explored with one cast after another. Good areas followed bad, but that didn't matter to me; I was a bass fisherman, and writers like Jason Lucas, Robert Page Lincoln, Homer Circle, Ray Bergman, and Wynn Davis were at my elbow guiding every cast.

It seemed as if hundreds of casts fell, and were chugged and burped. Yet nothing moved to the plug. I was beginning to question the advice of the writers. When my first bass struck, it came as fast as a bolt of heat lightning creasing a hot summer sky. I was completely bewildered, but only for a second.

The writers hadn't specifically cautioned me to set the hook, but I reared back out of sheer fright. The barb sank home. There was no give and take, as advocated in outdoor periodicals. I just leaned back and cranked hard on the reel handle until something gave. Luckily, the 3-pound bass gave in before my weak line.

I committed the cardinal sin of grabbing the line and lifting the fish into the boat. The horseshoe of good luck must have been with me that day, because the bass soon lay flopping on the floor. It was a beautiful sight; all green with dark streaks, with a mouth seemingly wide enough to swallow the boat; and it was mine.

I pumped hard on the oars and was soon proudly showing the fish to my parents. The delight in their eyes, and in mine, has scarcely dimmed since that day. When a nice bass fails to kindle a fire inside these bones, I hope I have enough sense to hang up my rods and watch sleep robbers on nighttime television.

Many years passed before I looked back on that childhood experience and decided that I hadn't changed my fishing style for twenty years. I was still plugging the shoreline and hoping for a good strike on surface lures. I only fished during summer evenings, when whippoorwills called, nighthawks boomed, and frogs croaked. Water skiers had put their toys away for another day, the swimmers had gone to bed, and then I'd fish; hot nights, cold nights, or rainy nights, it made little difference to me. I would work the shoreline and pound consecutive casts at docks, swimming rafts, and lily-pad areas. And I'd catch fish. Something was missing, though, because for every good night there would be a dozen bad ones.

I knew bass thrived in the lakes that I fished, but I never got my act together. Hit or miss was the nature of my fishing, and the misses far outnumbered the hits. Then I began hearing about structure fishing, and how fish moved onto structure (not necessarily shoreline structure). I read avidly everything I could on the subject.

One of the first articles I read was written by Buck Perry. Though I've never met him, he has had a profound, lasting impact on my fishing.

This was in the days before the widespread use of sonar units. I checked the depths of many lakes with a heavy lead weight attached to a strong cord. I made notations on a hand-drawn map of the water, and I marked dropoffs, tapering points, deep-water weedlines, submerged weedbeds. Each area was triangulated with shoreline markers for easy reference. I continued to study, ordered detailed gamefish studies, noted their habits and habitats, and I began catching more fish. It wasn't an overnight circus of smashing strikes from freewheeling gamefish. I landed more fish, but it wasn't a slaughter then and it isn't now. I worked for each fish. It became progressively easier to catch bass but there still remained many days when a fat zero marked my score after ten hours of fishing.

I next began to learn that weather conditions influenced fishing success, or the lack of it. I kept a diary of pertinent facts, and would record the time of day fish struck and were landed, depth of water, cloud cover, air temperature, wind direction, barometer reading at the start and end of a day, the lure that produced, and how long it had been since a cold front had passed through my area. It required three years of record keeping before I decided that weather conditions—and the amount of cloud cover—were the best guides to when and where bass might strike. Weather conditions and cloud cover affect fishing success, more than ten tackleboxes of good lures.

The largemouth bass is the most widely discussed gamefish today. It has captured the imagination of millions of anglers across the country. Literally hundreds of new lures have been invented in the last five years, and more will be developed in the future just as surely as spring follows winter. Many lures are often touted as being best for largemouth bass. The good ones stay around, while the dogs go begging for business and wind up in the financial boneyard. The fact is that a firm knowledge of largemouth-bass structure, their seasonal movements, and a few clues about how to fish at these times will go far in filling a limit. Chances are good that a dozen lures designed to be fished at various depths will do the job.

It should be noted that the following patterns of movement and fishing techniques will vary somewhat from one region to another. The spring spawn may occur in March and April in southern states, while it seldom takes place in the Midwest before May, June, or even July. The exact timing isn't nearly as important as is the fact that seasonal movements are nearly the same regardless of where they occur. It's easy to trace such movements if you know when optimum conditions occur. We'll take an in-depth look at the seasonal movements of largemouth bass. Then we'll examine some of the best areas to look for fish and the best tactics for catching them.

Spring

Three specific time periods apply to spring largemouth bass fishing —prespawn, spawn, and postspawn conditions. Each has a direct bearing on where the majority of bass will be found.

Much of the same information here that applies to bass found in natural lakes will apply to reservoir gamefish as well.

The taking of prespawn bass is often so easy that many states protect the species from overharvest by opening the season after spawning is completed. Other states allow bass to be taken year-round.

Some areas, particularly in the South, have a longer growing season and more fish. Such areas can withstand the pressure of prespawn fishermen. Northern states, with a shorter growing season, can damage a bass fishery beyond repair if they allow fishing for largemouths at this time.

Water temperature is the major factor that brings soon-to-spawn bass into shallow spring water. Certain areas may contain the proper water temperature for prespawning bass (59 to 60 degrees F.), but if the lake bottom isn't suitable for spawning chores, they won't be there.

One of the areas to observe closely are shallow bays or indentations off the main lake. If these areas are shallow, and contain black silt or decayed organisms, then you're on the right track. Such spots warm faster due to the heat-attracting powers of black-bottomed waters. Bass will filter into such areas whenever they begin feeling their oats.

Largemouth bass tend to stay in one or two such shallow areas during prespawn conditions, and ignore other, similar waters. The other shallow areas may not have direct access to deeper water, or perhaps something else is wrong. But bucketmouths apparently can sense a good spawning area and avoid a poor one. Only a small percentage of any natural lake or reservoir will have shorelines suitable for spawning fish.

Bass fishermen often probe every foot of shoreline with casts in hopes of finding a good area. This type of fishing may be fun, but it's seldom productive. The bulk of the fish will be found in only a few small areas. The balance of the shoreline is worthless. A trick I've used is to cruise slowly along the shoreline, standing in the bow of my boat. I look through polarized sunglasses for bass signs. Mark each area in your mind, continue a search for bed-making fish, and leave the fish alone until you've covered the entire lake or a major portion of it. Then return to the productive spots and begin fishing.

Prespawn bass are often restless and subject to in-and-out movements whenever a cold spell settles in. A drop of one or two degrees in water temperature can send fish heading for deeper water or weedy cover. They will remain there until inshore waters warm again. It's hard to take fish on artificials at this time.

Spinnerbaits or shallow-running surface lures can produce deadly results during prespawn conditions. Many fish will be protective of bedding areas and will actively pursue a lure, which is one of the reasons why this type of fishing is outlawed in some areas. It's very easy to remove the bulk of any natural lake's breeding stock during this period.

Some largemouth bass are skittish, and the first cast anywhere near them will result in the fish spooking from shallow to deep water. Persistent casting efforts are rarely needed because a bass will often strike the first lure that passes near it.

Other hotspots on any natural lake, especially a eutrophic lake, will deliver fast action. Look for shallow flats rimmed with reeds and a sandy loam bottom. A shallow bay dotted with cattails or lily pads can be productive. It's not uncommon to find bass bedding in water under docks or beneath tethered boats. This type of cover gives fish access to shallow, undisturbed water, and some protection from overhead predation. I've caught many fish by slanting a cast in under a dock or between a dock and a boat.

Spawning conditions are very similar to prespawn conditions, except that bass are actually in the act of reproduction. While fish will be fanning spawning redds in water from 6 inches to 3 feet deep during the prespawn period, both males and female will be present during the spawn. A cautious observer is likely to see a female and more than one male fish. The largest males service the female frequently. Other precocious male fish hang around the fringes, waiting for an opportunity to dart in and fertilize the eggs.

Large male fish are often hooked at this time. They lash out at anything within reach, possibly due to constant harassment from smaller males. One of the easiest ways to catch big males, and the occasional pot-bellied female, was shown to me on Lake Okeechobee in southern Florida. My guide and I waded the shallows. Every time we stepped into a bass bed (the water was dingy and we couldn't see but

Spinnerbaits are effective during the prespawn period. This angler carries a sizable collection in his tacklebox. Note the sonar unit in the stern.

could feel the depressions with our feet) we broke off a cattail stalk near the bed. We marked several dozen redds in this manner. We retraced our steps and cast black Johnson Silver Minnows near each bent cattail. The lures were allowed to sink only for a second and then brought back as rapidly as possible with short up-and-down flips of the rod tip. This caused the lure to hump up and down as it traveled over the bed. A fin would often crease the water and the lure would disappear in a fountain of spray. Nearly every fish we hooked was a male, although my guide nailed one 10-pound female.

The postspawn period for largemouth fishermen can be one of feast or famine. It's not uncommon for bass to slide into deep water as soon as spawning chores are completed. The fish may scatter, or hole up together in small pods of same-sized fish. I have seen some cases where bass will follow breaklines into deep water, but will remain near spawning sites. I have also seen fish disperse widely. A very short spell of inactivity normally occurs and then bass will go on a feeding spree to ward off hunger and the pressures of spawning. If fish can be located, the postspawn period can be a good time to fish.

Summer

The summer, from June through early September in most regions, is the one period of the year when most anglers go largemouth bass fishing. The weather, for the most part, is stable, with mile-high blue skies and warm temperatures. The conditions are pleasant, but summer is seldom the best time to go bass fishing.

As already mentioned, water temperature is an important clue to bass behavior. I have also stressed that weather conditions play a major role. Many anglers, however, still pound shoreline areas where fish were taken during the prespawn, spawn, and occasionally during the postspawn spring periods. The areas that produced three months ago may still deliver a small bass, but bigger fish are in deep water much of the time except for short, periodic movements on *shallower* structure (6 to 20 feet deep), such as weedbed edges, narrow points, the bases of lily pad stems, or submerged weedbeds.

A buddy of mine, a really dedicated bass fisherman, used to fish some southern Michigan lakes during the day. His STST method involved trolling deep-running plugs near bottom. He would use the largest Spoonplugs, floating Rebels behind a 2-ounce Baitwalker, or a Bomber or Waterdog. He bumped bottom and caught fish. His secret was to probe every piece of structure that tapered or dropped off into 18 or 20 feet of water. He was very successful. His stringers usually weighed 15 to 25 pounds. He didn't fish every day, however. His efforts were most fruitful on those days when a frontal system moved into the area. He would then fish from daylight to dark and denounce the midnight fishermen that flogged the shorelines for a few fish. "The fish are there all day. They often aren't feeding, but will strike out of boredom or competition. I give 'em something to compete for," he said.

Summer fishing requires more than dragging lures along bottom, hoping to intercept a bass. You must make a thorough study of bass behavior, and how fish react to heat, clear skies, and lakeside activity. The summer months bring a concentration of fishermen and other pleasure-seekers to most lakes. Water skiing, swimming, dock parties, and other activities keep bass from the shallows except for an occasional after-dark foray.

To nail bass consistently, know the lake and where fish will be found in it. Southern bass often hole up under heavy mats of floating weeds. Northern lakes seldom have heavy weed layers on the surface, but they do have deep weedbeds of various thicknesses. Bass will normally head near bottom, and will be found either on the dark side or the deep-water side of anything that blocks out the sun. Feeding movements are often short on bright days, if a movement occurs at all. Peak fishing usually occurs on cloudy days, at dusk or dawn, or after dark.

I've found that night fishing can generate some of the liveliest action of the season. Unfortunately, many anglers simply don't know

Rebel Super R

Bomber

Sonic

how to fish a lake, reservoir, strip-mine pit, or farmpond once the sun goes down. They peg lures at the shallows, spend part of their time pulling rigs out of shoreline brush and too little time fishing in the proper areas.

A now-deceased fisherman took me to task one night on an Illinois lake. "What'n'hell you doing up there in the shallows," he yelled. We were the only anglers on the lake that night. I noticed that he was fishing out from me, but hadn't paid much attention to him. I heard a couple of splashes and knew he had landed some fish. But then, so had I. I was proud of my 1½-pounders, so I rowed over to talk with him.

He eyeballed my bass, grunted something under his breath about shore fishermen and small fish, and then pinned me to my boat seat with a statement I've never forgotten: "Kid, you're wasting your time pounding the shoreline." I started to protest but he interrupted with his next words.

"The big fish aren't in the shallows, except on occasion. Out here in 8 to 12 feet of water is where you'll nail jumbo bass after dark. These fish use the same migration routes at night as they do during the day. C'mere and we'll see as how I can teach you something." I jumped in his boat, did all the rowing, and he proceeded to give me a crash course in the basics of night fishing for bass.

He pointed out that clear-water lakes offered the best prospects for night action, much better than dark, dingy water. The strip-mine pit we fished had water as clear as air. The fish, he said, were prone to making horizontal movements on structure from deep water. The fish usually use the same structure and movements as they do during daylight, except that they move freely under cover of darkness.

The tops of submerged weedbeds, moored rafts or boats, and submerged wood or brushy banks are good spots to try in natural lakes. Strip-mine pits offer good sport near the first breakline into deep water. Late in the summer, bass in natural lakes will move to steeper banks and dropoffs. I have seen largemouth bass moving onto boulders and large rubble in some Arkansas lakes. In Greers Ferry Lake, for example, fish move into such areas after dark to feed.

One spot my new buddy showed me was a small point spread out over a narrow flat covered with 2 feet of water. The flat made a shallow break of another foot, extended into the lake for a short distance, and made a second sharp break into 8 feet of water. A weedbed lay just off this second break. A tiny finger of slightly elevated bottom ran from the second breakline out to the weedbed, which was 10 feet away. That narrow finger was the migration route from the shoreline flats to the weedbed. We anchored quietly and fished this narrow slot on the shoreward side of the weeds for just one hour. He caught six fish, and I netted four. The smallest bass was a 2-pounder that struck a spinner bait. We landed six fish that weighed from 4 to 7 pounds each. Such areas, with a pronounced access route to the shallows from deeper weedbeds, can deliver hot action, but few anglers fish them.

I've since learned that the deep-water edges of weedbeds can generate plenty of starlight excitement. These areas should be combed with sinking lures, spinnerbaits, or small spoons. I try to carry a variety of lures that offer bass a color contrast against the night sky. Sonic lures are good choices for a variety of reasons. On some nights, the fish home-in on underwater vibrations easier than they do to lure movement. I have landed several after-dark largemouths that were hooked outside the mouth. Their aim was off just slightly, but enough to miss inhaling my lure. Of course, such foul-hooked gamefish were returned to the water.

A friend fishes exclusively in the Great Lakes states. He doesn't believe that sound, motion, or color are important for night-feeding bass. He fishes the same areas at night that he fishes during the day, except he uses a Texas-rigged purple worm. He works the breaklines just offshore with an unweighted worm retrieved at a steady pace, without the typical up-and-down movements. This method produces spectacular results for my friend occasionally. His best catches of lunker bass are normally made in 8 to 12 feet of water with the same rig, except he pinches on one No. 7 splitshot 18 inches ahead of the plastic worm. It is allowed to sink near bottom, and then he retrieves slowly with a flipping up-and-down rod-tip movement. The hook is left

Bing McClelland poses with a trophy largemouth bass taken on a plastic worm at night.

exposed, and he gives a mighty set whenever the worm stops. Most of his fish are caught within inches of bottom.

The only other trick my friend uses when he's plastic-worm fishing is to occasionally raise his rod tip to a near-vertical position. He quickly drops the tip, and a bass often hits the hook as it drifts down.

One spot where I have enjoyed very good after-dark fishing is near fields of lily pads, *provided that* they are situated with good structure nearby that drops into deeper water. I probe such areas several times each night in an attempt to hit that one short period when largemouths are in shallower water. If the pad stems are in 5 or 6 feet of water, you stand a better chance to take fish. I like to use crankbaits like Roger's Big Jim or a Norman N in spots like this. A slow-sinking jointed Rebel can be very effective. Savage strikes are the rule in these areas. Do yourself a favor, and cast far past a suspected bass area. Then reel the lure into that water. A lure dropping in on a shallow-water largemouth is like a beaver slapping the water next to your boat on a dark night. It's guaranteed to scare the hell out of you, and it does the same to the fish.

Summer fishing requires other tricks besides night fishing. I've known many sportsmen who simply will not fish after dark. These anglers need to learn some of the migration routes that bass take from deep to shallower water. Remember, deep water is home to most decent-size or trophy bass. They are seldom in the shallows except for brief forage-finding trips. These shoreward migrations follow a reasonably distinct pattern. The pattern may change somewhat from area to area, reservoir to reservoir, or strip-mine pit to strip-mine pit. A contour map, a sonar unit, and a little savvy will help you find these migration routes.

Largemouth bass often use a deep-water weedline as the contact point for inshore migrations. This fact is particularly true in natural lakes, but it applies to reservoirs as well. The weedline on the deep-water side often holds fish day and night. They may not be in a positive feeding mood; in fact, they may be resting. But resting fish may still strike, provided that a lure comes by *on bottom.*

Deep-running lures are often the ticket for taking fish at these sites, which may vary from 15 to 25 feet in depth. A trolled Spoonplug bumping and wiggling along bottom is an excellent lure. Cordell's Big O is a dandy.

One technique I prefer in this situation is a jig. The jig can be tipped with a worm, minnow, or any one of the twister-type plastic tails. The Reaper tail is an excellent choice. I enjoy casting a jig off the tips of deep-water weedlines. I allow the lure to free-fall to bottom, and then work it slowly along the outside edge of the weeds. This tactic calls for precision casting and a thorough knowledge of the weed locations, but it can deliver fast-paced excitement during most summer periods. This weedline area is one of the hottest spots for bass fishermen, and it's also one of the most overlooked areas.

Recognition of lake breaklines can increase your catch of summer bass. Many largemouths tend to stay in areas near the first dropoff *if* they aren't found off the deep-water edge of the weedbeds. If the deep spot fails to produce, move shoreward and fish near cabbage weeds along the first breakline. This spot is nearly always a perfect fishing location for fast action. The water depth enables faster fishing, and easier fan-casting to strain the water. A careful angler can even troll or backtroll live bait along bottom and take fish.

One last tip for summer bass: most clear-water lakes will contain bass from depths of 20 to 25 feet. Dark-colored lakes with a dirty tinge will usually offer the best bass fishing at depths of 15 feet or less. Darker water blocks out the sun, and allows the fish access to shallow areas. Clear lakes don't. Look for bass near weedbeds comprised of cabomba, broadleaf cabbage, coontail, and eel grass. Aisles between patches of weeds, along the deep-water edge, or just below near-surface streamers of coontail or cabomba are the top areas to fish for bass in summer.

Broadleaf Cabbage   Cabomba

Broadleaf cabbage and cabomba are thick, heavy weeds and afford good midsummer cover for largemouth bass, as well as other gamefish. Anglers should concentrate on the fringes of such weedbeds or cast to holes inside the beds, using lures that will rip through the cover.

Fall

The fall is a period of weather changes. One day it's likely to be spitting snow. The following day it may rain. On the third day, it might be 70 degrees outside.

Most lakes, particularly in less temperate areas than the South (although southern lakes do cool off to a lesser degree), are undergoing a remarkable change in this season. Cooler air temperatures lower the surface temperature of the lake. Northern lakes continue this cooling-down process until the surface water approaches its maximum density (at about 39 degrees). Then this water sinks to bottom, forcing the bottom water up to the surface. This is the fall turnover, a critical time for largemouth bass fishermen. Fishing won't be good until the condition stabilizes. Not until the water is the same temperature from top to bottom do largemouths become active again.

Colder water can seriously affect fishing. A bass with a lowered metabolism feeds little. He'll often take live bait or a lure presented directly to him but isn't apt to travel far for a meal.

During this fall coldwater period, aquatic vegetation begins to die off. Some shallow weeds are the first to go. Largemouths start leaving the shallower weedy areas, and begin a *slow* descent into deeper water. The knack of taking fall largemouths is to find deeper, still-living weedbeds. Largemouths will often be found tucked away in these areas. Fishing success depends solely upon an angler being able to penetrate such areas with lures or live baits.

Research indicates that once the water temperature falls to about 50 degrees, most small bass stop feeding. Larger males feed only a little. But females, those heavyweights that you couldn't nail during the summer, are often very aggressive and strike well in fall. Fisheries biologists reason that the sows are feeding heavily in order to put on pounds to carry them through the winter season, and to give them enough strength to survive spring spawning.

In northern parts of the Midwest, such as Indiana, Ohio, Illinois, Wisconsin, Minnesota, and Michigan, some of the biggest largemouth bass in any mesotrophic or eutrophic lake stay near any green weeds or weedbed areas, which are usually in deeper areas. Don't bother fishing brown weeds—those that have died. Bass don't like them.

One mesotrophic lake I fished in central Illinois during late October four years ago had already begun to show a weed die-off in the shallows. Many weeds were brown in shallow coves, but superb stands of coontail and cabomba were still present in 10 to 14 feet of water. These green weeds were home to many 4- to 6-pound bass. I would drift and cast jig-minnow or jig-eel combinations, and work them very slowly along bottom. The few male fish I caught would merely nip at the lure until hooked. Big females (the largest fish we caught) would slam into the rig like they hadn't eaten in a week. The battles I had with these bass were dogged, but they lacked the spectacular aerial antics of summer-caught fish.

I experimented with crankbaits for suspended fish along or just inside the edges of green-colored weeds. Virtually any crankbait would

Isolated green weeds

Dead weeds

Isolated patches of green weeds in late fall often contain largemouths. Crankbaits worked through the beds will produce strikes.

work, provided that it was reasonably small and fished as slow as possible, and was still able to obtain depth and keep the built-in wiggle. I found that crankbaits worked through and near green weedbeds located on a steep dropoff proved to be the winning combination, both for numbers and size of bass taken. We all reached our limit that day, which proves a point: fall largemouth fishing can deliver the best action of the season if you can find the fish. Finding green weeds is the first step. Then look for weedy areas near a steep dropoff or a small depression on bottom. The outside edge of the weedline forms a distinct breakline in many cases. Such areas can be marked with floating buoys. The fishing is much easier than during the summer.

Look for large concentrations of bass during the fall. The fish tend to hang together; the area inhabited may be small, in some cases no larger than an average bedroom. I've seen lakes where most of the big fish were located in an area 10 feet square. Such largemouth communes can provide outstanding fishing.

Fluttering a spinnerbait over the tops of heavy weed growth and then allowing it to sink into open holes in the weeds is a productive technique.

Lure presentation is important in fall. I've used the STST system, and taken several lunker bass from cold water. But I believe that a slow, careful presentation of a crankbait or jig is the better system, allowing you to search green weed areas. Casting from a motionless boat is much warmer than scooting down the lake making trolling passes. A warm, comfortable fisherman is more apt to feel the light takes of male fish and be able to cope with the savage slashes of big females.

The colder the water, the slower an angler should fish. Jig-eel and jig-minnow combinations are very effective just before freeze-up. These rigs can be crawled slowly along the bottom. Refrain from making the typical jigging lifts of the rod tip. Reel as slowly as possible, and let the jig do the rest. Strikes are soft and difficult to feel. A light line will help you detect a strike.

Small spinnerbaits, those with single blades rather than tandem spinners, can work well during the period preceding ice cover. They should be fished very slowly and allowed to free-fall, with the spinner blade revolving above the lure. Some anglers call this tactic "helicoptering," which means the blade flutters above the sinking lure. Bass will often sneak in under the spinning blade to grab the lure. Male fish often strike the blade, while females tend to engulf the entire rig. This tactic works well in sparse weedbeds or along the edges.

Winter

Some midwestern states have year-round bass fishing. Many lakes have open-water areas even during the winter. The water temperature normally hovers between 32 and 40 degrees. Only dedicated anglers brave the cold to fish under these conditions. One mistake can cost a fisherman his life.

Largemouth bass in most northern lakes will do one of two things during open-water winter periods: the fish will either be in very shallow water (often under the edge of shoreline ice cover) or in deeper holes near any remaining green weeds. I have caught many large bass in

This angler fished a small Rapala close to floating weeds to fool a largemouth. The bass, one of a school, was feeding on small shad.

both areas, but my steadiest success has come in the shallows. Such areas are easier to explore and fishing can be done at a more rapid pace.

In northern areas, the same jig-eel or jig-minnow combination that works during the fall will work in winter, but the speed must be motionless or close to it. Some anglers have told me that they have had fish grab a motionless jig. They prefer using stand-up jigs baited with an eel, nightcrawler, or minnow. An occasional slow movement will often attract fish.

Minnows that are fished slowly near green weeds in fairly shallow water (about 4 feet) can work well during these cold-weather periods. The bass will often grab a tethered minnow, since it represents an adequate, easily obtained meal. Shiner minnows in the 2- to 4-inch class are table treats for most bass. They seldom refuse minnows fished near green weeds in shallow water.

I'd just as soon do my winter bass fishing in Florida, where one can sample the pleasures of fishing in 70-degree weather. I don't enjoy freezing in an 8-ounce snowmobile suit on a wind-whipped northern lake.

CHAPTER

Smallmouth Bass

Largemouth bass and northern pike offer great sport, but if someone is looking for pure explosive action with a gamefish that packs a wallop like a mule and jumps like a tarpon, then I'd have to rate the smallmouth bass as one of the worthiest opponents found in fresh water. This species has a wide range, grows to admirable sizes, and fights until his last ounce of strength is gone. Even then, he comes to the boat with fire in his eye.

Smallies are great fun. I've had the pleasure of fishing for them in shield lakes in northeastern Minnesota and western Ontario, throughout the Great Lakes, and in many inland lakes. I've also caught them in Kentucky, Tennessee, Iowa, Nebraska, North and South Dakota, most northeastern states, as well as in Quebec and New Brunswick.

Smallies, like their bigmouth cousins, prefer certain types of structure during each of the four seasons. These migration patterns along structure have been well documented by fishermen. I've fished for smallmouth bass for thirty years. Only during the last ten, however, have I paid any attention to the structure preferences of this species. My success ratio has soared since I began structure fishing. I have caught more—and bigger—fish. I was once content with catching smallies of just-legal size, but after battling 5-pounders, I no longer want to fool with the runts.

The following seasonal information, structure preferences, and movement patterns may enable you to enjoy the satisfaction of outwitting a trophy smallmouth bass.

Spring

One of the major problems to overcome during spring fishing is clear water. Many lakes that hold smallies are gin-clear, and the fish in them are extremely wary. A spring freshet in the headwaters of a tributary stream may dirty some lake water near the outlet, but most of the time anglers must work in crystal-clear water. It's tough.

The prespawn and spawning seasons are two of the best periods to seek smallmouth bass. The fish seem less wary at this time because of upcoming spawning chores. This period usually begins when the water temperature is from 45 to 50 degrees F. The fish start moving from the depths into shallow, rocky areas, where they spread out over other bottom formations.

In most smallmouth lakes, it's possible simply to glance at the shoreline and locate good areas for prespawning smallmouth bass. This is particularly true if the water temperature is 50 degrees, or slightly warmer. Most shallow flats can be eliminated at first glance. Look for any shoreline area that offers a change in conformation. Such changes might be wherever baseball-size rocks (or larger) are found near sand, gravel, clay, or marl. The areas with large rocks will usually be the best spots to make contact with scrappy bronzebacks. Many lakes are composed mainly of such rocky areas. If rocks are abundant, you'll have to narrow down the choice of fishing areas still further. Deep waters near such rocky areas are far better fishing spots than are spots located some distance from deep water. If the entire shoreline is rocky, then look for additional breaks in the form of brush, reeds, submerged pilings, and so on. Michigan's Crystal Lake is a smallmouth haven, but most of the fish are caught along the south shore, where several cribs and old pilings are found. Smallies like the extra cover. These areas also provide good food: crayfish. Rocky or gravel points are very good, provided that they are at the mouth of a bay. Narrow bays have sharper points and produce better fishing.

Smallies, as they leave deep water, normally head for the shoreline with the sharpest breaklines and the most breaks on structure. In many Canadian lakes, the first smallmouth contact point is a sharp point at the mouth of a bay. The fish move up from deep water, contact the lower edge of the sharp points, head up the breakline, encounter several breaks in the form of boulders and large jagged rocks, and continue up until they reach water 2 to 6 feet deep.

Smallies will often remain off sharp points at the mouths of bays until warmer water triggers their spawning urge. This may require four or five weeks. The fish then move into the shallow bays, provided that they are made of a hard bottom strata of sand, rock, gravel, or small boulders. A small amount of silt or marl may cover the bottom, but smallies don't mind this if the strata under the debris is hard. They will not spawn in soft-bottomed areas so this can serve as a starting point in your process of elimination.

Light line is needed for spring fishing. The anglers who bring the most fish back to the dock are usually rigged with 4- or 6-pound monofilament. Use small jigs in clear, springtime water. I like Burke's Wig Wag Mino, Gapen's Ugly Bug Plus, or a Beetle Spin, all in $1/8$- or $1/16$-ounce sizes. Yellow, white, and black have been my most effective colors, although I've taken a number of fine smallies on brown, purple, and other colors.

More important than color is the method of presentation. Most of

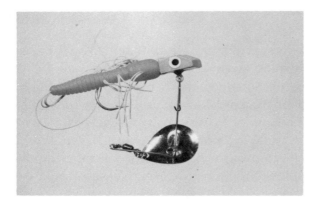

Ugly Bug Plus

Wig-Wag Mino

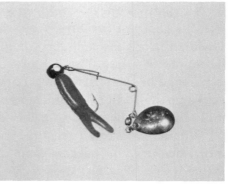

Beetle Spin

Countdown Rapala

the fish will be in water less than 10 feet deep. Some fish will stay near boulders with their tops out of water. Some of my fastest action took place several years ago on a Wisconsin lake when I hand-picked a limit of 4- to 5-pound smallies from water less than 3 feet deep. I caught fish on a dozen different artificials, but the presentation method and retrieve were the same.

Look for visible targets to cast toward. Large boulders, submerged brush, reeds, or piles of gravel or rocks are examples of likely targets. Cast small jigs, tipped with either a plastic grub, twister tail, or live bait, alongside the object. Reel very slowly, in a steady manner, and keep the lure bumping along bottom. This is where the fish are located. They won't strike an erratic retrieve (one that is traveling too fast), or anything off bottom.

Driftfishing is a very efficient technique because a breeze can power the boat downwind. There is no engine noise in the shallow water, and nothing will spook fish except inept retrieves. Cast downwind, and aim toward boulders or other breaks on structure. Wear a pair of polarized sunglasses to cut the surface glare of the water.

A strike on a small jig in cold water is very light. The line will often move sideways as a fish grabs the lure. An experienced angler can often spot the flash of a fish as it engulfs the jig. Set the hook lightly; cold weather and big fish can snap light mono.

Actual spawning normally takes place in fairly shallow, hard-bottomed bays. The choice of spawning sites can often be narrowed down to those bays with some ledge rock or submerged timber present. Smallmouths seem to prefer submerged logs or trees near their spawning sites.

By the time spawning occurs, the fish are occupying warmer water and are more active. Small crankbaits such as Mud Bugs, Deep Wee-R, or countdown Rapalas are excellent lure choices. Light lines should be used. It's often possible to pinpoint spawning fish by the characteristic whitish bed fanned from the bottom. Cast any of these lures past the bed (even if you can't see fish), and bring it past the spawning redd with just enough speed to bump bottom and bring out the built-in action.

Small jigs with a twister tail can work very well at this time. Cast beyond the bed, and fish it back with a lift-drop motion of the rod tip. Attempt to drop it directly into the spawning bed. Most smallmouths will swarm all over the lure.

Sometimes a cold front will push smallmouth bass from the shallows, out over the breakline, and back into the depths. They seldom go out as far as their midwinter sanctuary, but they may hold along the first or second sharp breakline. This is especially true if some breaks such as large boulders are present. Trolling or backtrolling seems to be the best way to nail fish at this time. It allows a slower lure or bait presentation to wary fish.

I fished Lake Erie's Bass Islands several years ago, when a cold spring kept fish deep. We trolled very slowly with several deep-running lures. The only time we caught fish was when the lure was actually bumping the sides and tops of boulders along the breakline. This technique, although costly in lures lost, proved entirely satisfactory because we managed to catch ten fish among three anglers. The largest fish was a stunning 5-pounder. The others ranged from 2½ to 4 pounds. All were taken in 12 feet of water. Other nearby boats fishing shallow shoals and reefs were skunked. It does pay to experiment with depth and speed, and lures, when fishing gets stinko in the shallows.

Summer

Most anglers believe that summer is a tough time to catch smallmouth bass. This may be true if you visit the same areas you fished in the spring. However, good fishing can be done if you read the weather patterns and know more than your neighbor about summer fishing. The trick to taking summer bronzebacks is to locate them. That may sound like an insurance salesman's double-talk, but it's the truth. Fish, regardless of species, can't be caught if they can't be found.

One problem confronting smallmouth bass fishermen is that they tend to fish for smallies in the same manner as they do summer largemouth bass. By doing so, they defeat themselves before they make their first cast or trolling pass. The name "bass" is the only thing these gamefish have in common. The two are as different as apples and oranges, and each demands specialized fishing techniques in summer.

Summer days, especially those during a cold front with high, clear skies, are the bane of summer anglers. Smallmouth bass get nervous during this type of weather and in a clear lake will often go very deep in an attempt to escape the effects of the frontal system.

One of the best methods that I've found for summer smallmouth fishing was shown to my wife and me by Dan Gapen, a tackle manufacturer and light-tackle enthusiast from Minnesota. We fished a series of small lakes near Gunflint Lake in northeastern Minnesota. A cold front had passed through the previous day, and Dan predicted poor fishing. He was right.

On our second day of fishing (the third day after the front passed through), clouds appeared on the western horizon. We fished Saganago Lake, and Dan brought out one of his new Baitwalkers—a lead weight with an offset wire arm that holds a leader. They come in various weights to meet different depth conditions. We tooled the rig up with a 4-pound mono leader measuring 24 inches, and a No. 8 longshank hook. Our bait was a leech. These squirmy critters look as appetizing as once-digested dog food, but smallmouth bass like 'em. They were hooked through the suction cup, and the rig was lowered over the side.

"There's a good breakline along here," Dan said. "It's down about 25 feet, and is fairly stable for 100 yards before falling off rapidly into 30 feet of water. Several small patches of boulders and rocks are found along the breakline. I think we'll find fish." He was more optimistic than I was because he had fished with leeches before. I hadn't.

Small puffs of breeze rippled the surface and reduced surface glare above and below the water. We trolled very slowly. The Baitwalkers were ticking the bottom when Dan's rod bucked. He's a happy-go-lucky angler, and his grin spread from one ear to the other. "Oh, the kid's done it again," he said, in a mock salute to his fishing ability.

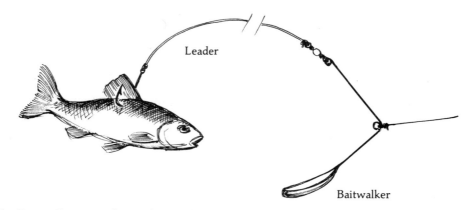

Leader

Baitwalker

The Baitwalker rig is designed to work along bottom, presenting live bait such as minnows, leeches, nightcrawlers, or salamanders to gamefish. The spring-wire holding the 12- to 18-inch leader keeps the bait off bottom. In clear water, the leader can be extended to 36 inches.

I started bringing my rig up from the depths when something nailed the leech and started for deeper water. I scrambled under Dan's rod and kept the line tight as I walked the rod tip around the bow of the boat so that we could battle our fish on either side of the craft. My 2-pound smallie came to the surface, jumped once with the Baitwalker bashing him alongside the head, and then rolled over in submission. Dan's fish was more rambunctious and required some clever rod work before it gave up and came to the net. His grin got wider as he netted a 4-pounder.

Kay got into the fray next and boated a 3-pounder. We nailed five more fish along that breakline. It's an amazing tribute to a trolling weight when you can fish in deep or shallow water, or among rocks and boulders, and never get hung up on bottom. That stretch of water would have eaten up other trolling weights, but the Baitwalker kept the rig near bottom at all times while the baited hook and leader trailed just above the rocks. This was the key point in our success that day. The leeches, of course, didn't fare too well, but so what. I don't like the slimy things anyway. They do lure fish, though.

Kay Richey admires a 3-pound smallmouth bass taken on a leech fished along bottom near boulders in 10 feet of water.

Some of the finest summer smallmouth fishing can be done very early in the morning. Water temperatures are often cool at this time. Big fish work up from the depths at night to feed, and are in shallower water at sunrise. The early-bird fisherman can pick up some nice bass just as the world comes to life. Dawn also offers some good straggler fishing. Stragglers are fish cut off from the main school; these fish often feed along the shoreline.

Good spots to fish for early-morning stragglers are along rocky shorelines or areas with steep dropoffs or sharp contour changes. The area must be close to deep water where bronzebacks can head if danger threatens. The areas must have some shallow water next to shore. It should be a short distance from shore to the first breakline. Avoid areas with steep cliffs and dropoffs next to shore that fall away into 40 feet of water. You'll not find smallies there.

A dropoff with small rocks or broken boulders is prime smallmouth habitat. Crayfish and minnows gather here and fish can feed near deep water.

Steep dropoff from shoreline

Small broken or eroded rocks down dropoff.

A tail-hooked crayfish or a brown-colored jig like Gapen's Ugly Bug can be deadly when used for early-morning smallies. Fish them slowly along bottom, and impart a jerky, short, lift-drop movement to the lure. The point is to imitate as closely as possible the crabbing movements of a crayfish. Make the lure work from rock to rock in a realistic manner. Smallmouths in the shallows at this time are hungry, and feeding voraciously. They attack anything they consider edible.

Some summer hotspots may be at depths of 20 feet or more. These fish-holding areas are often small and difficult to fish in conventional fashion. Backtrolling with a Lindy rig and a leech, nightcrawler, or small shiner or spottail minnow enables the angler to adjust his speed control and present the offering in a precise manner. Use just enough weight to get down to bottom. Keep tension on the reel spool, and backtroll slowly over rocky humps, submerged sandbars, submerged islands, or other structure. Keep to the dark side of the structure on sunny days. It may also be necessary to fish slightly deeper than on an overcast day.

One of the tricks to any fishing, and particularly smallmouth (or largemouth) bass fishing, is to find a pattern for the day. Avoid being a one-method fisherman. Instead, learn to use a dozen different techniques. Sooner or later one will pay off. It requires some time to determine the productive pattern for the day.

One technique that is popular if backtrolling doesn't produce is to anchor or drift and cast deep-running plugs. Select lures that are designed for a specific depth. If fish are holding at 15 feet, you certainly shouldn't use a lure that goes down only 5 or 10 feet. I prefer carrying a small arsenal of deep divers like the Bomber, Mud Bug, Spoonplug, Bagley's Diving B, or Bomber's Model A. These lures are great for probing the depths of most lakes. I like to use deep divers for working the different levels of stair-stepping ledges until I establish a pattern. It's possible to start out at 5 feet and work down the ledges until fish are located. You'll have then established a pattern that will continue to produce throughout the day, provided that weather conditions remain the same.

A small, rocky island with quick access to deep water can be a magnet for smallmouth bass. The jumble of small rocks provides an ideal habitat for crayfish and minnows. Such islands can be connected to the mainland, to a string of islands, or may be isolated in midlake.

One technique that is seldom considered for smallmouth bass is night fishing. I do it often in Michigan and other upper midwestern states, and I have caught lots of big fish. Manistee Lake, in lower Michigan, is a tributary of Lake Michigan. Each summer it receives hordes of spawning alewives. August is a great time to pick up smallies —and walleyes—that feed on dying alewives.

I prefer to troll floating Rebels along the first breakline. These lures will dive about 2 feet. That's enough to trigger strikes from big smallmouth bass. I troll the edges of sandbars and points, and into log-filled bays. It's truly exciting when a big bronzeback unloads on the lure and jumps several times under a full moon.

Casting with sinking River Runts is another accepted midsummer technique that pays off with big fish. Many anglers catch a mixed bag of smallies and walleyes. Points, dropoffs, gravel or sandbars, and submerged crib docks or pilings are excellent places to fish when smallies move shoreward from deep water.

Fall

Fall can be a great time to go smallmouth bass fishing. The air is nippy, and lake waters are undergoing the fall turnover where surface water intermingles with bottom water. The fall foliage is often magnificent. Better yet, bronzebacks often go on a prolonged feeding spree in autumn.

Smallmouth lakes are often different from waters inhabited by other species. The best lakes for this species are rock-lined, and are usually characterized by gin-clear waters and very little vegetation in the water or along shore. Such lakes are common in midwestern states such as Michigan, Wisconsin, Minnesota, as well as throughout western Ontario.

These top smallmouth lakes have many rock piles or bars rising out of the depths. Rocky ledges and lip areas abound in the shallows, sandbars are fairly common, and the lakes *may* have a small amount of vegetation that extends down to about 20 feet. Of prime importance are the rocky formations. A shield lake is comprised mostly of rock, but

River Runt

some of the top bronzeback lakes have lesser amounts of rock piles. This tends to concentrate gamefish during fall months. The key ingredient in this mix is deep water; it must be found near any rock piles that bass inhabit. Smallies use deep water as a sanctuary, and move up along breaklines to the rocks to feed.

It's common for smallies to feed avidly on these rock-pile formations during the fall turnover, which often occurs at the same time as the leaf drop from nearby hardwood trees. After the turnover is complete, the bass continue a shoreward movement and stay near underwater points covered with small to medium-size rocks. Baitfish commonly use these areas, and smallies fill up on them to get through long winter months.

A superb late-fall location is a long, sloping bar or point that *slowly* tapers down before dropping off into deep water. Several friends of mine claim that the longer the tapering bar or point is, the more smallmouth bass it will contain. A bar or point only 20 feet long will hold a few fish, but nothing in comparison to those sloping points or bars 100 feet long that drop off into some of the deepest water in the lake. If the bar has lots of rocks or small boulders, it may attract some of the biggest smallmouths in that lake. These rocks on the bar offer breaks on structure (hiding places in shallow water), and the fish flock to such areas.

Early morning, late afternoon, and during any period of cloud cover are the best times to find smallies feeding on minnows in such rocky areas. Don't fish on warm, sunny days. Bronzebacks will often leave the prime feeding zones provided by jagged rocks and boulders, and move over the lip of the first major dropoff. Then they will hold in shadowed areas until the weather stabilizes and cloud cover returns. For a smallmouth bass fisherman, stable weather is vastly different from the clear weather favored by most people. A period of cloud cover that filters out the sun is considered by smallmouth fishermen to be ideal. Good fishing can be had all day on cloudy days. But short, sporadic feeding movements occur only at daybreak, and again just before dark, on those days with high, clear skies.

The ultra-clear waters of fall place great burdens on anglers. I've had to fish with 2- or 4-pound mono in order to obtain strikes. The line thickness depends upon the clarity of the water in your particular lake, but I'd never use anything heavier than 6-pound mono.

Fishing techniques vary from one lake to another, but the two best ways to catch bronzebacks in fall are jig fishing, and slow trolling with live bait.

Jig fishing can be done from an anchored, drifting, or backtrolled

Dan Gapen hoists a jig-caught smallmouth bass aboard while fishing a shield lake in northern Wisconsin.

boat. The common drill for live-bait fishermen is to backtroll over rocky formations, but few jig fishermen try it. This tactic encourages precise lure control while allowing the angler to put the jig exactly where he wants it. I prefer Gapen's Pinky Jig, Mister Twister's Sassy Dad, Lindy-Little Joe's Fuzz-E-Grub, or an Ugly Bug Plus. Live bait also attracts smallies in the fall. I prefer tipping my jig with a shiner or small redtail chub. Hook these baitfish through both lips, and send them down into the rocky areas. It requires a slow lift-drop fishing method to turn on fall smallies. Competition for food is keen. I've seen several cases where other fish followed a hooked bass in an attempt to take food away from him. Although competition is heavy for available food, smallmouths are more likely to hit a jig-minnow combination moving slowly through the water. Fast, jerky retrieves are seldom productive.

One of the best places to look for smallmouth bass is among jagged rocks right at the lip of a dropoff. If this fails to produce, work slowly up the sloping bar and deliver short, accurate casts to visible rock formations.

Trolling is the other accepted technique for autumn smallmouth fishing. It often works extremely well in the mid-South. Shiners and redtail chubs are used often as bait in some of the mid-South's TVA lakes, such as Percy Priest and Dale Hollow in Tennessee.

Use a fine-wire hook. Insert the point through the minnow's chin and out through the top lip. A 3-foot, or slightly longer, leader is used with a Mister Twister sinker, a Lindy Rig sinker, or Gapen's Baitwalker rig. Use a sinker just heavy enough to get the minnow down below the boat when backtrolling. You'll be defeating your purpose if you have a long line strung out behind the boat. Keep it short; this will enable you to feel the soft pickups of fall fish.

Backtroll along the dropoff edge and allow the rig to bounce lightly off the tops of rocks. The fairly long leader will allow the minnow some freedom of movement; this action should attract feeding smallmouth bass.

Backtroll along both edges of the point, conduct another trolling pass across the jumbled rocks at the tip, and then work the long, sloping edges of the bar or point. Save the shallower, rock-studded portions for later fishing.

Winter

Little smallmouth bass fishing is done during the winter in the northern states or Canada. The lakes are tightly frozen. Occasionally, a smallmouth is taken on tipups or by anglers jigging for walleyes. The season is often closed at this time for these species, anyway.

The best winter fishing is done in southern lakes with good smallmouth populations. The conditions on these waters are similar to those on northern smallmouth lakes in the fall.

The fish are usually found fairly deep, often at 20 to 25 feet over rocky points and near stair-stepping ledges that contain breaks of small fist-sized rocks or boulders. The techniques listed above for fall smallmouths will help you take some southern smallies during the winter.

A buddy of mine fishes Dale Hollow often in winter. He spends most of his fishing time riding around gazing at his depthfinder. He looks for good, rocky structure along the face of long, fast-sloping bars that fall off into deep water. Once he finds this, he anchors nearby and casts a long line, free-spooling a 6-inch Ding-a-ling plastic worm into the depths. He then literally "crawls" the worm through the rock piles. He gives the plastic worm many long pauses, moves it an inch or two, and pauses again. This is very slow fishing, but areas such as this are often hotspots. The strikes are often soft and deliberate, but a solid set of the hook can give you plenty of action guaranteed to warm winter-chilled bones.

Panfish

Panfish are the most widespread, prolific gamefish in North America. This broad grouping of species includes bluegills, sunfish, rock bass, warmouth bass, yellow perch, white and black crappies.

Pinpointing the location of these gamefish during the four seasons they are available to anglers isn't easy. Each adopts migration patterns from deep to shallow water. Only a few fishermen, however, try to determine the patterns of these fish so that they can predict where they are located from day to day. Shallow-water fishing along the shoreline satisfies all but the most ardent angler. In this chapter we'll discuss the habits of panfish in deep water as well.

173

Spring

Most panfish spawn in the spring, although yellow perch often spawn before bluegills. This is a good time to locate and catch large numbers of panfish. The fish are concentrated in shallow, inshore areas. Competition for available food is keen. It's not difficult to reach your limit for a particular species when it enters shallow spawning sites.

Spawning temperatures vary according to species. Bluegills will usually spawn in late May in water between 65 and 70 degrees. They prefer nesting in gravel and sand. Bull (male) bluegills are pugnacious during prespawn and spawning periods and will hit almost anything presented to them.

Yellow perch normally spawn after dark in brushy or weedy lake areas where water is several feet deep. These gamefish will also spawn in streams or other running water if it is available. They prefer temperature of 45 to 50 degrees. One ripe female perch can lay up to 75,000 string-like eggs.

Most sunfish species follow the same basic spawning patterns as bluegills. They fan saucer-shaped nests in sand and gravel. The male fish guards the nest. Males often attack lures at this time, for they are territorial and very protective.

The prespawning schools of black crappies may number in the hundreds. Spawning normally occurs in late spring. Spawning beds are often shaped like clusters of grapes. Much of the egg-laying is done in vegetation such as weeds or reeds. Crappies also spawn actively in cattails and other emergent weed growth.

Rock bass normally spawn when water temperature is between 60 to 70 degrees, usually in May through early July, depending on latitude. These gamefish prefer to live in areas filled with small stones, rocks, and rubble.

Most panfish species are weed-oriented to a certain degree. In spring they move from deep-water weedbeds up to and along the first breakline. One productive area to fish shortly after ice-out, and before inshore waters warm, is the tip of any weedbed that works up to the first dropoff. Here, most panfish will hold and feed until the shallow spawning waters warm.

Small jigs or jig-minnow combos are deadly for crappies when fished near heavy weeds or brushpiles. This fish weighed nearly 2 pounds.

It's not uncommon for panfish to work tentatively into the shallows, wander aimlessly in an apparent attempt to locate good spawning sites, and then drop back into deeper water when and if a cold front moves through. They will remain in the shallows only after several days of continuous warm weather.

Shallow coves or bayous are superb spawning sites for many panfish, but not the yellow perch. Bluegills and sunfish favor black-bottomed areas from 2 to 5 feet deep. These areas usually warm much faster than open-water portions of the main lake. I've been able to locate such areas and make limit catches of big gills on a fly rod for three or four days in a row. The fish can be very spooky in shallow water after having spent months in deeper areas. Keep a low profile, and try to keep hooked fish from splashing too much. Small, sponge-rubber spiders (green) work well with a fly rod. I've also taken a number of doubles by fishing a wet fly on the tippet point, and a dry fly as a dropper. It's lots of fun catching two slab bluegills at a time. They often tug in opposite directions, and it's not uncommon to lose one or both fish during the fray, sometimes because of a broken leader.

Many sunfish and bluegills spawn in shoreline shallows along the main portion of a lake. This spawning often occurs one to two weeks later than it does in shallow backwater bays. Look for whitish beds in honeycomb clusters along the shoreline. Spawning will take place in about 2 feet of water, although some big bluegills will spawn in 4 to 6 feet of water along the first dropoff if the bottom is firm. These deep-water spawners will frequently hit No. 0 or No. 1 silver Mepps spinners. Cast far beyond the bedding fish, allow the spinner to sink near bottom, and retrieve slowly. Then drop the spinner in the bed. Almost every bull bluegill in the lake will pick up a spinner and try to carry it away. Set the hook, and then enjoy the fight.

The secret to crappie fishing in spring is to watch the weather and locate good spawning sites near submerged or emergent weeds. Cold fronts can ruin spring crappie fun. High, blue skies and cold weather, or cold rains, can lower water temperatures significantly, and turn off romance-minded crappies.

Rock bass, true to their name, prefer areas where there are rocks and rubble. They feed actively on minnows and grubs.

If the weather is stable, some cloud cover exists, and the waters have had a chance to warm, a good spot to look for crappies is near weedbeds in fairly shallow water. These gamefish will spawn in weeds by fanning out nests wherever they can find room on bottom. It can be great fun fishing in bulrushes or cattails because the frantic action of spawning fish will activate the tops of this emergent growth. It's a sure sign of spawning activity below. A minnow dappled on a short line between clumps of weeds can trigger savage bites. I tried this tactic one time in Florida, and the fishing was so good I hated to quit. I caught limits of crappies daily for two days.

Channels between lakes can hold lots of crappies in spring. These gamefish often move from a main lake into a connecting channel shortly after ice-out. They mill around and feed sporadically until the water warms enough for spawning. Channels often have good structure such as bridges, pilings, boat docks, ramps, and submerged brush. Any of these sites will normally produce good crappie fishing in the spring. In northern areas, the best spots to fish any crappie lake are usually found on the northeast, north, or northwest shores. These shorelines receive the full benefit of the sun, and warm much faster. Remember this next spring.

Summer

Fishing for panfish in summer can be truly exciting. The average lake fisherman, whether he fishes a reservoir, natural lake, farmpond, or strip-mine pit, still fishes the shoreline—the same places he fished when panfish were bedding in shallow water. He has his back turned on some of the finest action available, because it's located behind him in deeper water.

Warm surface water and bright sun force most large panfish deep during summer months. As water begins to warm, and spawning is completed, panfish of all species begin a slow descent into the depths, where they find cooler temperatures and some protection from overhead predation and the sun. They also find abundant forage near weedbeds.

Submerged brushpiles near shore are hotspots for spring crappies and perch.

During the summer, panfish must evade predators such as large bass, walleyes, northern pike, and muskies. Most panfish prefer to stay close to weedbeds, although crappies often favor brushpiles, tree limbs, and other piles of submerged timber. Fishing in these areas is sporty and productive, although you may lose some terminal tackle.

Few anglers realize that some panfish species, especially crappies and yellow perch, will suspend at some distance off the bottom during the summer. It's not true that these gamefish are *strictly* bottom-oriented. All panfish species will suspend to some degree, but yellow perch and crappies do so almost all the time during the summer.

Crappies normally suspend anywhere from 8 to 20 feet off bottom, usually along the deep edge of weedlines or along the edge of the first dropoff breakline. Certain weeds attract crappies more than others. One of the best areas to fish is low-growing sandgrass. If crappies are comfortable in a certain area, they may stay there day after day. They may move somewhat due to constant fishing pressure, but they usually maintain the same suspended depth. If fish quit biting, it's usually necessary to move only 20 feet away. Continue fishing in the same manner, at the same depth, provided that the fish are suspended and the weedline or dropoff remains constant.

Food sources are one reason why crappies and yellow perch suspend, although perch are more nomadic and tend to follow forage fish. They will suspend at or slightly below the level occupied by baitfish. Schooling tendencies are followed by both perch and crappies. If one or two fish in a school find baitfish, other fish from that school will join them. Crappies don't move as far in search of food as perch do, however. If you catch one crappie, you probably have found a school. Good fishing should follow.

Bluegills and sunfish are more apt to be bottom-oriented than perch and crappies. They may suspend just inches or a foot off bottom, or along a major breakline dropping into deep water, but that's about as far as they'll go. It's much more common to catch these fish near bottom than at mid-depths.

Among schooling fish such as crappies, the largest fish stay at the

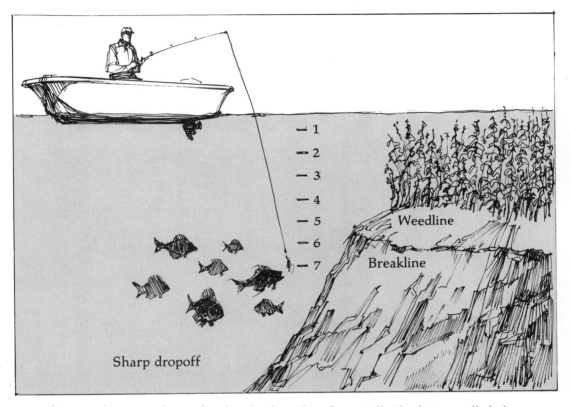

Crappies often suspend near the edge of a sharp dropoff, especially if it has a weedbed along the lip of the breakline. This is a good place to use jigs, counting the jig down as it sinks, to pinpoint the depth of the fish.

bottom level of the group. The average suspended fish may be down 15 feet, and may weigh 1 pound. If you fish a foot or two deeper, you may locate slabs weighing twice as much. Never pass up an opportunity to try slightly deeper waters once you've located a school.

Rock piles, brushy areas, and deep weedbeds are key places to fish for summer crappies. Note that the key word here is *deep.* The fish are not found near shallow rocks, brushy areas, or weedbeds. They must have direct access to deep water, a fact overlooked by many fishermen.

David Richey, Jr., the author's son, admires a nice yellow perch taken while fishing deep during the summer.

When fishing deep lakes with such structure, you may find both crappies and bluegills suspended—if the conditions are favorable. The typical movement of these gamefish is to be near the tops of such cover early in the morning and again just before dark, when less light penetrates the water. In late morning, fish are probably suspended vertically and horizontally along the first breakline. As the sun gets higher, these fish tend to move deeper alongside the structure and may go almost all the way to bottom. Overcast days will usually bring fish to the top or alongside the upper levels of the rocks, brush, or weedbeds, but always on the deep-water side.

One hotspot for summer crappies is in lakes where sandgrass or cabbage beds grow *near* deep rock piles. These two areas provide everything a crappie needs for survival.

Summer panfish anglers that fish lakes containing few rock piles or brushy areas must fish near weeds because they are the only cover available. Look for any irregularities in the weeds such as open spots, indentations, or areas where growth is sparse. An area with small humps or depressions near bottom and near weeds offers some of the best spots to fish. I must again stress the importance of locating fish, and the structure preferences they prefer. This is where anglers can find the hottest fishing action.

Some of the most exciting crappie fishing that I have experienced was in northern Florida last winter. We fished minnows on short lines, and dabbled our bait into hyacinth openings. The fish were feeding actively and would smack any minnow dropped into the water. These fish were large; many weighed 2 pounds or more. Structure? These crappies were found midway between the surface and bottom, snuggled in tightly against the hyacinths. The overhead canopy of plants blocked the sun and gave good protection to the fish.

One of the best crappie rigs, particularly for suspended fish, is a small jig. If one jig is good, then two are better. I commonly use two $\frac{1}{16}$- or $\frac{1}{32}$-ounce jigs, and fish one 2 feet above the other off a dropper line. Fish that are feeding heavily will spot the twin jigs coming, and it's possible to catch two fish at once. Lindy's Fuzz-E-Grub or Gapen's tiny Ugly Bugs are good choices in black, brown, white, green, or pink. Use dark jigs on overcast days, and light-colored jigs on bright days.

Try tipping a small jig with a small minnow. The smell given off by minnows, plus the flash of the minnow's sides, will bring in lunker crappies. Fish in an erratic manner with frequent jerks and stops. Some crappies will strike only when the lure travels at a steady speed. Experiment with retrieval speeds and various actions until you've established a daily pattern.

One technique that works well in midsummer is to troll near bottom with tiny jigs. Crappie lakes normally deliver the best action when a $\frac{1}{8}$- or $\frac{1}{16}$-ounce jig tipped with a 1-inch minnow is backtrolled near bottom. Choose sites near weeds or other structure. Bluegills will hit plain jigs better since they seldom feed on shiners. Comb the outside edges of weedbeds, backtroll into any indentations in the weeds, and set the hook whenever it stops.

Vertical jigging is a productive technique in summer, but few fishermen do it. This tactic works very well when you're going after suspended fish. I prefer a small jig, a tear-drop icefishing spoon baited with a minnow (for crappies), or a small piece of worm (for bluegills). I also use a small silver-bladed Mepps spinner. Locate the exact depth where fish are suspended and position the boat over the fish. Lower the rig into them, and move it up and down in slight movements. A rhythmic motion is needed. It's important to keep the rig working at all times. One of the biggest problems is pinpointing the exact dimensions of a school. Keep jigging vertically as you wind-drift. When the strikes stop, move back upwind until you make connections. After one or two passes, you'll know where the fish are located, and at what depth. The same technique works on yellow perch, too.

Fall

Fall is also a fine time to take panfish. Cooler weather, and increased appetites, can be expected. Some of the above-mentioned techniques work in fall, but anglers should change their tactics with the season.

In autumn, panfish are often on the move. Instead of allowing minnows and aquatic insects to come to them, they move off in search of chow in anticipation of winter's shorter food supplies. This often means it's harder to find them. You may catch one or two fish, but then the action stops because the fish have moved on. This is particularly true of crappies. It also applies to yellow perch, and, to a lesser degree, bluegills and sunfish.

Panfish often move shoreward in short feeding sprees, and then filter slowly out to deeper water. One good spot to try for them is over or alongside any submerged weedbeds growing in 10 to 15 feet of water. Panfish use weeds for cover, and as a guideline for inshore migrations. Points of weeds are best, but work all outside edges. Food for panfish is often found in these areas, and the water temperature is more to their liking.

Avoid flat-bottomed areas without cover. Panfish will avoid these areas and seek visible structure such as weeds, brush, or rock piles. Yellow perch will move across barren flats if their food supply heads that way.

Most panfish will begin a slow retreat toward deep water in October in northern states. By the time this gradual descent ends by ice-up, they will be holding at 20 feet or more.

Lure control is very important during the fall. A slow, pumping retrieve with tiny jigs is one of the best tricks you can use for fall crappies and bluegills. The lure must be presented at the proper depth, and activated by slow, upward lifts of the rod tip. Allow a short pause of one second between movements. Make sure you keep the jig in the proper zone. Most fish will strike during the pause. The take can be very light and difficult to feel, unless you're using light monofilament and a soft-action rod.

Another technique that works well is a very slow, steady retrieve. This tactic produces fish when they are reluctant to strike anything else. It triggers an instinctive strike. Just remember to keep the lure down at the fish's level, and move it at a snail's pace.

Reservoir fish follow an old stream channel whenever possible because it is often the deepest portion of the lake. Any brushy spots on

Small lures such as tiny jigs, sponge-rubber spiders, and little poppers are the best choice for bluegills when they move into the shallows in fall.

the outside bends of channels may hold fish. Just check enough locations until you find concentrations. The "panfish-disappearing act" almost always occurs just before freeze-up in northern lakes. In southern waters, panfish head for slightly deeper locations if some structure changes are available, such as brushlines, depressions, deep weedbeds, humps, or other breaks on structure.

Winter

Winter anglers must icefish for panfish in northern climates or try slightly deeper water in southern areas. If you're fishing through the ice, weedbeds are usually the best places to start. The water around weedbeds contains more oxygen. Yellow perch are about the only panfish that don't utilize weeds to any extent during winter. They need to keep moving to find food.

Crappies often suspend alongside weedbeds during winter months. They like green weeds; dead, brown weeds don't attract panfish. Bluegills are usually found near bottom, although they will suspend as well.

Submerged brushpiles are hotspots for winter crappies. Heavy brush or logs offer cover and hiding places for forage fish. Fishing near brushy areas is difficult, so a vertical jigging technique is recommended.

Bluegills often make vertical up-and-down movements. The amounts of snow cover on the ice, the thickness of lake ice, and the intensity of the sun can directly affect where fish will be found, and at what depth. Look for fish to be near bottom on bright, sunny days if the ice is free of snow. Overcast days may find fish feeding just below the ice.

My favorite fish-finding method on ice is to bore eight or ten holes about 20 yards apart. If one hole doesn't produce, I'll move on to another until fish are located. I fish at all depths, from top to bottom. I'll give one hole about fifteen minutes, and then try another.

Start jigging near bottom. Forget the violent up-and-down jigging movements that some anglers use to move their jig 3 or 4 feet at a time. A delicate, shivering lift-drop movement that moves a jig or ice-fly 2 or 3 inches is plenty. Begin near bottom, fish there for a minute or two, and move up 1 foot. Keep moving upward until you've explored all depths. If you haven't moved a fish by then, pick up and try a different hole. Repeat the technique until fish are located.

My favorite lures for crappies, sunfish, and bluegills are tiny $\frac{1}{32}$-ounce jigs or ice-flies. Teardrop spoons in silver, brass, or chartreuse

This fisherman dug his hole near the deep-water edge of a weedbed. The blue-gills were there, ready to strike his jig.

also work. A small shiner minnow is quite effective when used for crappies. Bluegills and sunfish prefer corn borers, wax worms, elmwood grubs, goldenrod grubs, mousees, and other insect larvae. I use Russian Hooks for perch. These small jigging spoons often weigh up to ⅛ ounce, and can be 2 inches long. They are teamed with a perch eye or small emerald shiner for yellow perch. The design of this rig enables it to give off a solid flash or glitter at depths of 20 feet.

Daytime is best for gills and sunfish, but some of my finest winter hours have been spent fishing at night for yellow perch and crappies. These fish seem to acquire a strong feeding urge once the sun goes down. I've spent many evenings in a shanty, huddled over a catalytic heater, and jigging for both species. The success rate often doubles when you fish the same areas after dark.

Pike and Muskies

Northern pike, and the various subspecies of muskellunge, are among the largest predatory gamefish available to most fishermen. They are mean, difficult to hook and land, and often as wary as a large brown trout in an overfished stream.

Pike and muskies are savage feeders that prefer to wait and ambush smaller fish or animals. Sneak attacks are the name of the game for these species. The time of day or night, or the season, doesn't matter. These wolves of the weedbeds and other structural cover subsist on live prey. It takes a healthy meal to satisfy their appetites. Structure patterns, seasonal movements on structure, and diet preferences at different seasons are as important to successful pike and muskie fishing as they are to other types of fishing.

191

There's something about hooking and landing a big pike or muskie that fires my imagination. My biggest northern weighed 29½ pounds, and was caught in High Rock Lake, Manitoba. The heaviest muskie I've caught to date weighed 35 pounds. It was landed in Dale Hollow Reservoir on the Kentucky-Tennessee border. I have seen much larger fish of both species. The biggest muskie I ever saw, on Ontario's Lake of The Woods, followed a crankbait to the boat. I was fishing with Les Sandy, a full-blooded Ojibway Indian, and owner of Sandy's Monument Bay Resort, Angle Inlet, Minnesota. Les has pet names for big muskies in his area. This one was the "Coca Cola Bay" muskie. He guessed its weight at 50 pounds.

The fish had been feeding heavily near a weedy area that dropped off to 20 feet of water bordered by rocky shoals. We had cast a thousand times with crankbaits, spinnerbaits, and jerkbaits. I nailed a 15-pound muskie on a spinnerbait. The big one kept savaging smaller gamefish but it wouldn't strike. Relentless casting finally produced a follow and a side-of-the-boat strike. I missed, and the muskie missed. He sank slowly into the depths. I'll long remember that savage snout, long, graceful body kicking up from bottom, and the upheaval of water that literally showered me when the fish made his attack. This year I'm going back to that bay for a return bout with that fish.

The sighting of a big muskie or northern pike keeps anglers chasing—and dreaming about—these gamefish. I get little pleasure from catching hammer-handle pike or muskies. They are often so gluttonous that they become deeply hooked and can't be released. I prefer using those tactics that will catch bigger fish. That's what the rest of this chapter will cover.

Spring

One of the peak times to gather in a truly big pike or muskie is during the spring. Fishing seasons are often set to coincide with the end of the spawning period. Some states set year-round seasons. In these areas, anglers may find good action at any time. Spawning efforts are directly affected by climate. Remember this.

Knowing the structure and habitat preferences of pike and muskies in spring are more important than going to a known "big-pike" lake. One point should be stressed: many lakes across the country contain pike and muskellunge, but only a handful hold truly big fish. A lake, for example, that produced big fish ten years ago may not have any today. Conditions change. A buildup of smaller fish and fewer trophy specimens can alter the predator-prey relationship drastically and reduce the possibility of taking big fish. Only fish those lakes that are *currently* (for the past two years) producing lunkers. You'll find only a small percentage consistent in this respect.

In spring, shallow water is the best place to fish for both species. It's not uncommon for northern pike to spawn before ice leaves the lake. This places them in the shallows very early. Muskies spawn somewhat later. Shallow, muddy bays are ideal locations for spring muskies, while northern pike often favor the shallows inshore of deep weedbeds. Northerns will be found near any tributary stream that allows migration or spawning. Muskies will spawn in tributaries occasionally, but not as often as some people think.

The important point here is that both species move shoreward shortly after ice-out, and sometimes before, swimming up from deep water. The shallows may be barren one day and full of prespawning gamefish the next. Pike and muskies are jittery in the shallows and heavy fishing pressure can force them back to deep-water sanctuaries. This is one reason why it's so important to find big-fish lakes that are not overfished. Too many people casting or trolling in the shallows can ruin the sport for everyone.

Cold spring waters affect the metabolism of both gamefish. They are more intent on spawning than feeding. The prime fishing action for both species occurs a week or two after spawning is completed. An angler lucky enough to be on the water at that time can take huge fish regularly.

Since these fish favor shallow water during spring many anglers believe that pike and muskies are in or near the shallows all the time. This isn't true. Fishermen should realize that inshore gamefish movements are geared to seasonal weather or habitat changes, and to spawning activities. As soon as the spring spawn is completed, these gamefish head for deep water to recover, feed, and use the depths for sanctuary. You'll have, at best, a one-month period (usually much less) of good shallow-water spring fishing.

The best fishing for muskies *normally* takes place a week or two after spawning is over, although the following techniques will produce some fish during the spawn. Muskies normally spawn in shallow, muddy bays with little cover. Trolling a long line with a magnum Rapala has occasionally worked for me. One year, several friends from the Detroit area fished Michigan's Brevort Lake when the season opened on May 15. We had had a very late spring that year; muskies were still in the shallow spawning grounds. A magnum Rapala, trolled slowly with an occasional zigzag motion, helped us catch several 30-pound fish. We haven't enjoyed similar luck since.

The postspawn period is one of the best times to fish. One of the finest places to locate big feeding muskies is in lakes with good cabbage-weed growth. It's often called muskie weed and will grow to 20-foot depths on clear lakes, and about 10 feet in darker, dingier water. It grows from a firm bottom. Muskies and northern pike use cabbage-weed edges for feeding areas during the postspawn season.

Try to locate cabbage beds that are just beginning to grow. The edges should be covered in a thorough manner. It pays to cast lures, or troll over the tops of the beds in areas where trolling is legal. Some states, like Wisconsin, have archaic laws on certain lakes where trolling, positioning of the boat, or any motor—gasoline or electric—can't be used for muskie fishing.

One reason why cabbage beds attract spring muskies is that they deliver excellent food supplies when muskies are ravenously hungry after spawning rigors. They also serve as good, shallow-water bases for fish that prey from cover.

One springtime tactic that has produced jarring strikes for me, and delivered several fish, is to rip lures over and through young cabbage weeds. A muskie will often lie near bottom and pass up lures that swim merrily along outside edges without encountering the weedline. It can

Bob Schaefer uses a gaff on a muskie taken in Michigan's Brevort Lake. The fish struck a Magnum Rapala trolled slowly over a shallow mud flat during the spring spawn.

be a different story when a spinnerbait or jig-eel combination is cast into the weeds and *ripped* through the cabbage at the fastest possible rate. It makes the fish think an easy meal is getting away. I have seen many big muskies throw a wake like a surfacing torpedo as they home in on the lure. A few muskies that I've caught in this manner nailed a lure festooned with streamers of cabbage weeds.

In any weedbed, concentrate your efforts along the deep-water edge. Most of the muskies taken during the spring will come from this area, but it always pays to fish the inshore edge of such areas as well as over the tops of young weeds. An exceptional area along the inshore edge of any weedbed is a break on bottom where fish can hide or follow it from deep to shallow water. A fallen tree, sunken boat, or brushpile on bottom *at* the shallow-water edge of the weedbed is probably the prime spot in that location.

Another spot overlooked by many spring fishermen is a dock that juts out into the lake from shore. Spring muskies like such areas and often feed here because the shallows, and docks, also afford some cover for small forage fish. The dock areas that offer the best fishing are usually those that extend far enough into the lake so that they are very close to a cabbage bed. Muskies found in these areas are often feeding heavily. Any spinnerbait, crankbait, or jerkbait capable of being fished in shallow water can take fish. A jig-and-eel (5-inch) combination fished on bottom is very effective.

The way to fish these areas is to wind-drift through the shallows first. Cast ahead of the boat and fish near rocks, shallow weeds, reeds, dead submerged branches, docked boats, boathouses, or the docks themselves *if* some cover is found nearby. Two anglers can cover such areas adequately if one man fishes the edges of weeds (and the tops of cabbage), while the other works the shallower areas.

The second wind-drift should allow you to cover the deep side of the cabbage. One man can fish along the outside edge and over the top

Kay Richey grits her teeth as Les Sandy nets a big muskie on Lake of the Woods in western Ontario. The fish struck a spinnerbait (inset) fished near a rockpile.

of the weeds. The other angler fishing the weeds should try to make some lure contact with the cabbage tops, and try to make his lure look like a minnow or gamefish in trouble.

Spring pike are also oriented to shallow water during cold-water periods. Shoreline shallows *close to deep water* are key spots to fish for trophy pike. Areas near islands; shallow, marshy locations; or brushy spots near shore are prime spots to look for cruising fish. An inflowing stream mouth that spreads out into a shallow, weedy bay is a hotspot for feeding pike after the spawn.

Look for any shallow bay or marshy area where nearby rock formations are thick, heavy, and composed of slab rock (mostly in Canada). Such spots will attract early-season northerns. Remember, the area *must* be located near deep water. If it isn't, the fish will seldom cross large, open flats to feed in shallow water. Spring pike prefer to ease up from deep water, follow a tapering bottom contour into the shallows, knock hell out of forage fish, and return by the same route if undisturbed.

I've taken a number of jumbo Canadian pike by standing on rocky outcroppings and flinging almost any medium-size lure into shallow areas. Remember, pike are found near shore during the spring *but only in select areas.*

Lures needed for spring pike fishing can vary from tandem spinnerbaits, Mepps spinner in No. 5 or muskie sizes, Dardevles, or other proven lures. Lure color or size isn't nearly as important as when and where you cast it.

Summer

Summer can offer good pike and muskie fishing, provided that anglers follow a few simple rules and understand how these gamefish react during warm weather. More anglers fish for these species in summer, but the catch ratio is lower because these fish may be much deeper than many fishermen realize. It's not uncommon to catch muskies at 30- to 40-foot depths, and northern pike below 20-foot depths.

Many anglers fish for pike and muskies during this period in many of the same areas as they did during the spring. Their reward for countless days on the lake is a mediocre catch of small fish that, when filleted, are barely capable of stinking up a frying pan. Shoreline fishing isn't the answer.

The following techniques are not geared for catching large numbers of fish, but those taken will be dandies.

Some of the best northern pike lakes in North America are not necessarily those nestled in some Canadian outback. Instead, they are found in the upper Midwest, from Michigan to North Dakota. The big-fish records from these states indicate a smattering of pike over 20 pounds and a few over 30. The better waters for these fish are lakes with 500 to 1000 acres; fertile waters with reduced visibility and an abundant forage base. The lakes should be at least 50 feet deep, the water greenish, to reduce visibility.

Many fishermen believe that prime pike and muskie lakes must be isolated. Actually, some of the finest fishing that I've had for these species was on lakes rimmed with cottages and boathouses, and filled with other boats, even water skiers. The trick is to fish those areas, and depths, where overhead commotion doesn't bother the gamefish.

The STST fishing method described in an earlier chapter is one weapon that summer pike and muskie fishermen can adopt. Trolling proved lures alongside or near excellent structure, at the proper depth and water temperature, is one of the best ways I know to get a big fish.

On deep, fertile pike lakes look for deep-growing weeds near underwater islands or dropoffs falling from 10 to 20 feet. Big fish can usually be found near rocky points in deep water, the deep edges of weedbeds, or submerged bars and rocky flats.

I'm not a troller by nature but I've found that it beats inactivity. One of the best lures for systematic straining of good pike water is a Spoonplug. Select sizes geared to reach bottom in the area you're fishing. A faster trolling speed than is considered normal will usually turn the trick.

The late-summer period will find most big pike ranging from *about* 15 to 25 feet below the surface. When fish are this deep, it's difficult to fish them in many lakes because the area to be fished is often small and

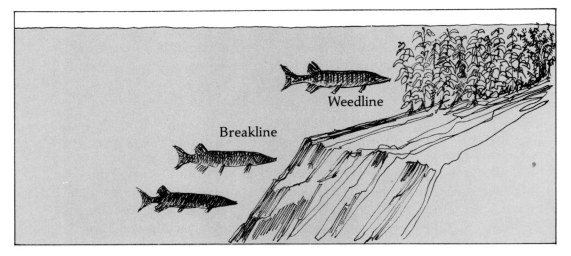

Pike in a positive feeding period will often hold near a weedline at the edge of a dropoff where food is available. As the sun rises higher in the sky they'll usually drop over the edge, seeking cooler water and protection from the sun.

ringed with deep weedbeds. The STST method produces good fishing if it's possible to troll a long run without getting fouled in weeds. A situation I've encountered is one many of us have been faced with . . . short, narrow areas where stillfishing is a better bet.

I'd rather watch grass grow than stillfish with live bait. To get big northerns, try deep-water jigging with spoons. It requires a fairly heavy spoon to jig effectively in 20 feet of water or more. I like Dardevle's Rok't Devle or Bass Devle, especially in red with white stripes. Lower it over a rocky hump or a narrow alley between weedbeds. Another good spot is off the deep-water tip of a weedbed, where a breakline forms as the bottom falls over the dropoff. Lower the spoon to bottom, and begin an up-and-down vertical jigging by raising the lure a foot or two. Then allow it to flutter down on a slack line. Most trophy pike will nail the spoon on the flutter-down, and you'll seldom feel the take. A slight line movement may be noticed, or you'll feel the fish as you begin the up-stroke. Set the hook hard and often.

A similar technique works with heavy leadhead jigs. I prefer those weighing nearly 1 ounce. Yellow or white have been my best colors. I like to tip them with a 2-inch fathead or shiner minnow. A strip of meat sliced from the side of a 6-inch sucker minnow will also work. Lower this rig to bottom and jig in the same manner. This is a very effective technique for those small areas where trolling is impossible. If a big pike grabs either the deep jigged spoon or jig-minnow rig, he'll be hooked deep. You'll not catch lots of fish this way, but many will weigh 10 pounds or more. My largest taken with a jig-minnow combination weighed almost 18 pounds. It struck in 25 feet of water.

The one time of year when pike really smack jigged spoons or jig-minnow rigs is when ciscoes and tullibees are present in deep water. These fish are the mainstay food in many northern pike lakes, and in some Canadian lakes as well. The pike are used to seeing these species at deeper levels. A jigged spoon or jig-minnow can be an effective tactic, especially in midsummer.

The next chapter will outline the fact that walleyes often suspend in or very near the deep-water edge of weedbeds. Muskies are also often found in these areas. Muskies feed on small walleyes—those fish in the 6- to 12-inch class. Small walleyes use the weedbeds for cover, and muskies work right into such areas in search of food. Look for walleye-feeding muskies along the outside (deep-water) edges of cabbage beds.

One of the prime muskie areas during midsummer is a weedbed edge fronting a gradual dropoff. The big fish are following small, cigar-size walleyes. These flats can be good spots to find fish during July and August. Look for small weedbeds on long, sloping flats that tumble over a dropoff. If other structure or breaks are found on these flats, so much the better.

Deep-diving crankbaits are an excellent choice at this time, although everything depends on the depth and location of the flats and weedbeds. Such areas require anglers to fish bottom areas with a jig and large minnow; intermediate regions near weedbeds for suspended muskies; and the edges of the cabbage beds with spinnerbaits, tandem bucktails, or with the STST method involving large spoons or spinnerbaits. Trollers often have more success at this time, provided that speed-trolling techniques are used in conjunction with lures capable of attaining a depth of 15 to 25 feet. Big muskies are often deep during the midsummer heat. You'll have to adapt your methods to meet this challenge.

Deep-diving lures work well during midsummer. Some of my favorites include the Swim Whizz, Pikie Minnow, Cisco Kid and large Spoonplugs. When casting, make a figure 8 after each cast is retrieved to the boat. Some anglers insert their rod tip into the water up nearly to the reel handles. This trick brought in several big muskies for some friends of mine last year. I'm a stand-up-and-cast angler. The figure 8 produced two nice fish for me last summer and several heart-stopping smashes that left me with a wide mouth and little else.

Some popular muskie lures (from top, clockwise): Suick, Swim Whizz, Rapala, Mepps Musky Killer, Daredevle.

Push rod into water
almost up to reel seat.

Muskies often follow lures to the boat and turn away without striking. To give them an added chance, anglers submerge their rod in the water almost to the reel and work the lure in a figure 8. A muskie often zooms up from bottom and strikes.

Night fishing is often ignored by muskie fishermen. I had heard a few wild tales from bass fishermen about huge fish smacking surface Jitterbugs or other lures, leading me to believe that muskies are often on the prowl at the same time. One evening I nailed a couple of 12-pound northerns. If pike were actively feeding, I thought, then muskies should be as well.

I then read an account of how a pair of muskie addicts had trolled the St. Lawrence River at night. They caught their share of trophy fish, and that encouraged me to try it. I've since caught a few big muskies after sundown. Here's how I do it.

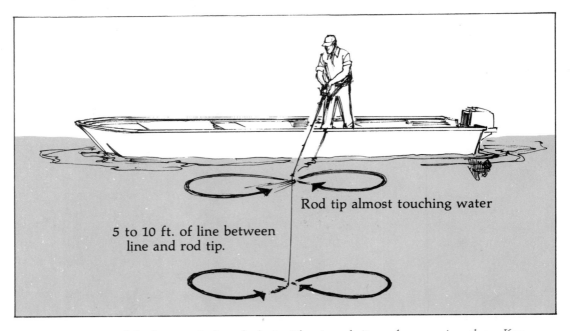

Rod tip almost touching water

5 to 10 ft. of line between
line and rod tip.

A variation of the figure 8 that works best with spinnerbaits or deep-running plugs. Keep 5 to 10 feet of line below the rod tip, lower the tip near the water, and keep working the spinnerbait deep.

I troll the same areas I fish during daylight hours, but I use weighted tandem muskie spinners. The trolling speed is very slow, just fast enough to bring out the throb of the spinner blades. These fish are sight feeders by nature, but I believe they also home in on sound vibrations produced by some lures. A big tandem spinner with flopping blades gives off a powerful impulse through the water. The best color for me has been black, with orange blades.

Full-moon periods are often best for after-dark muskie fishing. Fish the same areas you do during daylight hours, but at shallower depths. If a shallow pass fails to produce a strike, add a small weight 12 inches ahead of the spinner, and work the area again. Pay close attention to edges of cabbage beds, shallow flats with some low weed cover, or deep-water breaklines with some brush or rock piles present. These are hotspots for midnight muskies.

Most of the fish that I have caught were hooked at a depth of 10 feet. Fingers of elevated bottom with gently sloping sides that taper down into deep water can be good areas to troll. Casting can work well near boat docks, swimming rafts, or other man-made structure. Check each area thoroughly. As with daylight fishing it often pays to return two or three times each evening to spot-check such areas.

Fall

Muskie action continues at a rapid pace as leaves turn gold and the air becomes nippy. It has been said that this is one of the best times of year to catch big fish. It can be if you know when and where to fish. Not everyone does!

Changing weather patterns of fall have a tremendous effect on big muskies—particularly egg-carrying females. They feed with reckless abandon in preparation for the winter when food will be scarce. It requires plenty of food to build enough fat to nourish eggs for the spring spawn. It's possible during September, October, and November to catch the largest fish of the year. Look for unseasonably warm days that continue for some time, only to be blown helter-skelter by a cold front. This is *the* most important time to fish. Big fish often go crazy. The best spots to fish aren't those that deliver plenty of legal and slightly above-legal fish. Head for those lakes that hold few muskies, but huge fish. If you can plan on fishing two or three days during this period, you may land a 30- to 40-pound fish. Such weather changes are often predicted far in advance by newspapers, radio, and television.

Lakes with ample populations of forage fish such as ciscoes, herring, tullibees, or whitefish often hold lots of big muskies. These forage fish spawn in fall, and muskies are seldom far away from any concentration of such species. Forage fish spawn on gravel or sandy points located near deep water. Such areas are easily found if you consult local bait dealers or study a contour map. A drop in water

1.

2.

3.

Casting rigged suckers for muskies is hard work, but it can be a productive method. The diagram shows one way of rigging a sucker with a hook in its mouth.
1. Thread end of 1-ft. length of heavy, black Dacron line through sucker's mouth and out through gill.
2. Bring line across sucker's back; thread through other gill and out mouth. Insert a 10/0 Mustad sucker hook through top lip.
3. Snug line across back of fish and tie the ends to the shank of hook with several overhand knots. Clip ends short.

temperature is the key to spawning movements by forage fish. Keep close tabs on the weather and fish a lot when the water drops to 45 degrees or lower.

Any green weeds still available will attract muskies. Cold weather kills most shallow weedbeds; this is indicated by brown-colored dead or dying weeds floating on the surface. Concentrate solely on green weeds, which, incidentally, also attract forage fish.

Other fall muskie hotspots include sandbars, rock or gravel points, submerged logs, long points with some timber on bottom, or sharp dropoffs with any combination of the above found along bottom. The closer such breaks on structure are located to deep water, the better the fishing.

Crankbaits are one of the deadliest rigs known to fall muskie fishermen. I like to use big Pikie Minnows, the Smitty jointed diver, Cisco Kids, Swim Whizzes, and Bombers. They should be worked slowly because of coldwater temperatures. Reel rather quickly to get the lure down to optimum level, and then slow down the retrieve. Fall muskies often follow for long distances, provided that the lure isn't moving too fast. Believe me, muskies can turn on the speed if they wish, but a slow speed normally produces more strikes in fall.

Jerkbaits can work well, if the angler can keep the lure under the water without moving it too fast. Keep the rod tip low to the water. Reel just fast enough, and apply a jerk often enough, so that the lure stays down and doesn't bob to the surface.

Fairly large jigs like Grassl's "Swim Head" muskie jig dressed with a 3- or 4-inch minnow are good to use when worked slowly along bottom, particularly over submerged rock piles located near green weedbeds.

Autumn is also a good time to nail a trophy northern pike. Some of the finest lake-fishing action will take place after the fall turnover (about the time hardwood leaves fall). It will then last until the lake freezes. A savvy angler can often locate big fish at this time. If his presentation of lure or live bait is correct, it's possible to zap a true trophy fish.

This giant muskie, from Ontario's Georgian Bay, weighed over 45 pounds and fought like a tiger for 30 minutes.

The key factor in fall fishing is locating lakes with ample populations of big northerns. Some lakes contain only small fish, while a few are home to some enormous pike. These are the best choices if they are located close to home and readily accessible. Why travel two days to fish a northern pike lake? Careful scrutiny of catch records of lakes near your home can often reveal waters that have a history of holding lunker fish.

The best lakes for fall northern pike fishing are those with a sizable population of forage fish (whitefish, tullibees, ciscoes, or herring). These fish spawn during fall months, as was explained earlier in this chapter, but few anglers realize how extensively northerns rely upon these species for food. Lakes with good populations of these fish often hold pike weighing more than 20 pounds.

Weather patterns apply as much to pike as to muskies, although the calm days seem to deliver better northern action. Try to be on the water on a warm, cloudy day. Fishing in early morning and late evening is basically a waste of time. Some of the best fall pike fishing occurs at midday, when temperatures are warmest.

Good lures for pike include jig-minnow combinations fished along the edges if green weeds. Fish both the deep and shallow edges if some breaks are found either between the weeds and shore, or the dropoff. I prefer a ½-ounce plain jig dressed with a redtail minnow or other forage fish native to the area. This rig is useful when fished slowly along bottom. Good spots are along sand-gravel points that slope off rapidly into deep water near shore.

In late fall, it's quite common for small northerns and big northerns to trade places. Food availability is apparently the reason. The smaller pike will leave shallower areas and move into deeper water, while bigger fish will tend to move shoreward to feed on spawning whitefish. If you're catching small pike in deeper water regularly during the fall, then this shift has probably taken place. The larger fish will be found in shallower water.

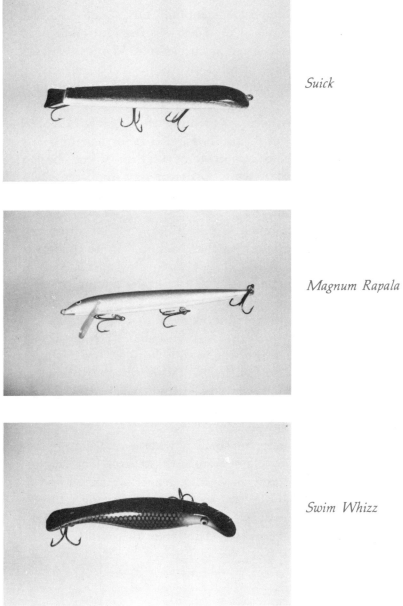

Suick

Magnum Rapala

Swim Whizz

Musky Killer

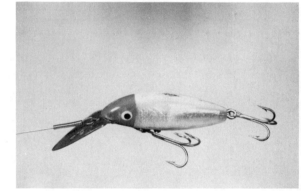

Cisco Kid

I enjoy fishing crankbaits for northerns during this period. Some of my better lures have been Bombers, used for fish 12 feet deep. I like the frog finish, although I've never seen a northern with a frog in his gullet. Other lures that produce well include Rebel's Super R and Bagley's Diving B. Try Spoonplugs or Countdown Rapalas—the latter is useful in shallow water. The time-honored red-white Dardevle is an appropriate choice if it's allowed to flutter down near bottom and is retrieved at slow speeds. I've also had excellent success with brown and shad-colored Mud Bugs.

Spearing northern pike is legal in some states, but check regulation before trying this sport.

Winter

Some big pike and muskies are caught in winter. Most of the fishing is done through the ice. Two methods—spearing and tipup fishing—are used.

Spearing is frowned upon by many lake fishermen because they feel it reduces the number of big fish in any lake. Research has proved that spearers don't catch more big pike or muskies than do tipup fishermen.

Some of the best spots to spear or tipup fish for muskies or northern pike are along deep-water edges of weedbeds, or in channels or depressions along the bottom. Winter fish seem to hold near bottom; they're frequently caught 25 to 30 feet down.

Spearers position their shanty over such areas, although they prefer slightly shallower water. Visibility is important. Clear-water lakes are best for spearing. A decoy (wooden or live sucker) is lowered near bottom and allowed to swim freely. A cruising gamefish that spots the decoy is lured in close, and the spear is dropped onto the fish's back. It calls for remarkable coordination and the ability to judge light refraction through a shanty hole in order to toss the spear into the proper spot.

Tipup fishermen also fish near bottom, but a small treble hook is inserted under the dorsal fin of a live forage fish native to the lake. Live smelt is the finest baitfish that I have used. I've taken more large pike (no muskies) on these baits than on any other. I prefer a No. 12 or 14 treble hook, which does little damage to the baitfish. It's strong enough to land a big fish, provided that the angler doesn't rush the landing job until the fish is completely played out.

It requires a depthfinder or a lead weight to determine the water depth in the area you're fishing. Exact depths are needed so that you can place the baitfish just off bottom. A baitfish lowered too close to bottom will hide in cover, and a pike won't see it. It's far better to position the minnow about 12 inches from bottom. Cruising pike or muskies will then be able to spot the minnow.

This youngster has just caught a northern pike on her tipup. Best method is to fish near bottom with a baitfish on a treble hook.

Weather conditions are as important during winter as during other seasons. Dark, overcast, and stormy days seldom produce much action. The fish seem to hold still, and do not feed actively. A two-day, or longer, break in the cloud cover, with accompanying bright sunshine, seems to trigger pike movement. A dark day with a fifteen-minute glimpse of bright sun is often enough to encourage fish to feed for short periods.

The majority of ice fishermen lose pike or muskies on tipups simply because they try to outpower the fish. My tipup spools are stocked with 150 yards of 30-pound braided Dacron or heavy monofilament. I never use wire leaders. Once a fish grabs the minnow I'll hold off setting the hook until the first run stops, and the predator swallows the bait. When the second run begins, I'll allow the line to tighten in my hands and set the hook with a short backward pull.

Play these fish gently, but with some firmness. They will often make a fake run toward the hole and mislead the angler into thinking they are through. Be aware of this and watch for another powerful dash under the ice. When the fish rolls up on his back under the ice, then try to land him. I prefer to use a three-prong gaff. Insert it under the jaw and lift the fish through the hole.

Walleyes and Sauger

These gamefish are seasonally oriented. The difference between success and an empty stringer hinges on knowing where they will be at certain times of the year. Much of their movement, from deep water to the shallows and back again, is dependent upon the availability of forage fish, upon water temperature, the amount of sunlight on the water, and other factors. Fishing pressure, except at night from a lighted boat, does little to push them from one area to another. Overfishing may cause fish to drop somewhat deeper, or move up or over on a bank. They don't leave traditional areas simply because someone is fishing for them.

Because walleyes and sauger are so similar in both appearance and habits, I have referred to the former throughout this chapter. But the techniques explained for catching walleyes will also take sauger. The major difference between these two species is that sauger prefer large turbid waters and can withstand more pollution than can walleyes.

Spring

Walleyes have three basic spring patterns—prespawn, spawn, and postspawn—during which they react differently. Anglers must understand how the fish behave in each period.

Prespawning walleyes may start migrating while ice is still on a lake. The major fact to consider here is whether a warmwater stream flows into the lake or not. Warm water can raise the lake temperature in that *vicinity* and get the fish charged up. Such movements normally occur only after dark. One test report based on actual observation in Michigan's Upper Peninsula (Lake Gogebic) proved conclusively that such inshore migrations do occur, but only after sundown. I've seen photos that reveal gleaming eyes everywhere; hundreds of gamefish that moved into the vicinity of a nearby stream or river that offered warmer water. Prespawning movements *normally* take place at about 40 degrees.

Spawning occurs mostly after dark; few fish spawn during daylight hours. Anglers who can brave the cold can often make good catches at night, provided that the season is open.

Most of the spawning activity occurs in water about 4 feet deep. If you have trouble catching spawning fish, try slightly deeper, *in the same area.* You might pick up prespawning fish waiting their turn to reproduce. The major portion of the walleye spawn in any lake will take place within seven days. I have encountered these fish in the shallows for nearly two weeks, but spawning will peak in a seven-day spread during the middle of this period. Only a handful of walleyes will use the shallows before and after the optimum time.

Walleyes will choose sand-gravel locations for their spawning. A firm bar of sand will attract some fish, but the bulk of the action takes place in areas containing a mixture of rock, gravel, and sand. Several year-classes of walleyes have been hurt because of bad weather during the spawn. (A year-class refers to all the fish spawned in one year.)

Biologists and research fishermen believe that cold weather, with a resulting drop in the water temperature, can cause walleyes to leave the shallows and not return to spawn.

The prespawn and spawning periods are of interest to anglers simply because they provide clues to postspawn fish movements, when the best fishing is available. In shallow, round-basined lakes walleyes disperse slowly after spawning. The males often remain in or very near the spawning grounds for periods of up to one month while females, usually the larger sex of the species, head for deep water to recover. It may be two weeks before the females begin feeding again. Male fish can usually be caught in the shallows with any shallow-water presentation, including trolling with the STST method. The scattering of big females poses a problem because they can be anywhere in a shallow lake. The opposite occurs in lakes featuring sharp breaklines or dropoffs into deep water. If these dropoffs are located near the spawning grounds, both males and females may swim promptly to deep water to recuperate. The fish then seek the deepest structure in the lake. Such lakes can be easy or difficult to fish, depending on how well you know the structure.

Some of the best lakes to fish for postspawn walleyes are small, fertile waters with abundant shallow areas. Never select a water of more than 1000 acres. Smaller areas can be thoroughly checked in a quicker, more efficient manner than can large waters. It allows more fishing time in locations more likely to hold postspawning fish. Fertile waters are usually late-mesotrophic or early eutrophic lakes. Fertility usually produces darker water, an advantage to anglers.

Jig-fishing has always brought in postspawn fish for me. I've had superb luck backtrolling with jigs tipped with live bait. I prefer to cast standing up and slowly work a dressed jig back to the boat, if I'm fishing an area where this can be done. Some spots are better for jigging than others. Redtail chubs, fathead minnows, or emerald shiners work well on jigs. Insert the point under the chin, out the top of the head, and fish them *very* slowly along bottom with short up-and-down strokes. Another trick I use often at this time is to forget the lift-drop

Leadhead jigs fished along bottom with a lift-drop action are dynamite for walleyes during the postspawn period.

Ugly Bug

Pinky Jig

method. Instead, I roll the jig-minnow along bottom with a steady retrieve. This method can deliver a soft, deliberate strike whenever the lift-drop technique fails. Try both systems.

There are many walleye jigs, but I favor Gapen's Ugly Bug or Pinky jig, Lindy-Little Joe's Fuzzy Grub, or floating jig-heads (fished on a slightly shorter leader) like those made by Mister Twister or Bill Binkelman. The floating jig-heads are best used while trolling behind a Lindy Rig or Baitwalker. They float up off bottom, and present nightcrawlers, leeches, salamanders, or minnows directly to fish that may be holding off a breakline. They are great during any period when walleyes suspend off bottom.

The presentation should be very slow, regardless of which bait or lure is being used. It may require two or three minutes to fish out a long cast. Trolling or backtrolling speeds should be kept to a crawl. Patience and persistence will pay off.

Summer

Summer is the time when most walleye or sauger fishermen expect to fill their stringers. Sadly, too many anglers return home with little to show for their untiring efforts except a catch of cigar-shaped walleyes. The reason why so many small walleyes show up in a catch is because the angler hasn't learned where bigger fish are found.

One tendency of schooling walleyes is to herd baitfish. Walleyes often herd small perch, ciscoes, or other forage fish tight in against a dropoff before systematically attacking them. Such feeding movements usually, but not always, take place in areas where walleyes can pin forage fish against a vertical or near-vertical dropoff. The only escape for baitfish then is to jump from the water. Since they can't fly, another walleye often nails them as they reenter the water. Such forays often take place after dark, but I've seen them occur on overcast days.

Mesotrophic lakes offer fine midsummer fishing. Ranging in size from 100 to 1000 acres, they are characterized by medium-clear to clear water, and a good growth of thick, shallow weeds. Look for cabbage weedbeds; they play an important role in summer walleye fishing.

Other structural lake formations found on meso lakes include some gravel points or bars, certain sections containing underwater rocks, and a shallow weed growth of junk weeds near shore with cabbage or cabomba offshore. These lakes normally are found through Michigan, Wisconsin, northern Minnesota (don't confuse them with shield lakes), and in other areas where farming or agriculture is found. They often hold largemouth bass, northern pike, and panfish in addition to walleyes.

Summer walleyes will usually be found *off* long tapering points. Look for fish to hold near any breaks on this structure. Breaks can be a

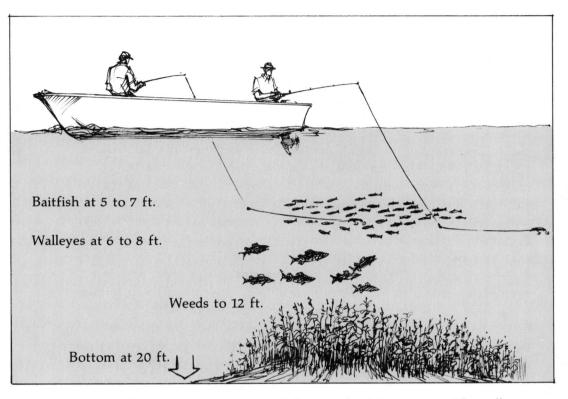

Baitfish at 5 to 7 ft.

Walleyes at 6 to 8 ft.

Weeds to 12 ft.

Bottom at 20 ft.

In summer walleyes often lurk above weedbeds where baitfish congregate. The walleyes, suspended below the school of baitfish, dart up from the weeds and grab a quick meal.

scattering of low weeds, rock piles, or gravel bars. A break could be an area where hard and soft bottom meet. Walleyes favor areas where something is completely different from the nearby environment. This could be a single rock on a flat, a small weedbed located on a point, or it could be a gravel bed with one soft-bottomed area. Look for those little differences that can be the key to midsummer walleye hideouts.

Avoid any area where sharp dropoffs occur. The fish may hold in such spots later in the year, but walleyes won't find anything there to hold them in midsummer. Select gradual, more sloping spots for summer fishing. You'll have better luck.

Weedbed areas are walleye hotspots. Such locations hold plenty of yellow perch and crayfish, two important ingredients in a walleye's summer diet. Look for fish along the deep-water edge, but don't overlook indentations, weed points, humps near the weeds, or any other *irregularity* along bottom. Some *big* midsummer fish are caught in 5 or 6 feet of water. Heavy weed growth cools the water, and provides ample shade and cover.

In oligotrophic (young) Canadian lakes walleyes like deep water. One lake I fished in northwestern Ontario contained a pair of underwater islands with 25 to 30 feet of water on all sides. A narrow elevated ridge ran between the two. It was 23 feet from the ridge to the top of the tallest island. It was 19 feet to the top of the shortest island. A current or wave action washed between the islands and attracted big fish. One hump, the tallest, had a flat top with a sharp break down one wall to a shelf, which lay in 17 feet of water. It was here, adjacent to deep water, that I would normally find fish. The tops of both humps were good spots, but the fish favored that island-top with the sharp break along one edge. I also caught many fish along the ridge that extended between the two humps. Walleyes in a negative feeding mood would often hold on the ridge. A lure had to be presented slowly, and right in their face, before they would strike. Fish holding on top or along the sharp break were always on the feed.

Another midsummer hotspot is wherever a flat extends far out into the lake. If the contour lines on your map run close together, and then parallel a broad, wide flat, it's likely that you'll encounter fish provided that some breaks occur on the flat. A small clump of weeds, rock piles, or a 2-foot drop may be all that is needed to attract fish to a flat. Some of the best breaklines on large flats are those that occur at 15- to 25-foot depths. Large bars or flats in fairly deep water attract and hold massive numbers of baitfish. This is one reason why walleyes favor such locations.

Keep an eye out for any unmapped submerged islands with rocky tops, found in 20 feet of water or more. If they have deep water, say 35 to 50 feet on all sides, it's possible you'll have something that no one else on your block has—a big-fish hotspot. I like to use a 1-ounce Baitwalker or heavy slip-sinker, 6-pound mono leader, and a leech, minnow, or nightcrawler hooked lightly through the lips or through the tip. I fish it slowly and carefully, work different angles, and use different presentation methods. I fish with the wind, against the wind, and across the wind. Sooner or later, I locate a concentration of big fish. Chances are good that only a few fish would weigh less than 6 pounds. Lakes with this type of underwater structure are common in Canada and northern Minnesota, Wisconsin, or Michigan. It's very important to keep your live-bait offering bumping the bottom. Work every break on structure from as many angles as possible.

Fall

In fall, walleye fishing is unpredictable. It's the one time of year when trophy fish can be taken regularly. It doesn't involve expensive gear (walleye fishing seldom does), but anglers must be able to interpret bottom conditions.

Most autumn fishing is done in deep water. This is especially true in the clearwater lakes of the North. On shallower, dirty-water lakes, still look for deep-water structure. "Deep" in such cases may only be 30 to 50 feet, but small humps, rock piles, sandbars in deep water, or other similar breaks in *water as deep as possible* should produce walleyes *if* any are present, and if the angler knows how to get down to them. The one thing I look for are deep areas that swing close to shore. A depthfinder can be used to pinpoint any deep-water edge of weedlines. Such areas hold forage fish and will attract walleyes moving up from the depths. Any small fingers or ridges that work from the weeds down to the dropoff could be a contact point where fish will move when working into shallower feeding zones.

A clean bar is not a tavern with freshly swept floors and tidy restrooms. To a structure fisherman, it's a sand or gravel bar with few breaks on structure. It extends from shore to the first major dropoff. Such areas can be good during the fall if the dropoff occurs at 20 feet

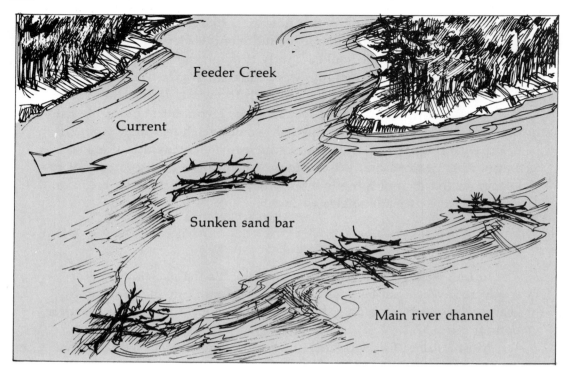

The edge of the sunken sandbar is often a hotspot for walleyes as they move up from deep water. Best spots to fish are near sunken timber or brushpiles along the edge of the bar.

or more. Walleyes can often find forage in such places. Or, they will contact the breakline, move up and over into shallower water, and continue a *short* distance to a weedline for food.

Backtrolling is a neat way to fish deep water for walleyes in fall. It allows precise speed and boat control and enables a fisherman to present his lure or live-bait rig *on bottom* and along the top or edges of underwater humps or similar structure. A forward troll moves the boat too fast, and causes line to string out behind. This necessitates the release of more line in order to get to bottom in deep water. It also decreases the "feel" needed by anglers to capitalize on a soft strike.

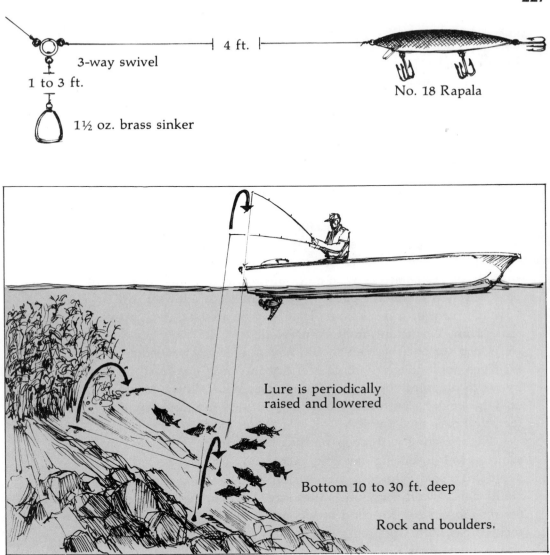

3-way swivel

4 ft.

1 to 3 ft.

No. 18 Rapala

1½ oz. brass sinker

Lure is periodically
raised and lowered

Bottom 10 to 30 ft. deep

Rock and boulders.

This 3-way swivel rig (top) with a trolling weight on a short dropper and a Rapala on a 4-foot leader is superb walleye-finder in deep water. Keep the sinker chugging along bottom by periodically raising and lowering the rod tip. Walleyes usually hit as the lure is lowered. Backtroll this rig along the deep side of weedbeds or over rocks and boulders.

I prefer backtrolling because it enables me to watch my depthfinder and back the boat's stern along an intricate path indicated by blips on the sonar unit. It also allows me to fish almost directly beneath the boat. This short-lining increases your sensitivity to strikes, and allows a more precise presentation of a lure or bait.

Jigs or slip-sinker rigs baited with nightcrawlers, minnows, salamanders, or leeches (in my order of preference) are superb rigs to use during fall months. Walleyes are normally feeding heavily at this time and are moving to natural bait. My preference for jigs or slip-sinker rigs would be slightly heavier than is needed because I want them directly under the boat on as short a line as possible. I find my catch success ratio climbs dramatically when I do this.

When backtrolling, learn to play the wind to your advantage. During a brief gust, a slow-down, or a gentle push by the wind, anglers should put their outboards in and out of gear to control each trolling pass better. A moment's pause in the right place allows a lure or bait to hover in front of a fish's nose. That may be all it takes to provoke a strike from a reluctant, nonfeeding walleye.

Deep-water fishermen should have a precise knowledge of where walleyes hold along any structure. Try throwing out small marker buoys to pinpoint edges of trolling passes. This allows you to do on-target fishing with every drift. If you miss the target by even 1 or 2 feet, you may miss the fish.

Night fishing with deep-running baits can be effective. I fish the same areas I do during daylight, except that I work somewhat shallower depths. It's cold fishing, so heavy clothes are needed. I troll Bombers, Hellbenders, Mud Bugs, and other lures that enable me to get down 12 feet or more. Look for good breaks around rock piles, especially those rocky areas with large rocks or boulders on bottom and smaller rocks above. Such areas form the breaks that autumn walleyes prefer, at least on clearwater lakes. Slow-trolling techniques pay off when the lure is bounced along bottom. Coldwater conditions slow a walleye's metabolism; fast trolling won't work. Use the smallest, lightest possible

Dan Gapen took this walleye on a Baitwalker rig and leech trolled along the bottom of a Minnesota lake.

lures, coupled with a light line, and you'll have a combination that is the best you could hope for during this difficult time of year.

Winter

The majority of winter walleye fishing is done on ice-covered lakes. Some winter sport can still be found in southern states, where the fish normally respond to the tactics used by northern anglers in fall.

In the heart of the North American walleye range (the northern tier of states and parts of Canada), winter brings ice and bone-chilling cold. Take time to learn the ins and outs of icefishing.

Move slowly and quietly over the ice on shallow lakes. Walleyes are extremely sensitive to sound or vibrations set up by running footsteps, snowmobiles, and gas-powered ice augers.

I normally set tipups parallel to the outside edge of a weedbed located in 6 to 15 feet of water. Use light mono line; avoid wire leaders. Use the smallest possible hook (single hooks are okay), and use minnows native to the areas. I prefer shiners, small suckers, chubs, redtail chubs, and wee smelt. Baitfish should be in the 2- or 3-inch class. Use only lively minnows; throw the floaters and bloaters onto the ice for the gulls to eat.

Suspend minnows on tipups so that they are 6 inches or less off bottom. Winter-weary marbleyes are likely to swim with anal fins dragging on bottom. A minnow swimming too far above their heads will not interest them. Don't use anything heavier than one or two BB splitshot on the line to keep the minnow near bottom.

Allow fish to run until they swallow the minnow (after they stop their first run). Set the hook as the second run begins. The fish shouldn't feel line drag or any resistance during the initial run.

Jigging for walleyes through the winter ice is great fun. I use a small, fiberglass jigging rod equipped with a baitcasting reel. My choice of lures includes small Swedish Pimples, ¼-ounce leadhead jigs, and jigging Rapalas. Fish will strike one lure today, only to pass it up for something else the next time you go fishing. Experiment with lures and jigging techniques. There are many times when the addition of a small minnow to a jigging lure will increase its effectiveness. It's worth a try when action is slow. A 2-inch emerald shiner is a good baitfish to use.

The best place to try winter jigging is within a foot of bottom. I'll usually fish near weedbeds, or along dropoffs with some cover on the break. Timbered lakes are often a good bet because fish cruise the dropoff, and work in and out of submerged timber. Experiment with various depths, locations, and jigging lures until you find one that pays off.

The period after first ice is often the best time to catch walleyes. Newly formed ice can be extremely dangerous, so play it safe. Check ice thicknesses before going out just after freeze-up. It might save your life.

Trout

T rout fishing is the spice of life for some anglers, but many fish only in streams and bypass some of the best sport left on this continent. Lake fishing for rainbows, browns, brookies, lakers, cutthroats, goldens, splake, and other species offers unparalled action.

Too many sportsmen think that trolling is the only way to catch trout. The truth is that trolling does work in natural lakes, beaver ponds, or other waters. These same gamefish can be taken on spinning or fly tackle, too.

I was introduced to lake fishing for trout many years ago, when Michigan angler Art Dengler took me under his wing. "Trout in lakes offer some of the best sport available anywhere today," he told me. "Most lakes are seldom trout-fished, and lunkers die every year without once seeing an angler's lure." My interest aroused, we set up a trip for the following week.

I'll not bore you with long-winded details but the fishing trip lasted four days, and we limited out daily; the first day, on rainbows; the second, on browns; the third day, on lake trout up to 15 pounds; and the last day produced five brook trout each. Those speckles weighed 3 pounds apiece. It was a trip that I'll always remember, not because of the huge numbers of fish landed, but instead for the knowledge I acquired at the hands of an old master.

Deep-water lakes are home to some of North America's largest trout. The primary reason why trout grow to awesome sizes is because they're not caught! The average angler doesn't understand trout movements, when the fish move onto structure, and how best to fish for them. Trout fishermen usually try to adapt stream-fishing tactics to a lake—it doesn't work. Oh, they may take an odd, small trout from the shallows, but stream techniques seldom work for fish weighing more than 5 pounds. The basic fact to be remembered is that trout, like all fish in lakes, use deep water as a sanctuary. Many trout are caught in 20 feet of water or more. A fisherman flogging the surface or inshore waters will be wasting his time, except for those few periods when trout move in shallow to feed, often under the cover of darkness.

All trout inhabit much the same areas, move somewhat the same way onto structure to feed, and leave the structure for a return to the sanctuary of deep water. The movements of gamefish are often altered, though, by the presence or absence of forage fish, water temperature, and time of year. Spawning, and times of water temperature changes, are two periods when an in-depth knowledge of trout species will offer clues to the whereabouts of these fish.

Spring

Some trout species spawn during the spring, while others spawn in the fall. Trout seldom feed well during the prespawn, spawn, and postspawn periods. That's why fishing for trout is tough at these times.

Rainbow trout normally spawn between March and May, depending on latitude. Fish at higher elevations usually reproduce later in the season. Browns, lakers, and brook trout go through the spawning procedure from October through early December. Golden trout, the gem of western alpine lakes, do their thing in August, a fall month at elevations above 10,000 feet. All of these species, plus any that weren't mentioned, will feed actively until about two weeks before the spawn. This two-week period is devoted to selecting a suitable spawning site; food is a low-priority item. Lake fishermen would be well-advised to fish rainbows during the fall, and browns, brookies, or lakers in the spring.

Most trout species will move into shallow water about two weeks after spring ice-out. They move from the depths into the shallows in search of food. The level at which they feed on structure is dictated, to a small degree, by the species involved. Rainbows, browns, cutthroats, goldens, and brook trout often hold and feed in water from 6 to 10 feet deep, provided that deep water or breaks on structure are located nearby to afford some protection. Lake trout and splake customarily feed just after ice-out in depths ranging from 10 to 20 feet. They seldom favor nearby deep water, although much of this inshore food gathering is done after sundown or during low-light periods.

The type of bottom structure will indicate where trout will be located during spring months. Western trout may hold near newly emerging weedbeds, where they feed on freshwater shrimp, sow bugs, or other aquatic food. In lakes of the East, Midwest, and portions of southern Canada you will normally find fish holding near the first steep breakline, if some breaks are found on bottom. I look for rocky areas with boulders for lakers and splake, or sandy points with stair-stepping ledges of sand or gravel near deep water for the other species. These are only basic observations. Each area must be studied in detail to ascertain the most probable location for trout during the spring. It's not the same on every lake.

Moving water really attracts spring trout. It warms lake water, and washes food downstream over the dropoff to feeding fish. Trout visit such areas shortly after ice-out. The first major dropoff at a rivermouth can be a key location for feeding fish, regardless of species.

The author lifts a handsome fly-caught brown trout from the mouth of the Lochy River on New Zealand's Wakatipu Lake.

In a typical dropoff near a river, the stream current crosses a sand or gravel bar. The combination of wave action in the lake, and dredging effects of the river current, to form a distinct, sharp dropoff, often falling from a depth of 3 to 6 feet, down to 6 to 10, depending on the stream size. A stream doesn't have to be trout water in order to attract trout from lakes. The current will wash nymphs, eggs from spawning forage fish, and other nutritional material into the lake. Dropoffs along rivermouths may vary from small holes to long, tapering affairs with several fish-holding ledges where trout will cruise in search of food. A rivermouth is the one springtime area where all trout species can be found from time to time.

Timing is important when fishing in rivermouths. A cold front featuring high skies and brilliant sunshine is not conducive to good trout catches in shallow water. Trout are curious about available food, but that curiosity is prevalent only during periods of low-light levels. Early morning, just before dark, and during overcast skies are prime times to fish for feeding trout. They tend to move shallower on any structure breaks. It's not unusual, at daybreak, to see dorsal fins splitting the surface in 2 feet of water. Use long, fine leaders, and small lures. Make a careful presentation whether with lure, fly, or live bait. A shadow, the plop of a lure landing too close to cruising fish, or a sloppy presentation will spook fish from shallow water.

I remember one time when brown trout moved in close to a Lake Michigan rivermouth. It was thirty minutes before daybreak. I was flyfishing with a No. 6 Gray Ghost streamer, trying to imitate smelt that the browns were eating. The casts were short 30-footers to visible fish. I landed two fish, each weighing 6 pounds. The sun was rising above the eastern hills when I spotted a giant dorsal fin of a brown trout that must have weighed at least 15 pounds. The smelt were leaping from the water as the fish slashed through the school. Duck soup, I thought.

My first cast produced a slapping strike from the fish, but no hookup. The brown had simply swatted the streamer in an attempt to kill it. I lowered the rod tip and allowed the fly to sink, hoping the fish would return to pick it up. A minute passed as I moved the fly back to my canoe, false-cast once, and hurried my forward cast. The fly slapped the water too hard on delivery. The trophy brown didn't hesitate; he left the shallow-water flat like his tail was on fire and never returned.

A fisherman in a small canoe, or wading, is mobile enough to move from one area to another. Trout sometimes move into a rivermouth but they are seldom motionless. They are constantly shifting positions in an attempt to find food. A school of forage fish represents chow time for hungry browns. These gamefish may herd baitfish schools to the surface, feed in one area, and then disappear only to surface again 100 yards away. The angler must move up or down the shoreline in order to stay near the fish. Do not crowd surfacing trout. Stay as far away from the fish as possible. Cast past them with a lure, live bait, or fly and work it back through the school. It may require a fast retrieve to turn on brown trout. Small spoons or minnow-imitating flies worked in a fast jerky manner work best on these fish.

Spring spawning trout will pick up (not necessarily eat) free-drifting roe from other spring spawners. For example, prespawning rainbows will often pick up and mash eggs in their mouth. During the fall, live bait or spawnbags rolled along bottom off a rivermouth are very effective for those trout species that will soon be spawning.

Summer

Summer is a difficult season for trout fishing. The fish are often deep and shallow-water catches are rare. It takes a detailed knowledge of deep-water habits, food sources, and lure presentations to take fish regularly. Some fishermen ignore this period and fish only during spring and fall. Summer can be a prime period, however, because fishing pressure is light.

The water temperature of any trout lake during June, July, August, and early September will determine the most logical place *and depth* where trout will be located. Most trout will be found in a broad temperature band ranging from 45 to 60 degrees, although certain species will be more commonly found at one end or the other of this range. Coldwater species such as lakers, splake, cutthroats, goldens, and some brookies favor colder temperatures than do rainbows and brown trout. An electronic water thermometer is needed to pinpoint the exact depths of a preferred temperature. In a pinch, one can use a bulb-type thermometer, although this method of temperature-taking is not as accurate and is more time-consuming.

Common baitfish in trout lakes include yellow perch, smelt, emerald or gray shiners, golden shiners, ciscoes, tullibees, and other species. Shiners and yellow perch favor warmer temperatures, while smelt, ciscoes, and tullibees enjoy colder water. A quick check of the temperature chart in Chapter 10 will reveal both the baitfish and trout temperature levels. If the two overlap, regardless of depth, any *sharp-breaking structure* will usually produce trout.

At certain times, trout suspend in any lake. This suspension normally takes place just below their optimum temperature level. Trout usually come up to strike, but seldom go deeper to take baitfish or a lure. This suspension happens a lot in summer. It's not directly related to bottom contours or other structure. The thermocline in any lake is often a narrow band of cooler water; the breakoff point between warmer and colder water is often distinct. Look for suspension of gamefish and baitfish just below the top layer of the thermocline.

Nevertheless, the normal place to find trout in summer lakes is near bottom or other sharp-breaking structure. These gamefish spend little time in shallow water because water temperatures along inshore areas are too warm and forage is located in deeper water. I look for sharp points extending from shore into deep water, with flats of hard-packed sand or small gravel off the tip. Trout will often pause near any rocks or submerged objects (such as small weedbeds in 20 feet of water) because they can hold and feed there for varying time periods before following the *deep-water edge* up into shallow water. It's possible to fish leadhead jigs along the edge of the point's shelf and pick up feeding trout.

In summer, trout often lurk at the deep-water edges of weedbeds.

Such areas, if found in about 20 feet of water, will have cooler water and an excellent baitfish population. The trout *normally* hold near bottom, in or along any depression or hole in the weedline. They then dart out to feed. Anglers who find suitable water temperatures in such areas can troll, backtroll, or cast jigs or small spinners. Many fishermen believe that trout in lakes are seldom found near weeds.

One method of fishing such areas is to try speed-trolling with Spoonplugs and the STST method. I believe that trolling, backtrolling, or speed-trolling are three of the most efficient methods an angler can

Jack Duffy swings a 14-pound brown trout into the boat on Lake Michigan. Duffy, using a fly rod and 6-pound mono, caught the fish trolling a flatfish 125 yards behind the boat near submerged rocks.

use on any summer trout lake. It allows a quick exploration of likely areas. A critical examination of a contour map will outline the best spots.

Trolling with Cowbells and minnows is a good method of catching trout. Select minnows native to the lake. Thread them on a small treble hook attached to an 18-inch leader. Use enough weight to take the Cowbell-minnow rig to bottom at very slow trolling speeds. Work in and out along edges of weedbeds. Keep the rig near bottom, and activate the throbbing beat of Cowbells by alternately raising and lowering the rod tip. I've caught more trout in summer with this method than with any other. Strikes are hard and sure. Slow trolling with this rig can deliver fish up to 15 pounds from waters sometimes ignored by area residents.

Other summer hotspots for trout are submerged rock piles or underwater islands. Every summer, I go to Bransons Lodge on Great Bear Lake in the Canadian Northwest Territories. Many anglers troll near shore in shallow water. They catch trout by using the STST method of fishing. Submerged rock piles some distance from shore are favored targets in midsummer, too. Flat-top rocky areas with 20 feet of water above them and deep water on all sides are my favorites. I'll often use a deep-diving lure such as a Ping-a-T, which runs about 18 feet deep on a very slow troll. I'll cover the edges and tops of these areas. I also look for large gravel or rocky bars some distance from shore, with sharp breaklines leading into deep water. The edges of these shallow bars can produce some gigantic trout. One must look for them because many guides will troll areas closer to shore unless directed otherwise.

In most coldwater trout lakes, lakers can be found in similar areas. If a lake contains only lake trout, and it is spring-fed, try fishing near submerged rock piles or shallow bars adjacent to deep water with jigs, spinners, or small spoons. Use a lift-drop method with jigs; a flutter-down, slow retrieve with spoons; and a slow, steady retrieve near bottom with spinners. Pay close attention to indentations in a bar or rock pile; they may harbor fish. Breaks on the breakline, which are often large rocks or boulders in northern waters, can hold fish.

Kay Richey strains to lift a 24-pound lake trout taken from Great Bear Lake, Northwest Territories. She caught the fish while trolling beneath the steep cliff in the background.

Greg Meadows lands a big lake trout on Great Bear Lake with the help of guide Charley Hamelin. Bransons Lodge can be seen along shore.

Fall

In autumn, trout repeat their spring inshore movements as waters cool. The major difference at this time of year is that brown trout, lake trout, golden trout, and other species are spawning. These gamefish show a marked reluctance to feed during this period, although they will strike to protect spawning redds or out of irritation.

Inshore structure movements often coincide with the leaf drop in northern areas *or* occur a month or so before freeze-up. Fall is a general term that can cover a period anywhere from August through November, depending upon latitude or elevation. Golden trout in western states may spawn in August, while brook trout in mountain areas of the Southeast may not spawn before October. It's all a question of location, elevation, and latitude. Ask fisheries officials in your state about the peak periods of spawning for the various trout species. Use these as guidelines, but still look for any differences in trout behavior in your local lakes.

Rivermouths, or areas such as a channel flowing between two lakes, are hotspots for fall trout fishermen. Any major lake between the spawning site and the midsummer home of these trout will be a good water to fish. Most of these connecting lakes will have an inlet and outlet, with deep water at each location. These should always be the first choice for structure fishermen looking for action.

Although inlets and outlets are easily recognized, don't end your search here. Instead, check any nearby areas for weedbeds fronting deep water, dropoffs, and isolated weedbeds or rocky areas in water 10 to 30 feet deep. Check any sharp-breaking dropoffs where gamefish have immediate access to deep water. Such areas attract prespawning trout like liver pellets attract hatchery trout.

Two methods are effective during this fall period. Baitfishing near inlets and outlets, or rivermouths, is a time-honored practice that usually succeeds. This method was discussed elsewhere and won't be repeated here, except to state that during the fall, feeding trout are usually spring spawners that gobble free-drifting eggs from spawning fish. Marble-size spawnbags fished on or within inches of bottom work well most of the time.

One method I use during fall months is the STST technique. Small Dardevles, Little Cleos, or floating Rapalas trolled just off the edges of sandbars, dropoffs, or submerged rock piles, weedbeds, and sunken islands will frequently bring in jumbo trout. I prefer slow trolling with a continual pump-drop-pump method of activating my rod tip and the trailing lure.

I've noticed one peculiarity about some trout species during the fall. If they migrate upstream through a connecting waterway or small

Flatfish

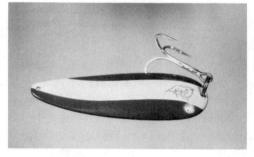

Daredevle

Rapala

lakes, they will often head toward green weedbed pockets. I'm not sure whether they use such areas for cover, or if they are actively feeding. The trout that I've taken in such spots are not fall spawners, but spring-spawning fish. I don't understand this phenomenon, although I've observed it a dozen times. Keep in mind that it does occur, however, often in October and November in northern areas, and possibly later in southern regions. This is a facet of trout fishing that hasn't been researched thoroughly. Perhaps detailed information on this weedbed movement will surface in years to come.

Trolling offers anglers their best chance at fall trout, but a few rules apply. Slow speeds are normally more productive. This is particularly true later in the season when the lake is cold. A slightly faster trolling speed can be used until the fall turnover (see Chapter 10) is completed. Afterward it's wise to throttle your speeds down to a bare crawl. Use lures that operate best at slow speeds. Ping-a-T's, Flatfish, Rapalas, and small spoons are my choice.

Winter

Trout fishermen in the mid-South can use the same tactics in winter as in the fall, but in the northern states and Canada, they must icefish.

This often means fishing deep for lake trout. Other trout species may frequent shoal waters or deep-water edges of weedbeds, but lakers are usually caught at depths of more than 100 feet. Lakers often favor flat-bottom areas, although they may suspend and feed at varying distances off bottom. Browns and rainbows are normally taken in much shallower water, often at depths of 10 to 35 feet. The one secret to icefishing for trout is to keep moving from hole to hole. Some anglers sit huddled over one hole hoping fish will come their way. They usually don't have much luck. I prefer spudding or drilling a dozen holes in various areas before fishing. If one spot fails to produce within fifteen or twenty minutes, I move my operation to another location.

One place in a lake that is often the site of fine shallow-water action is along a dropoff or the edge of a deep weedbed. I drill several

Richard Smith lifts a chunky brown trout from an ice hole. He caught the fish on a tipup baited with a live minnow.

holes paralleling this structure. Each ice hole will be about 30 yards apart. Many states allow the use of two lines, so I might jig-fish with a hand-held rod and set a minnow-baited tipup in another hole. I seldom move the tipups because they are baited with live minnows. The transferring of hooked shiners or other baitfish species may kill them. I just shift my jigging operation to a different area.

A Do-Jigger and minnow are a deadly combination for jigging through the ice for trout.

Tipup fishing has been discussed in previous chapters on northern pike and walleyes. The same tactics apply, although the baitfish used is smaller. Gray or emerald shiners are good, as are live smelt 3 inches long.

Jigging is an art. I favor small fiberglass rods with a levelwind baitcasting reel stocked with 6- to 10-pound mono. Lures might include Swedish Pimples, Do-Jiggers, small Dardevles, jigging Rapalas, or others. Use a small minnow or strip of fish flesh to flavor jigging lures. The combination of flash from the lure, and the scent of a minnow, is a double-barreled attraction few trout species can pass up.

Begin jigging near bottom along any weedline or dropoff, if it's located near deep water. Short, vertical lift-drop methods work best, as long as they aren't violent. A 3- or 4-inch upward lift and rapid lowering of the rod tip will produce the desired action. Work the bottom area for a few minutes, raise the lure a couple feet, jig again for a short period, and continue up until you're fishing under the ice. It often takes about twenty minutes to thoroughly explore all depths. If you haven't had a strike during this period move on to the next hole and repeat the routine. Sooner or later you'll contact fish along this structure.

Early morning and late afternoon are the best times to fish for ice-bound trout. I've had only sporadic action at midday. Some anglers prefer jigging after sundown. This is fun as long as the weather is moderate. Otherwise, a heated fish shanty can be a worthwhile investment for an ice fishermen.

CHAPTER 17

Salmon

The average angler considers salmon fishing a river sport, and usually thinks only about the Atlantic salmon. Many regions in North America offer excellent lake fishing for such species as: landlocked salmon, kokanee, coho, chinook, and sockeye salmon. Let's take a look at seasonal patterns and movements of salmon in freshwater lakes. You'll note a similarity in some respects, as well as major differences among species.

Coho Salmon

Coho (silver) salmon were introduced to fresh water during the mid-1960s when Michigan planted this West Coast gamefish in lakes Michigan, Huron, and Superior. Tributary streams were stocked, and then cohos descended to the Great Lakes. Here they found vast amounts of food, especially alewives—an oily, abundant trash fish. The trout became fat and sassy on a steady diet of this herring-like species. This was the first major successful planting of saltwater salmon into fresh water.

In spring, cohos will usually be found in the upper levels of a lake, and the inshore waters, from ice-out through early June. The inshore shallows warm more quickly than waters found far from shore. This warming tendency concentrates remnant schools of alewives, smelt, shiners, and other forage fish. Locate the principal forage species and then fish in the immediate areas with lures imitating these fish. It's certain that coho salmon will be nearby, and feeding heavily.

Excellent areas to fish early in the spring are any rivermouths or warmwater discharges. Many power plants or industrial sites discharge warm, treated water into the lake. This water may be only 5 to 10 degrees warmer than lake water, but it's enough to attract forage and predatory gamefish. Fishing will often be most productive in fairly shallow water and near outflowing currents of the discharge. I've had fantastic success trolling small Rebels, Rapalas, Sugar Spoons, Devle Dogs, or Little Cleos in water ranging from 6 to 20 feet deep. A rapid speed can be used if you troll a long line. I've discovered that trolling at least 60 yards of line behind the boat is best when fishing skinny water. This is not the time nor the place for heavy tackle; a 6-pound line is adequate. Many cohos weigh from only 1 to 6 pounds. These smaller salmon taste better now than at any stage in their three-year life. Strikes are hard and sure; spring cohos often dance from the water as they try repeatedly to shake the hook.

The color line is a clearly defined area off a rivermouth where dark, dirtier river water forms a noticeable line of different-colored water. The lake water will be clear (a bluish-green), but the river water will range from gray through dark, muddy colors. The exact line where clear and dirty water meet is the color line. Spring cohos will often cruise in clear water, but feed back and forth in dirty water on free-drifting food washing down with the current.

Trolling with the above-mentioned lures along this color line is one of the best ways to pick up spring coho salmon. A "snake trolling" or in-and-out pattern of boat handling produces more strikes than will a straight down-the-lake troll. Alternate your boat speeds, try different lures, and experiment with various depths until the daily pattern is discovered. I've discovered that alternate fast-slow speeds can turn a poor day into one filled with excitement. If two or more strikes occur as the boat slows down from faster speeds, then go slower. Frequent slowdowns often cause a lure to flutter down in an enticing manner.

One last tip: Keep hook points sharp! Coho often slap at lures or strike short. A dull hook simply won't deliver the adequate penetration needed to go through a tough mouth. Small trebles are more practical for hooking spring salmon than are the large hooks found on many commercial lures.

Summer coho fishing in the Great Lakes is an entirely different ball game. These fish are temperature conscious and usually suspend in the thermocline. They prefer a water temperature of about 54 degrees. I've seen some dramatic shifts in coho movement patterns, usually due to a thermocline shift. The Great Lakes often form a definite thermocline in June, but a cool spring, with cold rains, will keep the lake temperatures cool and the thermoclines may not form until July. Cohos will often be found in the thermocline and near any alewife schools.

Few fishermen are aware that cohos may suspend over very deep water in midsummer. It's not uncommon to locate salmon holding at 40 feet, although the depth of the lake there is 150 feet. Or, fish may suspend at 90 feet, over 200 feet of water. This is clearly the time and place for downrigger fishing—an innovation that has completely revolutionized deep-water fishing.

Dozens of downriggers are on the market. I use Luhr Jensen Auto Trac models. One long-arm, out-downrigger is mounted on each gunwale near the wheel. A short-arm downrigger is mounted on the stern corners. The downriggers allow me to fish lures at whatever depth salmon are located. A quick check with an electronic water thermometer, or the use of a chart-recording graph, can pinpoint the exact depth at which to set each rig. If salmon are suspended at 40 feet, it's wise to set the downrigger so the lure will pass 2 to 6 feet above the fish. Salmon will come up a short distance to strike but never go down for a lure.

Cohos often follow trolled lures for long distances, particularly during summer and early fall. A short speed-up or slow-down of the trolling speed or a sudden turn to port or starboard may generate strikes. A big coho has been known to break downrigger rods on the strike, if the drag isn't set properly.

Summer lures for coho salmon come in many sizes and all colors. Bright or fluorescent red, pink, orange, green, blue, or chartreuse are very effective, and chrome-blue or chrome-green can be hot on certain days. An all-black lure often turns the trick if salmon schools have been pounded steadily by fishermen. Lures such as the J-Plug, FirePlug, Flutter Spoon, Spring Spoon, Manistee Wobbler, and Ping-a-T are midsummer favorites.

Herring Dodgers or Cowbells are great to use during summer months when teamed with trolling flies. I prefer kelly-green Dodgers or Cowbells. A favorite combination is the green Jensen Dodger, followed by a green-black or green-white Michigan Rattlure fly. This is one of the hottest combinations for summer salmon.

Movement patterns must be recognized for success in summer. Cohos may feed heavily in one area for a week, only to disappear without a trace. Overnight movements often follow northerly patterns when fish decide to pack up and leave. If fishing is slow, raise the lures and move three or four miles north, and fish the same depth. If a storm hasn't turned the thermocline upside down, then a short move may result in fast action. Early morning usually provides the most spectacular action. The reason: fewer boats and less fishing pressure. One Michigan charterboat skipper I know likes to take his passengers out at 5 A.M. in order to get the best sport. He limits-out daily. Try fishing very early in the morning this year; it may just up your catch records for the year.

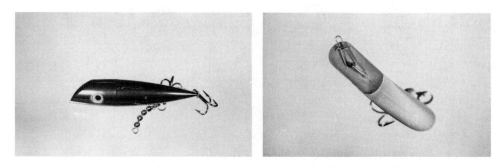

J-Plug   *Fire Plug*

Devle Dog

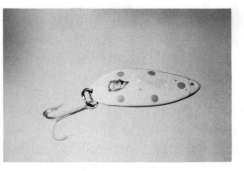

Spring Spoon   *Manistee Wobbler*

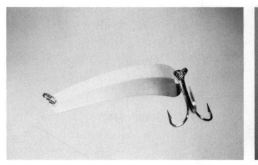

Fall coho fishing can offer the best action of all. Big fish (and plenty of them) plus good weather are commonplace during September and early October. The same basic lures work now, as they did during summer. The only difference is that coho salmon tend to live in slightly deeper water until the spawning urge strikes them. They then move inshore off rivermouths, where any of the spring, trout-fishing tactics can produce splendid action.

Once, cohos were stacked up in Lake Michigan between the Michigan towns of Onekama and Arcadia. One area—we called it "The Barrel"—was located in fairly deep water. The bottom contours were flat except inside the barrel, where the sides of this unusual, sharp-breaking structure made it look like an open grave site. Steep walls dropped off sharply. Salmon stayed inside the depression along the edge of the walls. Fish could be found only here, and the only way to catch salmon was to skim the bottom of the lake with cannonballs and lures until we reached the barrel. We rapidly lowered the cannonballs over the edge, and then trolled until we reached the opposite wall where our rigs were raised. Every pass through the area resulted in one slashing strike after another. One fish, a silvery coho weighing at least 25 pounds, slanted into the early morning sunlight, danced a tango on the surface, and ripped away on a line-grabbing run of 75 yards. We danced to his tune for twenty minutes before he was safely in the net. In that four-hour period of barrel fishing, twenty coho salmon were caught by four anglers. Each fish weighed more than 15 pounds.

Fall cohos tend to associate with sharp breaks on bottom structure. They stay in 54-degree water, and will often be found at that temperature level if it's located near a break on structure. Banks, those sharp-breaking dropoffs that fall swiftly into deep water, are favored locations. Some of the finest fishing that I've done has been in locations where a moment's error in judgment will result in the hanging of cannonballs and lures on the lip of a break. This necessitates the use of a sonar unit, and quick reflexes by the captain. If he lowers the cannonballs too soon, they will hang up on bottom. The fisherman will have to waste thirty minutes rerigging his gear. However, lowering cannonballs and lures at the proper time can drop the lure right into the holding area of cohos suspended along the lip of the breakline. If it's done, this tactic will result in a savage strike nearly every time. Experience is important. One slip, and fishing comes to an immediate halt.

Fall fishing is most productive early in the morning, before hordes of boats arrive on the fishing grounds. One captain I know makes a point of getting to his fishing area early. He often has a full limit for all of his anglers aboard before fishermen in other boats begin fishing. His secret is to be "the firstest with the mostest." He starts early, changes lures every fifteen minutes if they don't work, and he always takes the water temperature and marks the depth of the 54-degree water. He checks the water temperature three or four times each morning because wave action can move the soon-to-break-up thermocline up or down. This can ruin fishing. I've watched this skipper move right in on the beach, tracking 54-degree water. He claims that cohos will often be found in 15 feet of water, along sharp-breaking bottom contours, provided that the water temperature is right and there is an abundant food supply. He carries binoculars and scans inshore waters for sign of alewives or other forage fish breaking the surface. Wheeling gulls often signify the presence of forage fish and cohos are seldom far behind. I've watched him make limit catches of shallow-water cohos in thirty minutes, while other skippers are fishing offshore waters for nonfeeding fish in 90 feet of water. Next time you're coho fishing in fall, keep this in mind.

Chinook Salmon

If there's any single surprise left for spring Great Lakes fishermen, it's the chinook salmon. The average chinook (king) will weigh about 5 or 6 pounds, but once in a while an angler will tangle with a rowdy 25-pounder that leaves him with a sore wrist. Spring kings are wild; they strike hard and display a wild fury unmatched by any other gamefish except a muskie. They fight until their last ounce of strength is gone. Even then, they come to the net or gaff with fire in their eye and enough spunk left to make a shambles of shoddy equipment. Spring kings are the type of gamefish that anglers dream about in winter.

The same methods that produce fast action with spring cohos will work with chinook salmon. Faster-than-usual trolling speeds, snake trolling, and the presentation of lures along the color line or near warmwater discharges will generate strikes.

This species, the largest of the Pacific salmon, is sensitive to light. Cold fronts, with high skies and bright sun, will disrupt chinook fishing on the Great Lakes. It's far better to fish immediately before a spring storm, under an overcast sky, and take advantage of the slightly rougher water that decreases light penetration into the depths. Many anglers know that after-dark fishing works well just before the spawning run, but few have practiced it during the spring. It works!

One little-understood fact about chinook salmon is that they are more bottom or structurally oriented than cohos. Though cohos suspend off bottom frequently, the opposite is true with kings. They are more of a homebody than their smaller cousins, and they are more apt to hover, feed, and move on bottom structure. It's possible, of course, to catch suspended chinook salmon. This happens more often during summer than at any other time, however.

Sharp-breaking bottom contours located close to shore, rivermouths, or breakwaters at harbors are prime waters in spring for chinooks. Such areas offer a lot of food *and* the bottom contours these fish prefer. They tend to move in and out of choice feeding locations while remaining in the sanctuary of deep water.

A common error of summer chinook fishermen is that they work the same inshore areas they fished in spring. The fish aren't there because the water has warmed to unbearable temperatures. Fifty-four degrees is still the magic temperature. I try to locate this temperature at a depth where a contour map will reveal likely holding areas. I prefer those locations where the narrow band of 54-degree water touches a sharp-breaking dropoff close to deep water. Steep banks, gradual bars that break sharply into the depths, or depressed valleys on the floor of the lake are choice spots to begin your search. A contour map will reveal such locations, but finding them once you're on the water requires time and experience.

Downrigger fishing is also one of the best ways to contact summer chinooks. I'll often stagger my lures so that a 6-foot spread is found between the lowest and highest lures. This gives fish a chance to look over four or more lures at slightly different depths. A cruising chinook may decide to strike 5 feet off bottom one day, while the next day he may want dinner served at his table on the lake floor. Experiment with depths, lures, and trolling speeds until you figure out the daily pattern. Stick with that pattern until action slows, and then revert back to experimentation. Anglers who fish only one lure, one speed, and at one depth seldom bring in many fish.

Downriggers on the stern of this boat help anglers to troll at controlled depths for chinooks. Here a fisherwoman lands a hefty salmon.

Fall fishing tactics for chinook salmon are similar to those used in spring. The fish are usually lumped together in massive schools. One guy, fishing with me and watching my Vexilar Sona Graf, commented, "Those marks look like hogs wallowing around in a pen. I've never seen so many fish in my life." His words were barely out when a flatline with a Ping-a-T rattled in the rodholder. He then saw a silvery hen fish scramble into the air like a surface-to-air missile lifting off. "My gosh," he yelped, "that's one helluva big fish!" He battled the fish for twenty minutes before I could slide my custom-built tailer around the hen's tail and lift her into the boat. She was big—at least 31 pounds—and the fight she delivered that September morning is recounted every time my friend goes fishing. Chinooks have been known to break rods, jerk them overboard, and sprain wrists on the strike if someone is careless enough to be holding a trolling rod. The first prick of a hook sends

George Richey tails a big chinook for David Richey, the author's son, while trolling with downriggers on Lake Michigan. The fish struck a Jensen Dodger-Michigan Squid Fly over a sharp breakline in deep water.

Kay Richey grins over a 25-pound chinook salmon taken while fishing with downriggers. Note the cannonball dangling from the downrigger over her right shoulder; the line release is just above the ball.

them catapulting into the air in a series of jumps comparable to anything seen by saltwater anglers.

Slow-speed trolling produces the best action for boat fishermen. I prefer lures that generate a side-to-side wobble when fished at putt-putt speeds. Plugs such as the Ping-a-T, Flatfish, or Jensen Dodgers, fancied up with strips of Prism Tape and teamed with a green Michigan Squid fly, are very effective when trolled off rivermouths. The secret is to troll slowly enough so that plugs wobble and dig, or so a dodger rolls and wobbles but doesn't quite make a complete revolution.

When salmon are near the surface in August and early September, trolling for them with flat lines, at slow speeds, is the best strategy. Lures with a side-to-side wobble are productive.

A dodger trolled at these speeds will twist and jerk the trolling fly in such a manner that it appears alive. Drags must be properly set, not too loose and not too tight, because strikes are brutal. You'll have no doubt about a chinook strike, as line melts off the spool as an angry king moves away from the boat.

The color line is a likely area to find soon-to-spawn chinooks. Anglers often stagger downrigger lines, from bottom up at 10-foot intervals. They then troll in a circular pattern, testing every inch of the rivermouth. One technique favored by an expert Wisconsin angler is to troll against the grain or across the grain. If other boats troll one way, he'll work his lures in the opposite direction or cut across on a diagonal trolling pattern. This is impossible if too many boats are fishing, but it's a super method in areas that have little fishing pressure. Kings are used to seeing lures going in one direction only, but they will often snap at anything that moves off a different way. This little trick may help you reach your limit on days when other anglers found it difficult to hook a single fish.

Many states allow fishermen to use two rods for king salmon. This enables the use of four downrigger lines per boat, plus two flatlines, if three anglers are aboard. I fish dodgers and flies on the two out-downriggers, and Ping-a-T's and Flatfish on the stern downriggers. I trail chartreuse-with-red-dot Manistee Wobblers or Ping-a-T's on the two flatlines. This allows adequate coverage of all rivermouth depths. One day dodgers and flies may work best, while at another time the chinooks will hit only on flatlines.

Landlocked Salmon

Landlocked salmon remind me of a born-again Christian; he's the same fish he always was but he now has habits different from those of his sea-running brother, the Atlantic salmon. He's a stay-at-home fish and lives only in lakes.

Spring fishing for landlocks is a hit-or-miss sport. These fish, as temperamental as a new bride, are extremely finicky. Trolling with flies is the accepted technique, but few anglers know when and where to troll. Some prime locations for these gamefish are along rocky shorelines where boulders form breaks on a fast-sloping breakline. Points pushing out into deep water, particularly if rocks or boulders are found off the tip, are favored locations of this species. Also, the mouths of streams harboring spawning smelt. These forage fish are common in most lakes containing landlocked salmon. Try fishing off islands or over submerged shoals featuring rocks or boulders. Never pass up an area where ledge rock, with a generous sprinkling of rocks and boulders, butts up against deep water. Trolling fly fishermen, fishing from 6- to 15-foot depths, are often very successful.

Weather conditions play an important role in spring landlock fishing. The dirtier the weather, the better the fishing . . . up to a point. It's been proved that the downwind portion of the lake, if it contains some rocks and deep water, will deliver the fastest action. Trolling with flies is good if anglers stick with patterns that imitate forage fish. Some of my favorite ties are the Mickey Finn, Supervisor, Dark Tiger, Light Edson Tiger, or Nine-Three. Use a level sinking fly line, 100 yards of backing, and a 9-foot-long leader tapered down to a 4-pound tippet.

Smelt tend to move from the depths into shallow water during the night. Salmon will follow inshore migrations of forage fish; they can be found working in and around rocks and rivermouths at daybreak. A fairly fast trolling speed works best. I use the STST method to locate widespread pockets of fish. Chug the rod tip by pulling the rod forward and allow it to drop back. This practice causes the fly to jump ahead and then settle a few inches before the forward speed of the boat begins moving the fly again. Periodic chugging in this manner often induces strikes. Steer a zigzag course down the shoreline, and pay close attention to any bottom contours offering a sharp breakline. Spring is the best time to follow these gamefish into shallow water. Remember: any breaks on structure can serve as highways for forage and gamefish to follow from the depths into the shallows. Fish all breaklines, regardless of depth, and pay particular attention to any depressions between two ridges on bottom, especially if the depression contains rocks or boulders. Such areas are often overlooked, but capable of holding feeding fish.

Landlocked salmon are difficult to locate in summer, except around spring holes on bottom. During a hot summer that warms up the lake, a fisherman may get into sporadic early-morning shallow-water action. Spring and fall are usually better seasons to fish. Fall tactics for landlocked salmon are similar to those used in spring.

Kokanee Salmon

These gamefish are regionally popular in certain portions of the West. I've fished for them in several lakes in Idaho and Montana. They are more important to me, however, as a forage fish for trout than as a sportfish.

My kokanee experience has been limited to late summer months. I do remember one kokanee fishing trip I made several years ago. It wasn't the number or size of fish my partner and I caught; it was the method. We used small cowbells with tiny blades, a rubber snubber to absorb the strike of these tender-mouthed fish, and two small angleworms hooked through the nose on a No. 10 long-shank hook attached to an 18-inch leader. A small weight—a $\frac{1}{8}$-ounce bell sinker— was attached to the cowbells' keel. We spooled the attractor and bait out 50 yards behind the boat and trolled at slow speeds. We would chug the rod tip, steer a zigzag course, and alternately speed up and slow down to a crawl. The strikes were soft and delicate; many fish were lost during the scrap because hooks would tear free. Our fishing was done in open water, far from any bottom structure. The fish seemed to be prevalent in the top 10 feet of water.

The fishing was far from spectacular. In fact, I found it somewhat boring, although the fish seemed scrappy enough for their size. The fish we caught tasted good, but I must admit that the thought of fishing cutthroats in a nearby lake held my mind that day.

Baitcasting Tackle and Techniques

One of the most versatile outfits available for lake fishing is the baitcasting rig. Anglers can troll, cast, or jig-fish along rocky bars or other structure.

In fact, most kinds of fishing can be done with a quality baitcasting rod and reel. This gear is much smaller now than in past years, and the performance is much more reliable. Fishermen today enjoy smooth, effortless casting and a reliable drag system that enables them to play fish with a velvet touch. The reduced size of many baitcasting reels enables anglers to hold them comfortably in one hand for day-long fishing. They give a person a direct contact with the lure or bait, and this leads to more catches. I would rather use a baitcasting rod and reel for most of my lake fishing than any other rod-reel combination.

The quality of workmanship of the new baitcasting reels is superior to that found in spinning reels. Anglers seldom find frozen reel parts, sticking drags, or the other problems inherent in some spinning tackle.

One common misconception is that learning to cast with these rigs is difficult and time-consuming. Anyone with normal reflexes and dexterity can learn to cast within the hour. A novice must learn to "educate" the thumb of the casting hand to adjust needed tension to the revolving spool so that it doesn't overrun and cause a backlash. Today's modern reels are fitted with a mechanism designed to create or relieve tension on the reel while it's in freespool and ready for casting. This adjustment allows compensation for light or heavy lures. If adjusted properly so that the lure s-l-o-w-l-y falls away from the rod tip when the thumb is removed from the spool, the reel will seldom backlash when a cast is made.

If the lure falls rapidly from the rod tip as the thumb is removed from the arbor, the tension is improperly set and a backlash can occur if the angler doesn't thumb the spool correctly during a cast. This adjustment makes casting easy. Once this technique is mastered, a fisherman can cast confidently.

Casting

Casting with a baitcaster involves the use of the wrist and forearm. A properly set reel will enable you to make fast, accurate casts with a minimum of wasted motion. Reels out of adjustment, or not set properly for the weight of lure being used, will make casting with these rigs difficult. It requires only seconds to tune a reel so that the lure slowly falls away from the rod tip while it is in freespool and your thumb is off the arbor. Each time a new lure is used, the adjustment must be made in this manner. It leads to easier casting and fewer frayed nerves.

I'm right-handed, although I do cast with both hands. It's best if a right-handed angler can cast left-handed and operate the reel handle with the right hand. This eliminates the hassle of switching the reel from left to right hand for casting, and then back to the left hand for lure manipulation and retrieve. Most of the time, I cast with my right hand and then switch the rod to my left hand during the retrieve. It's simply more comfortable for me to do this. I alternate hands every other cast when fishing heavy jerkbaits for muskies. These heavy lures can make your wrist feel as limp as overcooked spaghetti at the end of a long day.

Casting with spinnerbaits, jerkbaits, surface lures, jigs, or other lures is easy. Point the rod tip at the target, and allow 2 to 4 inches of line to hang down from the tip to the lure. Bring the rod tip back to approximately 12 o'clock (directly overhead), and make a smooth forward cast. Raise the thumb off the arbor when the rod tip is slightly above your intended point of impact. The lure should sail out smoothly and without a backlash. The critical point in any cast is when the lure first leaves the rod tip, and again when it nears touchdown. The thumb is used to feather the lure into splashdown. But more importantly, it's used to supply a gradual, lessening pressure on the reel arbor as the lure gains velocity at the beginning of the cast.

One mistake made by baitcasters is to hold the reel in a horizontal manner. Baitcasting reels operate at peak efficiency when the cast is begun with the reel held in a near-vertical position. This reel position

Proper position when starting cast with baitcasting reel. The handle should be up, the reel vertical. This permits correct wrist movement and proper operation of the reel.

allows the freespool mechanism to operate smoothly, and it helps prevent line overrun. It requires some practice, but as stated earlier, almost anyone can learn the fundamentals of baitcasting in an hour.

Another problem inherent in baitcasting is "reaching." We've all been exposed to the problem; we'll be drifting down the lake and see a fishy-looking area. We'll make one cast, and then we've drifted by it. The natural tendency is to "reach out" with an extra-long cast in an attempt to work the cover just one more time. This reaching for distance upsets the natural power stroke of the cast, causes the spool to revolve faster, and our thumb usually doesn't compensate for the additional force of the cast. The result—a bird's nest large enough to house a mating pair of bald eagles.

Some of the backlashes are so bad that only major surgery can put you back into the fishing game. For example, a buddy of mine, a spinfishermen, once watched me hacking with my knife at one such mess. (We were fishing Norfolk Lake for bass.) I had stuck two fish, landed one, and just missed the other at the boat. I reached out with a long cast to some stickups, and the inevitable snarl occurred. My buddy was sympathetic. "Looks like trouble, oldtimer. When you finish cutting, tearing, and swearing, let me know and I'll let you use one of my spinning outfits. Until then I'll just keep fighting bass." He punctuated his remark by setting his hook into another bass, a 4-pounder. His snide comments and corner-of-the-mouth grin prompted me to perform an emergency operation on my line supply. I now carry at least two casting outfits at all times, so that the occasional severe backlash doesn't put me out of the ballgame.

The average backlash is easy to fix. It requires only a few pulls on loose loops to unravel. Anyone who considers backlashes a serious detriment to baitcasting has never spent much time trying to work twists out of mono spinning line. Now *that* gives me a headache!

Veteran anglers find it easier to manipulate a lure with baitcasting outfits than with any other type of fishing tackle. Max Donovan, an old fishing pal, once told me that a good man on a casting reel can talk to fish. "I've seen guys that can make plugs sing and dance, tailwalk, chug,

Cory Kilvert holds up his 22-pound northern pike taken on a Daredevle and baitcasting tackle. He used a fast, skittering retrieve across the surface to nail the fish.

pop, burp, wiggle, and wobble. The combination of rod-tip action while cupping the reel in the left hand enables fishermen to make lures perform at any retrieval speed, from slow to fast. A good man with one of these rigs is a joy to watch," Max told me. I've watched some pros putting lures through their paces, and I'm convinced that he's right.

Don Podraza, a muskie-fishing partner from Wisconsin, is a master with a baitcasting outfit. He stands while he is fishing; his hands and arms are in constant motion as he teases muskies up from the depths. "It's difficult to deliver the proper stroke to jerkbaits with spinning gear," Don maintains. "I like to give my Suicks or Bobby Baits a single jerk or double-jerk, and then follow up with a short pause before jerking again. Such manipulations with a spinning reel aren't possible because you're always pulling the reel handle away from your fingers. That's usually the time when a big muskie chooses to strike. A baitcasting reel performs this task much better," he said. It's impossible to disagree with anyone who has caught and released hundreds of legal-size muskies.

Trolling

Trolling is an art. It requires the teaming of rod, reel, line, and lure or live bait with a knowledge of the water, gamefish moods, and practical experience at reading the water in order to determine where fish hold. It means more than throwing a Dardevle out behind the boat and motoring slowly down the lake.

Baitcasting tackle is ideal for trolling because it allows an instantaneous release of line as bottom contours change. A hand-held casting outfit helps anglers strike feeding fish much more quickly. It also allows a more positive feel of lure action, changes in bottom structure and composition, and the soft, nibbling bites from gamefish.

Using the structure-fishing method on lakes while trolling with baitcasting tackle is one of the best ways I know to catch fish. The average angler trolls down the lake with his rod tip held at halfmast without a thought of what his lure or live bait may be doing. One time I fished Great Bear Lake, Northwest Territories, for lake trout and watched two anglers fish all day with lures skipping behind the boat. They didn't catch a fish, and it's no wonder. Skilled fishermen *know* what a trolled lure or bait is doing, and they know where their rig is at all times. It's difficult to learn these things with a rod tip poking holes in the sky.

Keep the rod tip low to the water. This position allows a deeper penetration of the bait or lure and helps you to detect strikes. I've given up on rod holders; they tend to foul your line while you're fighting a fish. It gives me greater pleasure to hold the rod in one hand and feel a powerful strike. A low rod tip also allows anglers to feel bottom if that is where you're fishing. Contact with weed growth is important with many lake-fishing techniques, but if your lure has gathered weeds like a junkie looking for a cheap high, you'll miss out on action.

Backtrolling or forward trolling are two fishing tactics that produce good results when going after a variety of species. Walleye fishing, for instance, often requires getting near bottom or along deep-water weedlines or other structure. A hand-held rod is more sensitive and

Trolling requires solid baitcasting tackle in order to battle and land big fish. This troller uses a level-wind reel, keeps his rod low to the water.

responsive to changes in bottom contours, bottom composition, rocks, boulders, weed growth, or a number of other structure changes. You'll soon learn to tell the difference between one or the other. Backtrollers often fish almost directly under the boat. A sensitive baitcasting rod will telegraph messages up to the angler in an instant and allow him to compensate for any changes.

Baitcasting tackle is extremely helpful when a gamefish slams a lure, and misses. It's easy to push the freespool button and release line to make the lure appear stunned, and unable to resist capture. I've taken many gamefish by dropping line back after a missed strike. A trailing fish will often turn around and slam the lure again as it flutters down. Try this with a spinning rig, and you'll probably be a day late and minus a fish. The trick is to release about 5 or 6 feet of line, and then reengage the spool. When the fish strikes again, he'll probably do so hard enough to rattle your teeth.

Jig-Fishing

One of my favorite lake-fishing methods is to use jigs with a baitcasting rig. I can think of nothing I enjoy more than fooling a bass, northern pike, walleye, or other gamefish with a jig.

I was once fishing northern Ontario just before the lake-trout spawning period. The lakers were schooled off a rivermouth entering the lake. It seemed as if every fish had starved itself for a month, while waiting for me to arrive. I had intended to fish for walleyes, and was armed with dozens of jigs. The lakers didn't care; they were happy over my lure choices.

My guide picked a promising area at the rivermouth current edge and told me to expect to catch walleyes. I loop-knotted a yellow ¼-ounce jig to my 10-pound mono and draped a cast over a nearby boulder jutting from 12 feet of water. I lifted the line off the rock, allowed it to sink near bottom, and struck hard as the line shifted sideways during the descent.

I'm not sure who was more surprised, me or the lake trout. I expected a walleye and found myself battling a 10-pound laker. I fought him for several minutes before the creamy-spotted fish came to the waiting net. The action repeated itself on nearly every cast. I caught ten lakers and returned seven.

Anyone with a spinning outfit could have duplicated that feat. But my lift-drop routine worked well with the baitcasting rig for some time on that lake. The action finally died, and I began experimenting with various retrieves. I finally turned the lakers back on with a rolling retrieve that crawled the jig slowly across bottom before inching up the dropoff. That retrieve prompted another half-dozen strikes. Such variations in the retrieve can be obtained with other types of gear besides baitcasting. But I prefer easy casting, an excellent feel of the lure and positive interpretation to bottom conditions. I firmly believe that a baitcasting rig offers all this and more.

A fisherman *can* detect a bite easily while jig-fishing with a baitcasting outfit. Jig-fishing isn't as easy as some outdoor writers claim; it's difficult to sense a fish mouthing the lure, and to differentiate between that feeling and a jig working the bottom. Ask any veteran angler about this; he'll probably rattle off hundreds of cases where he set the hook without knowing why. Most of the time a sixth sense tells you a fish has the lure. I've set a hook innumerable times without knowing why and often I'll finish my thoughts while battling a fish. It just seems to me that a baitcasting rig, held correctly, allows a greater feel or sensitivity to the passage of the lure over bottom. This is quite important when fishing with jigs.

Minnow Fishing

Anyone who has read my previous books knows that I'd rather watch ice freeze than fish with minnows. It's not that minnow fishing isn't a great way to take many gamefish species. It is. Thousands of anglers can't be wrong, but it's just not for me. I don't like to stillfish with live bait for any species. The largest fish in the lake could be starving for a minnow, and I'd spend long hours flogging the water with everything known to man before I'd minnow-fish.

Baitcasting tackle is often used for minnow fishing, however. Anglers can either stillfish with a husky baitfish tethered under a red-white bobber, or they can rig a minnow for casting. The latter method is one that delivers fast action for big muskies. My one and only experience with an old minnow-fishing muskie guide opened my eyes, but not my mind. He caught muskies while I caught a cold. He did it with a big rigged sucker that weighed nearly a pound.

Charley was nearing eighty when I fished with him in northern Minnesota. His eyesight was failing, but his casting arm looked like it should have been on a plumber. His arm had developed from slogging heavy suckers out into open cabomba and lettuce patches for some sixty years.

He sewed his bait with heavy cuttyhunk line after selecting a sucker minnow 12 inches long. He inserted a No. 2 treble hook through both lips, from bottom to top, and a 1/0 treble through the tail. He tied a strong 30-pound leader between front and tail hook, and then wrapped the cuttyhunk around the minnow and fastened that line to both hooks. It reminded me of wrapping strong cord around a rolled beef roast. I suspect muskies may have looked at the bait in much the same manner.

This trussed bait weighed nearly 1 pound. At the end of a long day of fishing, the bait must have felt as if it weighed 10 pounds. Charley was as fresh at the end of the day as he was at its beginning. "You've got to believe that each cast will bring a strike," he maintained. His optimism was less than contagious; to me it seemed like very hard work, with little reward in sight. My guide couldn't care less; he had caught thousands of muskies on the rig and was content to let me jerk and double-jerk my jerkbaits. He watched my efforts with an ill-concealed sneer on his face and muttered something about kids and their toys.

My guide had an unerring ability to find muskies. He hammered cast after cast into open pockets, probed the deep-water edges of weedbeds, and made that sewed sucker do tricks I never thought possible . . . and he did it with baitcasting tackle.

He often dropped his rod tip and whispered, "I've got a taker!" His toneless voice caught my attention, and I watched him punch the freespool button as a muskie moved off with the bait. He looked like an ancient dog riveted on point; his body was crouched, leaning forward, and his arms stuck straight out in front as he followed the fish's progress through the weeds. "Ah . . ." he muttered, "he's stopped to scoff down the minnow." The age lines in his face creased deeper as he waited for the muskie to make its move.

The line started moving again. Charley took up the slack, dropped his rod tip, and powered the hooks home with such force that I thought he would snap the muskie's neck. It didn't, but the violent set brought about a startling reaction. The fish powered itself from the water in a mighty, gill-rattling, mouth-open jump that displayed vividly the awesome power of this species. It made a short run of 25 yards, jetted into the air again, turned a cartwheel, and came crashing back down. This was repeated again before man and fish settled down to a slugging match in deep water.

Twenty minutes after Charley made the set, I slipped the gaff under a bone-hard muskie jaw. I grunted as I heaved the 30-pound fish from the water. The gaff slipped in my hands and the handle banged my wrist several times before I could grab it and hold on. We overwhelmed the fish and slid him into the boat. Charley cracked the fish's skull with a lead-weighted billy he carries for such purposes, and we then sat back to congratulate ourselves.

"Young man," Charley said, as he stared at me, "you've just seen what baitcasting tackle and minnow fishing can do. It's not a stunt, and it's not something everyone can do, but casting rigged suckers can deliver a brand of muskie excitement unequalled with any other technique. Don't ever forget it!" I never forgot Charley's calm expertise with that jumping muskie. I also never forgot the raw power needed to cast a heavy, live bait hour after hour to attract a big fish.

Spinning Tackle and Techniques

One of the major developments in fishing in the last hundred years has been the birth and growth of spinning tackle. Spinning reels have been heralded as the best thing since sliced bread. That may or may not be true, but I believe that spinning gear has helped many fishermen learn how to cast, and therefore how to fish. A novice, even a small child, can learn to cast with a spinning rig in minutes.

I prefer an open-face spinning reel. Most of my lake fishing is done with ultralight or medium-weight tackle. The lightest line I use is 4-pound mono for trout and other small species; the heaviest, 15-pound mono for big pike and muskies. I'm not a strong man, so I find it tiring to use two-handed spinning rods and huge reels that weigh nearly 2 pounds. I'm tired before I start fishing with such heavy tackle. My spinning is done with lighter rods and reels. I'd rather be tired from fighting a fish than from fighting heavyweight gear.

279

If the fish I'm seeking weigh under 8 pounds, I'll use ultralight gear and enjoy a superb battle. If my quarry weighs from 6 to 15 pounds, I'll use tackle that can handle up to 12-pound mono, and lures to ½ ounce. With fish ranging from 12 to 35 pounds, such as big pike, catfish, or muskies, I'll choose a reel that can handle 15- to 20-pound mono and lures weighing 1 ounce or more.

Spinning rods range from little cuties 5 feet long up to rod designer Dick Swan's noodle rods, which may be 15 feet long. They are made of fiberglass, graphite, boron, or boron-graphite combinations. I've even seen a few bamboo rods although this material is high priced and doesn't lend itself well to spinning rod construction. Brand names of rods that I've used successfully include Browning, Shakespeare, Heddon, Garcia, Lou Childre, Skyline, and Fenwick. Many modern rods place line and lure weight information just above the cork grip. This helps anglers choose the proper rod.

Reels, whether open face or closed face, come in many styles. The important item to consider is to purchase a reel of proved quality and of proper size to handle the type of lake fishing you plan to do. Look for smooth operation, a trouble-free full bail, and a smooth, nonsticking drag system. Reels I would endorse include Garcia, Shakespeare, Daiwa, Cardinal, and Ryobi. There are many others with a reputation for dependable performance. Some I've used sparingly, and others not at all. I refuse to mention any kind of tackle that I'm not familiar with.

Many anglers try to make one spinning outfit work for all types of lake fishing. They want something that can be used for shallow-water fishing, for trolling, and for slinging muskie jerkbaits hour after hour. There's no such animal being manufactured today. It's far better to purchase at least two spinning outfits, and probably three. A three-rod combination will enable anglers, if they wish to skimp, to purchase just two spinning reels with additional spools of line. This offers an instantaneous choice of line size by simply switching reel spools for a heavier or lighter line. My choice, if money is an important consideration, would be to buy an ultralight rod and reel, and a medium-action rod and reel with two or three extra spools. Load the

Kay Richey's ultralight spinning outfit proved equal to the task of fighting and landing this 5-pound brook trout.

spools with 15-pound mono. This rig can subdue the largest lake trout or muskie swimming in North American waters.

The reel you buy should have a positive antireverse and quick access to drag setting. When playing a gamefish, you often have to loosen the drag quickly. This must be done without fumbling because a big fish, making a long run, can peel line off a reel with the speed of lightning. One common mistake is to tighten the drag in hopes of turning a fish. The opposite is true; drags must be loosened before spool friction builds up and pops the line. A drag adjustment placed in an awkward position can cost you a big fish.

Medium-weight spinning tackle can even subdue big muskies if the angler takes his time. This one weighed 35 pounds.

Casting positions with spinning tackle are much the same as they are with baitcasting rigs. Sight the target with 2 to 4 inches of line dangling from the rod tip down to the lure. Sweep the rod sharply back to a 12 o'clock position and bring it forward without hesitation. Release the line from the index finger when the rod tip is slightly above the target. The lure and line should shoot away from the rod and sail out in a smooth arc. The angler can "feather" the line as it spins off the reel to slow down lure flight. With practice, you can drop a lure with accuracy and still get a dainty touchdown.

Spinning tackle is better suited to casting than to trolling, but many walleye fishermen use it for backtrolling. They hold the rod in their right hand, with the bail open and their index finger hooked over the line. A gentle nudge from a fish allows a prompt release of line so that the walleye doesn't detect resistance. They give the fish a moment of slack line, turn the handle to pick up the line with the bail, and set the hook when they feel the line tighten in the fish.

Forward trolling is another game. A fisherman must know where his lure is at all times. I favor a light-action rod and 6- or 8-pound line for much of my trolling. I want to know exactly what my lure is doing at all times. Don't use a stiff, pool-cue rod. A softer rod, with a good taper from tip to butt section, can reveal weeds on a lure, a soft or hard bottom, rocks, and boulders.

When trolling, hold the tip of the spinning rod parallel to the water and near the surface. This helps you feel soft strikes or changes in bottom contours if you're fishing with bottom-bouncing lures. It also allows you to set the hook once fish start nibbling at the lure. Many species follow and tap at live bait or lures several times without taking solidly enough to be hooked. A rod tip held low allows you to "feel" the lure.

Baitfishing with spinning tackle is a natural for lake fishermen. The difference between baitfishing and trolling or casting in a lake is in the manner in which the rod is held. Baitfishermen have a tendency to hold their rod tip at a 10 or 11 o'clock position while waiting for a strike. This high rod position allows a better feel of the bait and the soft, sucking strikes of gamefish. Whenever they detect a strike they drop the rod tip, allow a bit of slack line to develop, and set the hook when the fish takes up the slack. Many fish are hooked deep with this baitfishing method. The hook hold is usually solid, provided that the fish doesn't break the line.

Spinning tackle has completely captivated the angling public of North America. This fishing equipment has allowed novices and experts alike to enjoy the fruits of fishing. Long, effortless casts and sound reliability are just two merits of spinning rods and reels. Trouble-free drag systems allow anglers to battle—and land—giant fish. These are a few of the reasons why spinning gear is here to stay.

Lure Fishing

T he smallmouth bass were suspended off the lip of a double-bar dropoff. The bottom tapered gradually away from shore, fell from one short bar to another, and then dropped smartly down to a rubble-strewn bottom. The maximum depth was 28 feet, and the fish were holding at 16 feet.

I tried crawling jigs up over the shelf, and my partner, Pete Jones, was tossing hardware. Nothing worked, although the fish remained rooted in the same location as if waiting for us to get our act together.

We finally decided that crankbaits were the only answer. I put on a deep-running Lindy-Little Joe Thin Shad, while Pete used a Count Shad (by the same company) in perch color. His sinking lure was designed to work at controlled depths, while mine ran extra deep on a rapid retrieve.

285

Pete knew from past experience just how long it took his lure to sink to the 16-foot level. My lure splatted down, and a medium-fast retrieve brought out the peak wiggle and diving pattern built into the lure. I felt a half-hearted nudge on my first cast, struck, and missed the fish. I wheeled the lure in fast and shot another cast to the same area.

My buddy's lure reached the desired level, and he began his retrieve to keep the lure at the proper depth. A smallie slashed out from under the overhanging lip and whacked his lure. Meanwhile, my lure was passing through the small school. Another fish struck it, and was hooked. We battled our fish on opposite sides of the boat. We tried to hurry them as quickly as possible so that we could work our lures through the fish again before they sensed danger and retreated to deep water.

I lipped my 3-pounder from the water, tossed it on ice, and started another retrieve while Pete's smallie—a 3½-pounder—joined my fish. I nailed another willing taker on the next cast, as did my partner. We boated this pair of 3-pounders, and that was it for that spot.

Our luck, if you wish to call it that, wasn't due to the brand-name lure we used. Rather, it was the type of lure needed to get down to the gamefish. One major problem facing anglers today is they have too many lures to choose from and too little time to experiment with those in their tackle box. Fishermen would do well to invest some time in learning how a lure works, what practical depths can be attained with each plug, and when to use a specific lure. Fishing situations change daily, and anglers must learn to adapt fishing techniques, and lures, to various conditions.

Stan Lievense, a skilled Michigan angler, once told me, "If you're going to fish with lures, be sure to select one that works at the proper speed and the proper depth for the gamefish intended." His wise words of advice apply as much now as then. Space-age plastics, deep-diving lips, internal rattles, and other modern-day wonders of the lure industry have one thing in common: They equip a lure to be fished in a specific manner, at a specific speed, and at predetermined depths. It makes little sense to force a topwater lure to work deep water, yet I've seen anglers try this many times.

The bulk of today's lures fall into one of the following categories—surface, floating-diving, medium-depth, deep-diving, and bottom-bumpers. Each should be worked a specific way to bring out the best action.

Surface Lures

A surface lure is designed to be worked on the surface of a lake. Old favorites like the Jitterbug and Hula Popper fall into this broad classification. The endearing quality about these plugs is that they deliver topwater strikes that can be seen . . . and felt.

The basic surface lure was designed to be fished as slowly as possible. Hurrying a retrieve may turn on the occasional fish, but it leaves most species cold and frightened. The best way to get explosive strikes is to make topwater plugs imitate an injured minnow, rodent, or something edible. Gamefish often investigate a surface lure from a distance before moving in to deliver the killing strike. One mistake anglers make is to move the lure from its point of impact directly after touchdown. Allow the surface lure to remain motionless, often for periods of a minute or more before it is moved. This gives a curious gamefish, such as a largemouth bass, ample opportunity to recover from its initial fright and move over to investigate.

Each lure has a movement that produces a desired action or sound. Many surface lures gurgle, pop, or make other funny noises when activated by a slight rod-tip movement. It requires some testing to determine just how to bring out this movement and fish-attracting noise. Try to imitate a wounded fish or small animal on the water. If you watch closely, you will notice that they often lie motionless for some time before moving. The first movements are slow, deliberate, and somewhat tentative; this could be from fear of being discovered by a gamefish. Your surface lure should follow much the same pattern.

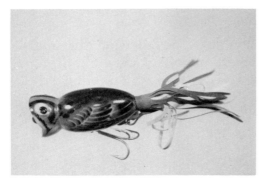

Hula Popper

Jitterbug

Zara Spook

I used to fish for largemouth bass at night on many lakes, from Michigan to Florida. Some of my greatest thrills took place with surface lures under star-speckled skies. I used two lures—the Jitterbug and Hula Popper—most of the time. Shorelines, boat docks, swimming beaches, and deep-water edges of weedbeds were my midnight prowling grounds. I learned to manipulate topwater plugs to obtain the maximum amount of action from a minimum amount of effort. It often required two to five minutes to fish out each cast. The longer I paused between chugs of my rod tip, the more fish I hooked. One night I had trouble hooking even junior-size bass. I decided to experiment and see just what these lures could deliver. My basic Jitterbug approach was to cast out, allow it to lay motionless, and inch it back very slowly with frequent pauses. This time I tried a slow, steady retrieve without pauses. A bass arrowed up from the weedbed, smashed the lure midway through the retrieve, and missed. I continued a steady retrieve, and the bass came back again. He struck, missed, turned on his tail, and struck again at the side of the boat. This time I managed to stick him, and we battled it out beneath a full moon for ten minutes before he tired and was netted. That fish weighed 6½ pounds; not a big fish, mind you, by Florida standards, but a beautiful largemouth from a heavily fished Michigan lake.

That smooth, gurgling retrieve delivered five other strikes. The fish that I kept ranged from 3 to 6½ pounds. It was a classic lesson in the versatility of surface lures.

Some lures, often called "stick baits," are manufactured to produce different types of actions depending on how you manipulate your rod tip. You can make these lures nod, jump, dart sideways, and do other tricks. Fish often move in for a closer look, and succumb to temptation as the lure quivers after a deft bit of rod work.

Hula Poppers, and other lures built along similar lines, demand rod-tip action to produce jarring strikes. I've found one of the best ways to fish this lure is with 1-inch-long rod-tip jerks. Some anglers may call this a jerkbait, but I disagree. Large jerkbaits, like the Suick, call for heavy rod-tip jerks to bring out their action. The long-lasting Hula Popper loses its effectiveness when twitched mightily across the surface. Small rod-tip twitches will deliver a gentle "plop" that seems to draw fish from far away. Space at least ten seconds between each "plop," and you'll find that bigmouths will often smack the lure just as you start your next movement. I twitch the lure all the way to the boat in 1-inch pulls. Many strikes occur next to the gunwale.

Surface lures are often used to catch largemouth bass. Their usefulness doesn't end there, however. One of the biggest northern pike that I caught came from a small, natural lake known for its bass fishing. The fish hammered a jointed Jitterbug puttered across the surface. Northerns seldom feed actively after dark, and infrequently on the surface, but this fish rose through 6 feet of water to splash heavily on top as it took the plug. It was an exciting battle. The pike weighed 14 pounds and jumped twice during the struggle. I have also taken jumbo bluegills, crappies, rock bass, smallmouth bass, and walleyes on topwater lures.

Floating-Diving Lures

Many modern plugs fall into this category. They float at rest and dive to depths of 3 to 10 feet on the retrieve. Such plugs have proved themselves in lakes where fish often feed near shore in depths shared by brush, heavy weeds, or other underwater obstructions. The angler can cast tight to shore and move the plug slowly until it wiggles to bring out peak depth and lure action. This type of lure is dandy for areas where the bottom contour slopes gradually away from shore. As the retrieval speed is increased, the lure digs deeper and tends to follow bottom contours out and over the breaklines. Such locations are prime feeding areas in most lakes or reservoirs.

Hundreds of lures fall into the floating-diving category. One of the first such lures I used was Heddon's River Runt floater. Fished slowly, it worked well on the surface, but the lure really came into its own when fished with a slow, steady retrieve.

A retrieve with lures like the River Runt and others of its ilk can be varied according to the situation. I've learned that these lures are adaptable to anything except an extremely fast retrieve. One trick that often works, once the lure has dived to its maximum depth, is to stop the retrieve for a moment. The lure will then begin rising to the surface. A short pause, and another period of reeling, will cause the lure to dive and rise and dive again. This stop-and-go, up-and-down lure presentation can trigger strikes from many gamefish. It's a natural when fishing for night-feeding walleyes and smallmouth bass. They follow the lure for some distance, often pecking at the plug, but a brief pause and the resulting upward lure drift often is just too tempting for some species. Strikes are hard and sure, and hookups are common.

One area on most kinds of lakes where floating-diving lures are deadly is over shallow (6 to 10 feet) sandbars or the tops of weedbeds. These lures can dive only to a certain depth; it requires a knowledge of just how deep each lure will go. If weeds grow to within 6 feet of the surface, you'll have to select a lure that will dive to about 5 feet. A plug that works any deeper is destined to deliver frustration and few fish, since more time will be spent pulling lettuce off the hooks than gamefish.

Lures that run slightly deeper can be used in such areas provided that the angler adopts the stop-and-go retrieve. Try to time each pause so the lure rises above the weeds before the next portion of the retrieve is started.

Deep-water weedbed edges are perfect habitats for feeding gamefish. These areas are ideal for floating-diving lures. I enjoy casting parallel to the weeds, cranking the lure as deeply as possible, and trying to skim the plug close to the weeds. If the weedbed edge fronts on a short flat and sharp breakline into deep water, so much the better. You'll be fishing an area that gamefish use as a highway from deep water into shallower feeding zones.

One trick that works with this type of lure is to approach a potential feeding area with casts from every conceivable direction. I've noticed a tendency for many species to strike lures delivered from one

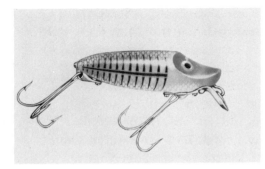

River Runt Spook

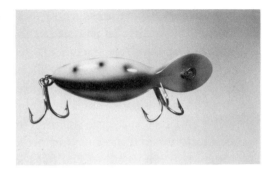

Tadpolly

Sonic

Hot Shot

Pikie Minnow

direction but not from another. This is often true when a breeze is blowing. Gamefish often feed into small currents generated by the wind ruffling the water.

Medium-Depth Lures

There are two basic types of medium-depth lures—those that dive to depths of 10 to 15 feet, and those that slowly sink to those levels and are then worked like conventional lures.

Countdown Rapalas or Lindy-Little Joe's Count are two examples of lures that will sink to a desired level. Fishermen who use these plugs should know just how fast they sink, and how deep the water is in that particular area. The best way to determine sinking time is to move into shallow water—say 6 feet—and make a short cast. Count "one hundred, two hundred, three hundred" until the lure touches bottom. If you've counted to "six hundred," you'll know it requires about one second for the lure to sink 1 foot.

Many so-called "crankbaits" are designed to operate best at certain depths. All the angler must do is to determine those depths he will probably be fishing, and then select a lure designed to work at that level. One old trick is to determine the forage available in each lake and select a lure color that approximates the food fish. Team proper color with a lure that works at the proper depth and you'll be one-up on many lake fishermen.

If you have a particularly long stretch of choice fishing water where the depth of the water remains constant, it may be wise to troll some medium-depth lures. A plug that works well at 10 feet can be very effective when trolled slowly along a 10-foot breakline. The fisherman can vary his speed, troll a snakelike "S" pattern, and present the lure to fish from various angles. Try to make three or four trolling passes along the same contour. Fish move on and off a breakline; lures may miss the fish on one pass, but make contact with them on another.

Spoons and spinners also fall under the heading of medium-depth lures. Many anglers fish these lures about midway between the surface and bottom, although in a pinch, they can be grubbed along the lake floor or skittered across the surface. The angler that experiments at various depths with spinners or spoons may find himself hooking more fish

Spoons.   This line is *normally* an elongated, concave piece of brass stamped with a certain design. The configuration of the spoon, and the painting or plating, is what triggers strikes from gamefish. The purpose of these lures is to imitate forage fish.

Baitfish flash and turn while swimming, or when in distress, and a spoon represents a moving minnow or one that is sick or injured. How the angler retrieves the lure is the secret to hooking fish on spoons.

Spoons have a certain speed when trolled or retrieved that brings out the correct action and throbbing beat of the lure. A lake fishermen must learn the proper trolling or retrieval speed for each spoon in order to make it perform to the best of its built-in ability.

Spoon trollers often adopt a chugging motion to activate a spoon. The rod tip is swept toward the bow and then allowed to drift back toward the stern. This causes the lure to increase its speed and wobble, and then it flutters down in the water until the boat speed catches up to the slack line. Following gamefish often strike on this "flutterdown."

Casting spoons is an excellent way to take many gamefish. One chilly spring day I was standing off a Michigan river mouth. Steelhead were abundant, but they were finicky about spoon color and retrieval speeds. It required most of the morning to figure out what they wanted. I was using a blue-silver Devle Dog—a ¼-ounce model—and would cast as far into the lake as possible. I allowed the spoon to sink to a count of five and started it back with a steady retrieve.

The trick I learned that day came about by accident. A steelhead struck, and missed. I started reeling much faster, trying to con the fish into thinking a minnow was trying to get away. Four high-speed cranks on my reel handle was all it took to jar that steelhead into a smashing strike. The fish hit, pinwheeled into the air, and headed across the lake with my reel screeching like a banshee with sore tonsils. Ten minutes later I netted a prime male steelhead, slipped him onto my stringer, and went back to casting. I tried the speedup again, giving my reel handle four rapid turns. Again it happened! This time the fish was so strong he popped my 6-pound mono.

The balance of the day was spent hooking one steelhead after another, losing some and landing some. The lure speedup and then slowdown was the trick that angered fish that day.

It doesn't always work, though. Sometimes fish require a very slow retrieve, with the spoon barely wobbling. Other times a flutterdown of 6 feet will work, as may a lift-drop of the rod tip while retrieving at normal speeds.

Catching fish with spoons at the medium depths is fun, and a challenge that requires constant experimentation. If fish are located, and known to be in a certain area, the experimentation time is usually shortened. Try different spoons, various colors, and different sinking times and retrieval speeds. It can pay off with plenty of action.

Spinners. I frankly admit to less than spectacular results with spinners at medium depths, except on muskies. For other species I've given large and small spinners equal time, but find that spoons often pay off better for me than do spinners.

Spinners are exciting lures to fish, though. There's something about the throbbing beat of the spinner blade that makes some gamefish ornery. Big pike and muskies, and the occasional largemouth bass, can be suckers for spinnerbaits when fished near prime cover.

One time I was tossing (does anyone cast tandem spinnerbaits?) to a weedbed that dropped off into 20 feet of water. It was on Ontario's Lake of the Woods where I was fishing with Les Sandy at his Monument Bay Lodge. We were trying for one of his named muskies, the "Coca Cola Bay Muskie," to be exact. The big fish was scouring the small bay, and baitfish were leaping from the water in confusion and attempting to get as far from the jaws of the predator as possible. "Try a dark spinnerbait," Les told me. "I've hooked that fish several times on a black Mepps Musky Killer, only to lose him on jumps."

These Devle Dogs are of different colors and designs to imitate various species of baitfish. Spoons must be given enticing action when trolled or retrieved.

A collection of spinners for smaller gamefish. These lures are meant to be cast and retrieved rather than trolled.

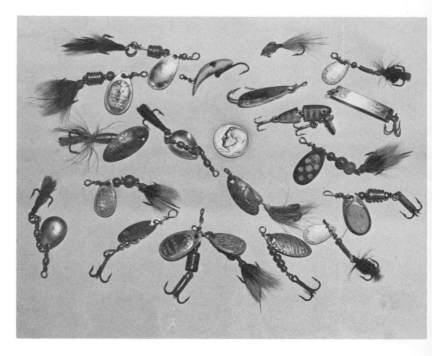

This fisherman uses an electronic water thermometer to determine the probable depth of bass. Then he goes after them with plastic worms in a variety of colors and sizes.

I snapped one on, led the cruising fish by 10 feet, and made a smooth cast. The spinner plunked down with the finesse of a dead elm limb falling off a tree in a windstorm. SPLAT, it went, and YANK went the lure. A fish had inhaled the lure on splashdown and we were off and running.

A short time later, following two beautiful jumps, Les netted an 18-pound muskie, hardly the monster I hoped to catch. The fish was firmly hooked, and dispatched before we brought it into the boat.

We hooked two other muskies that evening, landed one and lost one. The boated fish was only 14 pounds, lightly hooked, and we released it. The muskie named after the popular soft drink never struck, but continued chasing baitfish for an hour.

The fish we hooked (other than my first one) were taken at mid-depth as the spinner twinkled past a weedbed. Anglers have long "ripped" spinners through the tops and edges of weedbeds, simulating a baitfish in panic. We tried this trick several times when the sodapop fish neared the cabbage, but he ingored the spinner and continued feeding on the real thing. Perhaps he'd been hooked too many times on a black spinnerbait to play games again.

I've learned that the hooks on many spinners are seldom sharp enough when they leave the factory. I carry a small bastard file to triangulate the hook points, and feather them out to a razor-sharp point. The resistance of water pressure against a spinner blade reduced the direct pull needed to set the hooks.

Spinners, in my humble opinion, are meant to be cast and not trolled, either foreward or backward. The continual throb of the blade reduces your sense of feel, and a trolled spinner often comes back to the boat garlanded with weeds. Casting, however, enables the angler to maintain direct feel of the lure and what it's doing.

If fast sinking time is required for spinners to reach productive water, opt for a smaller blade. A large blade offers so much resistance to the water, it requires too much time to sink to the required depths.

The same experimentation with lure color and retrieval speed is needed with spinners as with spoons or other lures. I've seen days when gamefish will strike a brass spinner, but ignore or flee from silver spinners. My rule of thumb is to use a silver spinner on a dark day, and a brass or copper spinner on a bright day.

Plastic worms. One place where plastic worms come to the fore is when largemouth bass are suspended, often along a breakline or the edge of a weedbed. Then, the plastic crawlers can be fished at mid-depth instead of along bottom.

A trick I've used on largemouth many times is to Texas-rig the worm *without a tunnel sinker.* The hook point is inserted in the tip of the worm, pushed through about one-half inch, and turned out the side. The hook is turned again and buried in the side of the worm. This makes it virtually weedless.

Use light line and no weight. Allow the worm to flutter and undulate downward; this natural action of a free-drifting worm really turns on wary bass in clear-water lakes.

The line often will switch sideways in the water when a bass picks up the sinking crawler. Allow the fish time to ball it up in his mouth, and when the line starts moving off, allow it to come tight and set the hook.

Any make of plastic worm will do, although I favor the natural, purple, brown, bass, or dark blue for this type of fishing. I guess it's because I've taken more fish on those colors.

Deep-Diving Lures

This type is one of the most popular. It works extremely well during hot summer months when gamefish are more intent on resting than feeding. A deep-diving plug will often induce a strike when other lures fail. One reason is that deep-water fish often feel safe in the sanctuary of the depths. A lure that wiggles along near resting sites can trigger a strike from fish in a nonfeeding attitude.

There are countless lures in this classification. Many are easily identified by a long plastic lip. The lip causes them to dive and increases the wiggle. When purchasing these lures, look for an extra-strength bill and body design, and strong hooks. A lure has to be tough to withstand the constant stress of bouncing over the bottom.

Some of my favorites are Bomber's Model A, Young's Shad Lure, Bagley's Diving Kill'R B, Rebel's Deep Wee-R, and Super-R, and many others. A fast crank will send these lures toward bottom, and they seldom stop until they get there. Of course, plugs of this type can go just so deep before they stop diving. It's usually possible to obtain slightly more depth with 6-pound monofilament than with 15-pound line. Water resistance against the line is the determining factor. I've found that 8-pound mono is a good all-round line for most fishing circumstances, except when I'm fishing for heavyweights. Then I'll generally use 15-pound mono and sacrifice some depth for greater line strength.

The hard, fast retrieve-and-pause technique that works with medium-depth lures also delivers fast action with deep-diving plugs. A nonfeeding gamefish that spots a wiggling lure scraping along near bottom may not be inclined to chase and feed at that time. But a lure that wiggles along and then suddenly heads for the surface often triggers a strike.

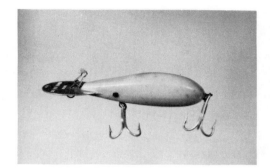

Little Dig

Lazy Ike

Arbogaster

Deep-Diving River Runt

Hustler

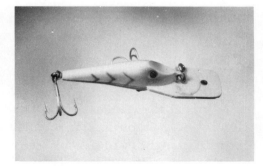

Deep-diving lures like this Swim Whizz are killers for muskies or other gamefish that take to deep water in summer.

Bottom-Bumpers

The nether-world of lake gamefish is one of near-darkness at all times. Little sunlight filters down into the depths, and many species take refuge in areas where the light is dim. Here, they rest, feed sporadically, and recharge their batteries after long bouts on spawning beds. Fish in deep water may rest for long periods, especially during the early days of a cold front. If anglers want action they must seek out fish in the depths with bottom-bumping lures.

Anglers who use the STST method rely on bottom-bumping lures. There are several that fall within this group. The Spoonplug (invented by Buck Perry) is one example. Mudbugs, Bombers, and similar lures have made their mark. Jigs are also productive when bounced along bottom.

That the leadhead jig is a proven bottom-bumper and deep-water lure goes without saying. If I had a choice of only one or two lures to bring along, this one would accompany me wherever I went. My faith in them is without bounds.

Leadhead jigs are meant for deep fishing, or bouncing along bottom where many lake gamefish spend countless hours. They are almost snagproof, something that cannot be said about many lures.

One of the techniques I frequently use is to wind-drift with a jig lowered to bottom. This fish-finding technique is simple: the wind provides propulsion and a short lift-drop of the rod tip gives action to the jig.

Everyone has favorite jig-fishing techniques, but mine is a short 6-inch lift-drop of the rod tip. This bounces a jig along bottom, sending up little clouds of silt. The sound of the jig thunking into bottom, or being dragged along bottom, must send out sound waves to feeding fish.

To me, a jig doesn't look like anything edible, but then, I'm not a gamefish. The up-and-down motion of the lure is what triggers strikes, although if a strip of fish flesh is added, the action and scent of the meat can trigger the feeding instinct in a fish.

One of the tricks I use, particularly for walleyes and northern pike, is to remove the throat latch from a dinner-size walleye. This V-shaped piece of meat is located on the bottom of the lower jaw, just ahead of the gills. Cut it free and attach it to the hook through the thick portion at the apex of the V.

This piece of walleye flesh will wiggle in the water when the rot tip is raised and lowered, giving action to the jig. Never handle the throat latch after filling gas cans or handling oily objects. The smell is transferred to the fish flesh, rendering it unfit for use.

I'll often catch four or five small walleyes for dinner, kill them and remove the throat latch. I carry a small Dixie cup, add water, and place the V-shaped baits in the cup. They remain soft and durable for long periods of time.

Jigs come in a variety of sizes, shapes, and colors. Some are dressed with bucktail, marabou, feathers, and tinsel; others have soft plastic bodies. Head shape varies from one jig to another. I've found the round or flat jig head best for most purposes.

Experiment with sizes, colors, and rod-tip actions. What entices a fish one day will fail the next. Keep trying new jig movements, retrieval speeds, and sooner or later you'll connect with these bottom-bumpers.

Spoonplugs allow trollers or casters to strain the water at any and all practical depths. A fisherman can comb the shallows, work into slightly deeper water, and then strain deep water with various-size Spoonplugs. This results in a fast, accurate presentation at all depths.

Crankbait fishermen have been using bottom-bouncing plugs for some time. Some of these lures, like the larger Cisco Kids or Bombers, have proved themselves to midsummer fishermen seeking big northern pike or muskies. Walleye fishermen, largemouth bass busters, and other lake fishermen also adopt the bottom-bouncing philosophy, and for good reason—they catch fish.

Other Tips

A common problem with many lures, particularly the floating-diving or deep-diving plugs, is that they may run accurately for some time only to develop an erratic action after a fish is hooked on them. Adjustments are touchy on these plugs. Jaw pressure from a fish, or the stresses from pounding constantly against rocks or a hard bottom, can turn a reliable lure into a worthless one.

Lure fishermen must be able to fine-tune every plug so that it delivers the optimum action and diving qualities. This is a simple matter, but one that many anglers ignore.

One of the best fishing tools available is a pair of needlenose pliers. This tool will enable fishermen to fine-tune any lure, and do it in short order.

Lures were designed to swim straight, and not to turn over on one side or run off on a tangent away from the line retrieve. Make *gentle* adjustments, not forceful adjustments that may do more harm than good.

If a lure doesn't run true, the line may have been tied to it incorrectly. A lure that consistently runs to the right should have the line-tie bent *slightly* to the left. The reverse is true if the lure runs off to the left. Make all line-tie adjustments in small doses; a strong bend one way or the other can ruin a fine lure.

It's possible to control a lure's wiggle. A tighter swing in the side-to-side wiggle can be attained by bending the line-tie up away from the lip. This little trick can make or break a lure, however. A correct adjustment will increase the beat of the lure, while an over-adjustment will kill the action. Make all adjustments sparingly until you obtain the desired action.

You can fine-tune a lure to deliver a slower wiggle by bending the line-tie down toward the lip. This technique may stimulate a lazy fish in summer.

Hook size can affect the action of many lures. I learned this while bass fishing in Oklahoma. A largemouth slammed my lure, danced through the stickups, and was quickly landed. The hooks were twisted and bent, so I replaced them. My replacements were slightly larger than those issued with the plug. The result was a lure that didn't behave normally. It didn't produce another strike until I found hooks of the proper size.

Some lures fail to deliver peak action when tied with an improved clinch knot or any other knot that jams tight against the line-tie. Rapalas or Rebels, or other minnow-imitating lures, operate best when they are tied with a loop knot that allows peak action. Many anglers don't do this. If your lure doesn't produce the desired action, try using a loop knot. If that doesn't work, then try fine-tuning it. If that fails to deliver the expected results, throw the plug away and try another.

Plugs issued from a factory are subject to quality controls. Even though these controls are stringent, and manufacturers wish to sell only top-of-the-line lures, it's possible to purchase a plug with poor action. One time I tested twelve lures of the same size and color, made by one manufacturer. Only two had the desired action. The others were useless. Some could have been fixed by fine tuning the lip or line-tie, but why bother? Some sporting goods stores will allow you to test lures on water, and others won't. I buy my plugs from those that will.

Lure fishing requires a fishermen to use lures designed for a specific purpose and depth. The techniques outlined in this book will be of little value unless you use lures in the manner for which they were intended.

CHAPTER

Flyfishing

About twenty-five years ago, I began to fish lakes with fly tackle. Bluegills, sunfish, and small largemouth bass were my quarry. These gamefish, especially during the spring, didn't care about the type of fly I delivered their way. They were in the shallows looking for food and the meaty-looking imitations I cast were good enough for them. I'd catch fish until my flies were tattered and torn. Fishing like this is still available today. The inland lakes, reservoirs, Great Lakes, farmponds, and strip-mine pits of North America are filled with gamefish. A flyfisherman can enjoy excellent sport if he knows how, when, and where to present his offerings.

The tackle required for flyfishing lakes can be as inexpensive or expensive as you choose. It doesn't require expensive tackle to flyfish in still waters; almost any well-balanced rod, reel, and line combination

307

will work fine. A passing knowledge of flies and flyfishing techniques will work wonders on most gamefish, provided that you hit them at a time when shallow water is their home. This normally means during spring or fall, or after dark on hot summer nights.

Here's basically what you'll need to get started on an enjoyable career of flyfishing the lakes.

Rods and Reels

My idea of a good flyrod for lake fishing is one that can handle a No. 7 flyline. Such rods are generally about 7½ to 8½ feet long and have a smooth action.

It doesn't require long casts to catch fish in most lakes. The average cast will be about 30 feet. Panfish anglers rarely cast even that far, and many fish are taken with short, accurate casts of 20 feet.

My first flyrod was a miserable piece of junk given to me by a well-meaning relative. "Here," he said, "now you can flyfish off your Dad's dock." I didn't know any better because I was only fourteen years old. I did know that something wasn't right when the flyline stuck together. When I made a 20-foot cast, the line landed in the water in tight coils. I stretched the line, cleaned it as best I could, and tied up some leaders. After much work it was still a bad piece of equipment.

That rod served only one purpose; it made me want something better, something well balanced and capable of casting—not throwing—a flyline far enough to catch fish. Oh, I caught a few bluegills that were village idiots, but it wasn't fun fishing with that clunker rod. It was so bad that when someone finally stole it from our car, I never shed a tear. Instead, I used that opportunity to buy a Shakespeare flyrod. It has caught more panfish, bass, and steelhead than any other flyrod that I've owned.

A lake fisherman needs a reel balanced to his flyrod. Most of the fish that are hooked and landed from lakes are played by stripping in the line until the fish can be netted or beached. There is little need for sophisticated reels; few species will be played directly off the reel.

Lines

The flyline is the most important part of a lake fisherman's outfit. A mediocre line, or one too heavy or light for the rod-reel combination, can turn off more anglers than any other factor. The flyline must be balanced to the rod and reel for smooth, effortless casting.

I've mentioned that I consider a No. 7 outfit perfect for most lake fishing. I've used heavy-duty rods, reels, and lines when tangling with huge chinook salmon, but wielding an outfit geared to a No. 10 or 11 line is too much work for me. I'm not physically strong enough to manhandle a big outfit like this all day. One or two outings have proved to me that I can land very large fish, including 35-pound king salmon, on a No. 7 outfit if I just take my time. Besides, it's more fun with a lighter outfit.

Flylines come in sizes from No. 4 to No. 12. There are floaters, sinkers, fast sinkers, lines with floating belly and sinking tip, lead-core lines (which I've used on many occasions when fish are deep), and level lines. If I've missed any, it's because I don't care about specialty lines. I use either a level or weight-forward flyline for most of my lake fishing. These two lines will handle nearly any fishing situation. I do prefer a floating line. Scientific Anglers' AirCel flyline is one of the finest for all types of lake flyfishing. It floats extremely well, and doesn't require constant dressing as do other lines. I just make sure that it's well dried after every use.

I use from 50 to 75 yards of braided Dacron backing on all fly reels. This fills the fly-reel arbor enough so that the flyline completely fills the spool. This eliminates having a half-full spool. Nail knots are used to connect backing with flyline and flyline with the butt section of the leader. A small coating of Pliobond will make these backing-flyline connections smooth and trouble-free.

Leaders

A leader must be tapered down from a fairly heavy butt section to the tippet or leader point. A leader that isn't tapered smoothly from large to small diameter can be difficult to cast because it doesn't roll out smoothly and deliver the fly delicately to the lake surface. I make sure that I tie properly tapered leaders.

Many anglers detest tying their own leaders. It requires them to measure all leader sections, and make sure each is properly tapered. This is a time-consuming process, and one easily solved by the purchase of tapered, knotless leaders. I remove them from the package, stretch them between two pieces of rubber to remove the coils and kinks, and dress them with a leader sink if I want the leader to sink slightly below the surface. Most of my fishing in lakes is done in shallow water. A floating leader is skylighted and can be seen by gamefish. This is one reason why my leaders are treated. They float in the surface film of water, and are invisible to feeding gamefish. Little tricks like this can really help you take more fish from inland lakes.

Leaders are available commercially in lengths from 7½ to 12 feet. Specialty houses that cater to flyfishermen often offer leaders up to 15 feet long. Most of my lake flyfishing is done with leaders ranging from 7½ to 9 feet, and tapered down to a 2-pound test tippet. If the fish are large, I'll use a leader of 9 feet with a tippet made of 4-pound mono. This will handle most bass, trout, and some northern pike if you play your catch carefully.

Flies

Your choice of flies for lake fishing is virtually limitless. This may explain why most flyfishermen carry too many flies. They waste valuable fishing time trying to determine which fly to use in certain situations.

I've learned that the following flies produce good results for various species of gamefish.

This angler waded along the lake shore, casting to rising fish, and hooked a beautiful trout.

Bluegills and panfish.   Flies tied on a No. 10 to 16 hook. **Wet flies:** Scarlet Ibis, Yellow Sally, Ginger Quill, Grizzly King, Parmachene Belle, Montreal, Claret Gnat, Royal Coachman. **Dry flies:** Adams, Mosquito, Red Quill, Pink Lady, and Leadwing Coachman. Various nymph patterns are productive as long as they are small and dark.

Trout.   Flies are tied on hooks ranging from No. 4 through No. 20. Many productive flies are local patterns. The ones listed here have been steady producers for me. **Dry flies:** Adams, Female Beaverkill, Dark Hendrickson, Gold Ribbed Hare's Ear, Red Fox, Male Beaverkill, Brown Bivisible, Pale Evening Dun, Borcher's Drake, Red Quill, Blue Quill, Ginger Quill, and March Brown. **Wet Flies:** Professor, Light or Dark Hendrickson, Cowdung, Wooly Worm, Black Gnat, Female Beaverkill, Quill Gordon, Light Cahill, Wickhams Fancy, Royal Coachman, Alder Fly, and Western Bee. **Nymphs:** Spring's Wiggler, Zug Bug, Breadcrust, Michigan nymph, Leadwing Coachman, Beaver nymph, Inch Worm, Strawman nymph, Isonychia nymph, and Quill Gordon nymph.

Pike and muskies.   These gamefish prefer large flies tied in streamer fashion to imitate minnows. Flies should have predominant colors of either red and white or blue and white. My favorites include Nite Owl, Red Trude, Muddler Minnow (an exception to the above rule), Warden's Worry, Parson Tom, Ambrose Bucktail, Royal Coachman, White Maribou, and Black Nose Dace. Flies should be tied on 1/0 to No. 2 longshank hooks.

Largemouth bass.   I've caught many largemouth bass on small flies while fishing for bluegills and other panfish. Some bass weighed as much as 5 pounds. The best flyrodding for this species is done on bass bugs. One of my favorites is the Devle Bug manufactured by the same people that produce Dardevle lures. It comes in several sizes and shapes, but the mose is one of the best.

Steelhead and salmon. These gamefish, upon entering fresh water, can be taken in tidal lagoons, wide places in the river, or in lakes through which they pass. They are generally receptive to flies tied in bright colors. Use flies tied on No. 2, 4, and 6 hooks, either weighted or unweighted. I prefer Dave's Favorite, Richey's Wiggler, Spring's Wiggler, Winan's Wiggler, Red PM Special, Orange PM Special, Crick, Royal Coachman, Copper Demon, Golden Girl, Platte River Special, Betsie Special, Skunk, Jock Scott, Umpqua Special, Burlap, and Golden Demon.

Techniques

Certain areas in a lake offer anglers good flyfishing. The inshore spawning waters are fine places to fish during the spring for panfish and bass. I prefer to wade softly and fancast through an area pockmarked with spawning beds. A wet fly (try a No. 14 Scarlet Ibis) can be very effective in spring. The water clarity enables me to see the fly and thus spot a soft take. I retrieve it slowly, with frequent pauses. The fly will settle slightly during the pause; this is usually when panfish grab on and begin that familiar water-circling battle that places their broad side against the pull of the line.

Bluegills are likely to grab slow-sinking flies when they hug the edge of a breakline after spawning. I favor a dark-colored nymph at this time. A 30-foot cast is long enough when you're fishing from a boat. Allow the fly to sink 6 or 8 feet and bring it back very slowly with inch-long twitches of the flyline. Watch the floating end of your flyline for a slight switch in direction. It usually means a fish has taken the nymph.

Northern pike and muskies are a separate challenge for lake flyfishermen. I once watched Stan Lievense nail several muskies on large streamer flies in Iron Lake, in Michigan's Upper Peninsula. He worked the edges of weedbeds and fished the streamer with fast, jerky strips. The fly undulated like a live minnow. Before the day was over Stan's arm was tired and his flies were ragged. He used a 2-foot length of 15-pound mono as a shock tippet, and to protect against bite-offs. When going after pike and muskies, locate a good fish and then keep after it until it nails the fly. I've done my best flyfishing for northern pike in some of the outback lakes of northern Canada. Rivermouths are good places to try in that country.

Trout are still another option for a lake flyfisherman. These fish are likely to eat whatever is available at a certain time. They may feed on freshwater shrimp one day, emerging nymphs the next, adult spinners dropping to the water to lay eggs, or minnows. The angler must be able to pinpoint feeding activity and determine just what food is being consumed.

The only time that I'll use dry flies for trout in lakes is when an obvious hatch is in the making. If the waters are calm, and trout activity on the surface isn't obvious, I'll use nymphs, streamers, or wet flies. If I think a hatch is due soon, I'll try to imitate the nymph of the soon-to-emerge insect. Try to make it struggle to the surface. Trout often cruise in search of food. One spot they stay at often is along the edge of the first major dropoff. In my area this may be close to shore, although in some lakes a boat may be needed to reach productive fishing water.

Don't make the mistake of staying rooted to one spot. Move every ten or fifteen casts and work up or down the shoreline. This is one good way to locate trout. I moved only 25 yards on some occasions, and began taking rainbows or browns after long periods of inactivity.

Trout will often roll on the surface as they feed on emerging nymphs. It's important to determine whether this rolling is significant, or if the fish are actually feeding on surface or subsurface insects. The answer to that question will give you the clue needed to select a fly— either wet or dry.

Experiment with retrieval speeds. Sometimes, trout in lakes prefer a fast-moving fly. At other times, they want a fly that moves very slowly or struggles toward the surface. One time I caught a brace of hefty brown trout by allowing my dry fly to rest without movement on the surface of a small pond. The trout would smash up through the water and take the fly off the surface in a lather of spray. Trout are unpredictable. This one experience proved to me that trout will take motionless flies, although it is unlikely much of the time.

Index